ACKNOWLEDGMENTS

I couldn't have written this book without the support of the following people. I want to thank them all.

Michelle Beckstrom - Painting on Front Cover
Dedicated to her daughter, Iris

Isabelle Shurman - All sketches

Marilyn Maddison *(Pictured right)* - Photos

Monica Marshall - Photos

Doug Goodman - Photo

USDA - Public Domain Photos

Unsplash.com - Photos

Brenda Patoine - Photos

JoAnne Dennee -Photos

Pat Jackson - Photos

Robert Resnik - Major Editing

Robert Maddison - Technical Support

Ellen & Paul Gittelsohn - Technical Support

Ray Kania - Layout Assistance
Great Big Graphics Morrisville, Vermont

OUTLINE

FOREWORD
Sarah Salatino Full Circle Garden vi

PREFACE
Ron Krupp vii

GARDEN NOTES
Tips on Navigating the Book. x

THE PLANT AND ANIMAL KINGDOMS xiii

CLIMATE CHANGE AND THE WARMING OF THE PLANET xvi

THE SEASONS 1

    Autumn 4

    Winter 43

    Spring 62

    Summer 111

THE END 179

APPENDIX:

    Useful Links and Other Valuable Information 181

    Woodchuck Garden Website Guide 183

AUTHOR BIO .... Inside Back Cover

TESTIMONIALS .... Back Cover

FOREWORD

I first met Ron on in 2006 when he presented his book, The Woodchuck's Guide to Gardening, to a garden club meeting I was attending. Who is this Woodchuck character who weaves into just one book gardening how to, poems, land and cultural history, shared gardening experiences from others, and personal musings? This began a friendship that has grown through serving together on the board of directors of the Friends of The Horticulture Farm. One of Ron's many newsletter articles addressed the compelling reasons to preserve the Hort Farm, calling it "The Jewel in the Crown" which read like an ode to the collections there, showcasing Ron's enjoyable writing style which you will find here. Since then, Ron has been an inspiration and advisor to me in forming and focusing the vision for my nursery business, Full Circle Gardens, to grow and provide perennials with a purpose for our pollinators.

This latest book in the Woodchuck series will not disappoint. Ron's expertise in writing and teaching and many years of gardening experience have come through once more in this lovely illustrated and informational ornamental gardening book. But there are two voices to be heard here. In all the books of the series the Chuckster has emerged as the irreverent other voice of Ron's. Together they help and encourage the new gardener to try new practices and explain the reasons why they work. For that is what gardening is about. If something isn't working, try something else. To read this latest Woodchuck's guide is to receive well researched and well experienced information that will lead to your gardening success in growing ornamental plants.

Through his highly informative book with its poetic musings and beautiful illustrations, Ron teaches us all to stop, observe, and relish our gardens. For that is what learning to garden is all about. Not just the process but the magic, the wonder, and the awe of the natural world. You may want to read The Woodchuck Travels Through the Garden Seasons slowly, ear-marking pages for later consideration as I have done with this and the other Woodchuck books. Keep it close as a handy reference. This is truly the "jewel in the crown" of all ornamental gardening books.

Sarah Salatino
Full Circle Gardens - Essex Junction, VT

PREFACE

We come from the earth,
We return to the earth.
And in between we garden.

-Anon

    My Garden Journal continues the journey that began in the spring of 1969 when I started gardening at Hill & Dale Farm on Putney Mountain in southeastern Vermont. I've always wanted a trilogy to call my own, and here it is - my third book about gardening in Vermont.

    What would our world be without the Plant and Animal Kingdoms? Could we live without spring bulbs, grasses, woodland plants, shrubs, perennials, climbers, groundcovers, trees and, of course, bees, butterflies and hummingbirds? Perhaps it would look like endless miles of desert on the prairie where the buffalo once roamed.

    I describe ornamentals and landscape plants with an emphasis on native species and pollinators. I'll reveal their practical nature and aesthetic qualities, all complemented with a variety of poetry and prose, sketches, photos and paintings.

When Bob Dylan wrote the song "The Times They Are A Changin'" in 1964, he created a warning of impending change, and also a call for action. This archetypal protest song on poverty and racism was an anthem of hope. It summed up the anti-establishment feelings of people who would later be known as hippies, myself included.

The times are still "A Changin'", and not for the better:

We are rapidly destroying the diversity of the plant and animal kingdoms. As a gardener who lives close to land, I witness this destruction daily, and hope that the damage is not irreparable.

Native species plants are those that occur naturally in a region in which they evolved. These plants are the ecological basis upon which all life depends. Without them, and without the insects that co-evolved with them, local birds cannot survive. What's clear is that the lives of insects and flowers comingle. Insects make buzzing sounds with their wings when they fly around flowers. It's been found for example, that nectar in evening primroses increase with the sounds of hovering bees.

The best way to create a sustainably designed habitat for songbirds, bees, hummingbirds, butterflies and insects is to provide a native pollinator landscape in your garden. Restoring native plant habitat is vital to preserving biodiversity. By the act of creating a native plant garden, each patch of habitat becomes part of a collective effort to nurture and sustain the living landscape for birds and other animals.

Unfortunately, habitat destruction and climate change has put the native pollinators at risk - and at the same time our entire food system. That's why we must suspend the use of environmentally-harmful pesticides which are killing the pollinators that are necessary players in the Earth's ecosystem.

*See more information on Climate Change, Global Warming and Disruption in My Woodchuck's Garden Website #11. Bill McKibben of Ripton, Vermont is featured.

Most of the landscaping plants available in nurseries are species from other countries. These exotic plants not only sever the food web, but many have become invasive, outcompeting native species and degrading habitat in remaining natural areas. But that's "a changin'" as more native plants are becoming available.

The Practical and the Ornamental

When designing your garden, select plants that meet both your practical and ornamental/aesthetic needs. My spirits are always lifted in early summer when I canoe down the quiet, slow-moving LaPlatte River - coming upon a group of blue irises on the muddy banks as blue herons hover above. Blueberries provide tasty berries in summer and good fall color and are a perfect substitute for the invasive burning bush, which is prohibited for sale in Vermont.

Sugar Maples provide shade in summer, leaves in red, orange, and yellows in fall, and sweet syrup in spring. Tamaracks come after the maples, with their yellow needles, which drop in early winter. Close by are the evergreens - providing a lovely contrast.

My neighbors converted a part of their lawn into a patio garden with containers of annuals like nasturtiums and lovely tropical trumpet flowers (Datura). Or how about transforming a shaded area with ferns, hostas, and a tiny pond with a fountain and a crab apple to boot for shade and relaxation. Why not add a sculpture and bench on which to sit and meditate. You may choose dianthus, a pink, stunning, sun-loving, wide-spreading groundcover for a small hillside or rock garden, a rosa rugosa hedge for privacy and screening and a yellow flowering forsythia shrub for beauty in spring.

Climbing plants like hydrangea and honeysuckle are deciduous perennials, which provide both practicality and beauty. In my front yard, they climb up lattice type trellises with their lovely blooms and provide shade in summer as well. As you can see, they serve both a useful and ornamental purpose. When you put the two together, you've got the plant kingdom all rolled up into one.

Some annual climbers are morning glories and flowering sweet peas. In many cases, morning glories drop seed and return the next year. The morning glories climb up the clematis in my front yard after the clematis has bloomed in purple-blue.

"Your mind is a garden. Your thoughts are the seeds. The harvest can either be flowers or weeds."

William Wordsworth 1770-1850

TIPS ON NAVIGATING THROUGH MY GARDEN BOOK:

MY WOODCHUCK GARDEN WEBSITE includes thirty two topics with detailed information on each topic. It complements the main themes of the book. Take for example - #5 – How to Select Perennials for All-Season Color – and see how it relates to growing perennials throughout the year. .

You can access the topics and information at **woodchuckgardening.com** or *https://woodchuck37.wixsite.com/woodchuck*. A guide to topics is located at the end of the book after the Appendix.

-My book is comprised of many personal anecdotes and stories side by side with an encyclopedic style filled with specific information. This detailed material can be seen in grey boxes such as this.

-My book is filled with both native and non-native plants. I attempt to emphasize the importance of native plants as they provide more nectar and pollen to pollinators and are beneficial to the environment. Pollinators have evolved with native plants, which are best adapted to the local growing season, climate, and soils. Non-native plants may not provide pollinators with enough nectar or pollen, or may be inedible to butterfly or moth caterpillars.

-I attempt to describe the plants in their order of flowering beginning in spring. This challenges me to hone my observation skills and to help the reader notice the blooming time of plants as they appear. You be the judge. I place a * next to the plant.

-Along the way, a Jester called the "Chuckster" makes fun of me on the garden path, and I respond in-kind to his trickery. At times, he has a woebegone look on his face. An alter-ego of sorts, he has been a constant in the Woodchuck series, including my last book, *The Woodchuck Returns to Gardening*.

The "Chuckster"

MY HOME AND COMMUNITY GARDENS

-Many of the plants I describe come from my two gardens - one in my home garden close to Shelburne Bay on Lake Champlain and the other at the 3-acre Tommy Thompson Community Garden near the Winooski River, which flows nearby into the lake. Both of my gardens are located in Zone 5 Plant Hardiness Zones as compared to Zone 3 in the mountains and colder locations of Vermont.

THE TOMMY THOMPSON COMMUNITY GARDEN

In commemoration of its namesake, a plaque at the community garden reads:
In memory of Tommy Thompson – farseeing-founder of
Burlington Community Gardens who spent his last decade
promoting community gardening around the globe.

"Someday when enough people see this joy or experience
it themselves, there just may be Gardens for All."
Byron H. "Tommy" Thompson - 1917-83

MY HOME GARDEN

As with my two other garden books, I follow organic methods without the use of harmful synthetic chemicals. I focus on composting, cover crops, organic matter, mulching, and soil fertility. In order to have healthy soil, you need to have a symbiotic association between fungi and plant roots called the mycorrhizal relationship. Photosynthesis lays the basis for this dynamic process.

Please follow me through the seasons of the year. My Garden Journal includes nature walks. These afternoon wanderings pass through the woods and down to Lake Champlain. My constant companion is my lab-newfie mix, Hercules. We listen for the sounds and sights of birds, especially the ever-present crows, ducks and even a soaring eagle now and then. As the day ebbs, I watch the sun sink over the distant Adirondacks on the lake's western shore. These treks lift my spirit.

Now and then, I throw in a curve - like when I write about the elemental beings: the gnomes who tend the earth, the undines - guardians of the water, the sylphs who aerate life and salamanders who infuse matter with fire. The "Chuckster" just shakes his head and says, "please be patient with Ron as he likes to wander off into distant lands."

Please use my journal as a way to check on a particular season and compare it with your own garden experiences. Skip around to the time of the year you wish. I travel as far back as 2013 and up through 2021, beginning with the earlier years.

There is no way I can describe all the plants growing in Vermont. That's why I have created "My Woodchuck Garden Website" that includes a list and detailed description of trees, native pollinators, perennials, and shrubs. There is an outline of the website in the website at the end of the book.

I consider myself a "learner in the learning process" as this book has taken many years to complete. I'm sure there are gaps in my musings and that is okay as my learned colleagues in the world of horticulture helped me plug the holes, i.e. "With a Little Help from My Friends." Dr. Norman Pellett, Emeritus Professor of Horticulture at the University of Vermont has been especially supportive.

THE PLANT AND ANIMAL KINGDOMS

THE PLANT KINGDOM

Native species plants are those that occur naturally in a region in which they evolved. These plants are the ecological basis upon which all life depends. Without them, and without the insects that co-evolved with them, local birds cannot survive. What's clear is that the lives of insects and flowers comingle. Insects make buzzing sounds with their wings when they fly around flowers. It's been found for example, that nectar in evening primroses increase with the sounds of hovering bees.

Entomologist Doug Tallamy has shown that native oak trees support over 500 species of caterpillars whereas ginkgo's, a commonly planted landscape tree from Asia, host only 5 species of caterpillars. It takes over 6,000 caterpillars to raise one brood of chickadees. The problem is obvious. Ginkgoes are not common in Vermont, but do grow in parts of southern New England. Ironically, the current Vermont champion ginkgo is in Bennington. The last time it was measured in 2003 with a height was 68 feet.

Native oaks and willows provide food for many species of insects, whereas redbud offers little food. The American native trumpet honeysuckle (Lonicera sempervirens) is a well-behaved species in the U.S., but Japanese honeysuckle (Lonicera japonica) is classified as an invasive species. Invasive honeysuckle provides low fat and poor nutrition to song, game and migrating birds, whereas the native American cranberry viburnum provides nourishment with its prolific fruiting.

Over the past century, urbanization has taken intact, ecologically productive land and fragmented and transformed it with lawns and exotic ornamental plants. The continental U.S. lost a staggering 150 million acres of habitat and farmland to urban sprawl, and that trend isn't slowing. The modern obsession with highly manicured "perfect" lawns has created a green, monoculture carpet across the country that covers over 40 million acres. This human-dominated landscape no longer supports functioning ecosystems, and the remaining isolated natural areas are not large enough to support wildlife.

For too long, native pollinator plants have been ignored in our landscapes, but that's finally starting to change. They are by nature hardier, better adapted to climate change and are able to provide critical habitat for wildlife. Plus, they have attractive flowers, colorful berries and fall foliage. Over winter, I love to observe the red stems of the native red osier dogwood in my community garden.

Dr. Douglas Tallamy describes in his book "Bringing Home Nature" how the use of non-native plants in landscaping sounds the alarm about habitat and species loss. He provides a narrative thread that challenges the dangerous notion that humans are "here," and nature is "someplace else." Tallamy's vision shows us how humans and nature can co-exist with mutual benefits.

Landscaping choices have meaningful effects on the populations of birds and the insects they need to survive. You can benefit birds and other wildlife by selecting native plants when making landscaping decisions. We have the power to support habitat for wildlife and bring natural beauty to our patch of the earth.

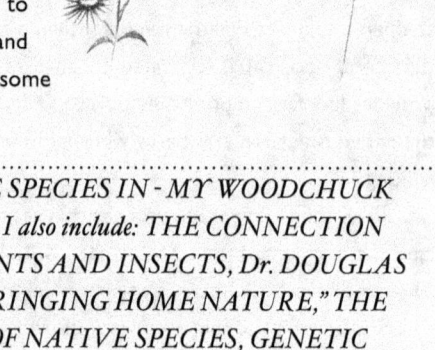

For the past five years, I've been planting a nectar-rich feast of native pollinator plants. My goal is to create a pollinator garden with a mix of flowers that bloom from spring through fall - providing pollinators with all the food, water and shelter they need. At the end of the day, I love to retreat to my garden for peace and relaxation, knowing I'm helping in some small way.

....

**SEE MORE ON NATIVE SPECIES IN - MY WOODCHUCK GARDEN WEBSITE #1. I also include: THE CONNECTION BETWEEN NATIVE PLANTS AND INSECTS, Dr. DOUGLAS TALLAMY'S BOOK - "BRINGING HOME NATURE," THE ORIGINS AND LOSS OF NATIVE SPECIES, GENETIC DIVERSITY AND LISTS OF NATIVE SPECIES IN VERMONT.*

....

THE ANIMAL KINGDOM

The biodiversity crisis in the Animal Kingdom is being dubbed the "insect apocalypse." The bounty of Earth's butterflies, beetles, bees and many other insects is slipping away. One of the results of fewer insects is smaller fish, as there are less insects for the fish to consume. This is due to the loss of pollinator plants, insecticides, pollution, deforestation, loss of habitat and climate change. Everything is connected.

We can thank native pollinators for one out of every three bites of food we eat. Without them, we could run short of foods we love, like apples, oranges, avocados and other crops. These beneficial pollinator species are responsible for the most crucial links in the entire world food chain.

Pollinators may be our planet's most ecologically and economically important group of animals. They provide stability for every terrestrial ecosystem in the world, because wild flowering plants all depend on native bees, flies, butterflies, beetles, moths, bats, birds and other animals to reproduce. Other wildlife then eat the fruits and seeds that result from pollination, spreading the seeds that in turn give rise to future generations of plants.

The Loss of Bees 2021 - The latest honey bee numbers are dire: Beekeepers across the U.S. just reported the second-highest annual losses of honeybee colonies -- for the second year in a row. The beekeeper who has hives close to my community garden had to replace all the bees from his hives. The year before, he lost over half. And it's not just honeybees. More than a quarter of bee species haven't been seen since the 1990s and other pollinators like monarchs are dying out. A key culprit in this catastrophic bee loss is Bayer-Monsanto's bee-killing neonicotinoid pesticides.

CLIMATE CHANGE AND THE WARMING OF THE PLANET

Climate change (or what some call climate disruption or chaos) is addressed in terms of how it affects the world of plants, wildlife, insects, birds, and humans. We can no longer ignore how the warming of the earth is having a profound impact on the natural world and our lives. Sub-tropical plants now grow outside at the Brooklyn Botanical Gardens like camellias.

David Schmidt, a fellow community gardener did not dig up his gladiolus in the fall of 2019. What was unusual is that the glads wintered over and flowered in the summer 2020. Something disruptive is definitely happening down here on earth.

Our warming climate has increased the spread of the invasives: Amur honeysuckle, buckthorn, wild parsnips, Japanese hops, rosa multiflora, and Oriental bittersweet can be found prospering in woods, fields and gardens. These non-native plants form clusters and thick masses and are difficult to eradicate. Let's not forget poison ivy and kudzu, a highly invasive warm climate loving plant, which has moved up from the deep southeast to Massachusetts.

Polar bears, the world's largest bear species, spend over half their time hunting. They rely heavily on sea ice to access the high-fat food supply they need to survive. As the ice sheets shrink, polar bears are forced onto land. They become undernourished and less capable of feeding their cubs. As the sea ice melts, polar bears are dying.

It's possible that the Earth's fragile arctic ecosystem could soon be filled with noisy drillers and extensive pollution. In the oceans -- oil spills cause fur-bearing mammals like sea otters to lose their water repellency. They suffer from hypothermia. Whales and dolphins inhale the oil -- impacting their lung function. Many die.

Elizabeth Kolbert has written a book we all should read. It's called The Sixth Extinction. Over the last half-billion years, there have been Five Mass Extinctions, when the diversity of life on earth suddenly and dramatically contracted. Scientists around the world are currently monitoring the sixth extinction, predicted to be the most devastating extinction event since the asteroid impact that wiped out the dinosaurs. This time around it's about climate change and how the cataclysm is happening because of human carelessness.

The summer of 2020 brought serious drought and dry weather to many parts of the country including Vermont. Out west, wildfires consumed many parts of California and the Northwest. California is suffering from extreme heat and drought and the "Golden state "is rapidly running out of water.

And in the far north, icebergs melted, and the seas rose higher on islands in the Pacific. A scientific report from April 2021 stated that the world's glaciers are melting faster than ever, losing 31 percent more snow and ice per year than they did 15 years earlier. Scientists blame human-caused global warming from fossil fuels. Half the world's glacial loss is coming from the United States and Canada. Alaska's melt rate are among the highest on the planet with the Columbia glacier retreating about 115 feet per year. In Iceland, a funeral was held for the loss of a small glacier.

2020 brought many examples of the deadly consequences of our failure to address climate risks. Record-breaking hurricanes, wildfires, and drought-on top of the COVID-19 pandemic-battered communities across the nation. Already in 2021, the heat wave in the Pacific Northwest has become the deadliest weather-related event in Washington state history. With temperatures near 120 degrees, power grids were overwhelmed, and hundreds were hospitalized for heat related illnesses. Dozens of heat related deaths have been reported in the region. Wildfires rampage throughout the Western states.
https://ucsusa.org/resources/killer-heat-united-states-0

The Red Alert - In August of 2021, the world's climate scientists just sounded a "Red Alert for humanity." The Intergovernmental Panel on Climate Change (IPCC), the Nobel Prize-winning body that synthesizes and summarizes the state of climate science, stating that the climate is already causing irreversible damage and the worst is yet to come. We must act immediately and on a massive scale to save lives and species from a planet beginning to spiral out of control.

From the U.S. to Brazil, Siberia to Turkey, Italy to Greece, we're witnessing fires raging across the globe, consuming forests, lives, wildlife, and our future. Fires have also razed natural savanna grasslands, burning within and around Indigenous territories. The combination of extreme heat and prolonged drought have led to the worst fires in almost a decade.

It's all connected. The burning season of Amazon forest has also begun. A historic drought, rampant deforestation, and lax environmental regulations mean this year is likely to be a devastating year for fires. However, unlike in the U.S. and around the world, fires don't occur naturally in the Amazon rainforest. They are set deliberately to clear deforested areas to make way for agriculture or renew existing pasture.

The coastal tourist village of Mendocino, California is almost out of water. The town has no central water system and is trucking water in. Ryan Rhoades, superintendent of the Mendocino City Community Services District, which manages the town's water, said he receives daily reports of homes with dry wells. "People are scared," he said.

The extreme heat is also impacting birds. In Seattle, more than 100 juvenile Caspian Terns perished when they fled rooftop nests, plunging to the pavement below. In eastern Oregon and Tucson, Arizona, hundreds of fledgling Cooper's and Swainson's Hawks have abandoned their nests too early because of extreme heat. Birds are telling us in the clearest way possible that we must act urgently to address climate change.

Heatwaves, floods, forest fires, and hurricanes are becoming common across the globe. Fossil fuel usage is driving this climate chaos. But financial institutions like pension funds are still backing them. These funds allow the oil, gas, and coal industries to pollute communities and harm wildlife. We need to cut off the money to Big Oil. Big Oil knew the dangers of climate change for decades and chose not to act, valuing profits over the future of life on Earth.

Nearly all public pension funds in the United States are invested in fossil fuel companies -- using tax dollars to support powerful polluters that are causing climate chaos. From tar sands and gas pipelines to fracking wells and offshore drilling -- retirement savings are being invested to support these projects. This polluting industry will not stop on its own.

THE JOURNEY BEGINS

Please join Hercules (Herk) and I as we begin our
Gardening Journey through the year.

No more time for Lollygagging - Heigh Ho Silver - Let's Get Going!

Autumn is a second
spring when every
leaf is a flower.

-*Albert Camus (1913-1960)*

THE SEASONS

I want to continue our conversation by sharing stories through the course of the year in Northern New England. I begin my journey with the shorter and cooler days of AUTUMN, my favorite season of the year. There is a distinct shift in the colors in the garden and nature and evening sunsets filled with strong hues. Everywhere there are warm tones of rich red, burgundy, orange, deep purple, gold, and toasty brown. Just drive along a country road in Vermont in September and see what I mean!

Maple leaves glow along with perennials like goldenrod and purple New England asters, painting the Vermont landscape in a palette of color. I can hear the buzzing of the bees on the five-foot asters in my community garden, and love watching joe pye weed, rosy in the evening light. I don't want to miss the lovely tall sedum "Autumn Joy" in pink.

Early WINTER arrives with cold rains, wind and then snow and ice. Yet winter is not without its beauty. On a sunless day, the grays merge to form a somber and peaceful landscape. Imagine the silhouette of a leafless tree as you sit by the warmth of your woodstove.

> "I prefer winter and fall, when you feel the bone structure of the landscape--the loneliness of it, the dead feeling of winter. Something waits beneath it, the whole story doesn't show."
>
> -*Andrew Wyeth (1917-2009)*

As the stillness of Winter ebbs and flows, I need to pause and appreciate the beauty of the frozen landscape as it reveals the sparkling wonders of nature. As I walk with my dog, Hercules, I marvel at the beauty of the varied shades of bark on a snowy day.

In early SPRING, mud season and the tapping of maple trees begins, and soon crocuses push up through the earth in their white, yellow and purple hues. It won't be long before the lime-green leaves of trees brighten the landscape, and the sounds of peepers present a concert from the wetlands.

While not the first bulb to bloom, the daffodil is the quintessential flower of spring. Representing the sun itself, the daffodil's stature and bright clear color announces the beginning of spring. They deliver a show in step with the following poem:

> I WANDERED LONELY AS A CLOUD
> I wandered lonely as a cloud
> That floats on high o'er vales and hills,
> When all at once I saw a crowd,
> A host, of golden daffodils;
> Beside the lake, beneath the trees,
> Fluttering and dancing in the breeze.
> For oft, when on my couch I lie
> In vacant or in pensive mood,
> They flash upon that inward eye
> Which is the bliss of solitude;
> And then my heart with pleasure fills,
> And dances with the daffodils.
>
> *-William Wordsworth 1770-1850*

The SUMMER days of June-blooming peonies waft their overpowering fragrance as the sun warms the soil and us. The peonies' large white blooms greet me as I walk up the steps of my front porch. Summer is the time when the sun reaches its highest position in the sky, and when we commune with nature. Many plants thrust out and open their flowers to the sun. As I relax in my community garden, the yellow calendulas, green dill and red poppies - having dropped seed from the previous season, return in color. They surround me, breathing out their essence in scent and drifting pollen as bees buzz.

Daffodils - Monica Marshall

As a young boy, I spent lots of time outside in the warmth of summer. I remember how the kids in the neighborhood stayed out until dark - our jeans caked in mud. My mom had trouble getting me to come back home. Here is a poem to that time.

> YELLOW LIGHT
> early summer
> getting dark
> late to home
> ran fast
> my mother's call
> fell to earth
> looked up
> saw yellow light
> from kitchen window
> home at last
>
> *-The Woodchuck Gardener*

A change appears in MIDSUMMER. The foliage of trees change color, sinking down from the bright green of spring into dark heavy shades, especially after a dry spell. In early summer, one can distinguish one tree from another by the shade of the foliage even at a great distance. But after midsummer, the color of trees becomes a uniform dark green, with slight variations of more silvery hues. We all soldier on during the dog days of summer with the daylilies. Soon, fall will come again. The act of planting daffodil bulbs in October is an act of hope. While much of the natural world sleeps through winter in dormancy, flower bulbs are storehouses of nutrients that send out roots and nurture new life within.

As Henry David Thoreau once said: "In wilderness is the preservation of the world." The quotation comes from his 1851 essay, "Walking."

Aldo Leopold (1887-1948) also put it well:

> "There are some who can live without wild things
> and some who cannot. I am one who cannot."

AUTUMN

SEPTEMBER, OCTOBER AND NOVEMBER

> The Harvest
> The silver rain, the shining sun,
> The fields where scarlet poppies run,
> And all the ripples of the wheat
> And in the bread that I do eat
> So when I sit for every meal
> And say a grace, I always feel
> That I am eating rain and sun,
> And fields where scarlet poppies run.
>
> -Alice C. Henderson (1888)

Early Murmurs and Musings

As the days get shorter and nights cool down, we welcome the sweetest time of year. Autumn is a season of profound and abrupt change. It's both dynamic and at the same time, one of foreboding, for we know what's to come. One could spend from now until Indigenous Day writing about Vermont's foliage and never tire. (Indigenous Peoples Day is celebrated annually on the second Monday in October as an enlightened alternative to Columbus Day.)

The summery September scenery around us has begun its tumble toward the warmer side of the rainbow with the colorful maple leaves. Later in fall, seeds form as the plants begin to fade, droop, and turn brown. By the first killing frost, many annuals and perennials have done their time, though not all.

Paddling on the Lake September 2015

In the evenings, I've been hanging out on the shores of Shelburne Bay on Lake Champlain, a five-minute walk down the hill from my home. The mornings and evenings are my favorite times. In the morning, the waters of Shelburne Bay glow in colors of the sun rising to the east. The September sunsets are even more spectacular. As the sun goes down over the Adirondack Mountains in the west, a red/magenta glow hovers in the sky and rainbow colors lap ever so quietly on the water. I love to paddle my canoe amongst the shimmering hues or swim, walk or simply sit as darkness begins to fill in the crevices of eventide. By the way, Mercury was in Retrograde that autumn, so if you're having trouble making decisions, that's the reason. The "Chuckster' just shook his head.

The blueberry plants in my community garden plots are just beginning to turn from green to a burnished red as a sign of fall. The maple leaves will soon begin their pigment changes into red, yellow and orange by the time of my annual canoe outing on distant ponds, where I celebrate the time of my birth on September 29th. (This is day of the celebration of Michaelmass, one of the four Christian festivals. St. Johns Tide occurs earlier on June 21st, along with Christmas and Easter in midwinter and spring respectively.)

The days have been hot - into the mid 70s and sometimes 80s, along with cool evenings and dew on the grass. There were a few frosts in the high mountain peaks, but none at all in the Champlain Valley where I live. Will this spell trouble for the "leaf peepers" - the touristas who flock to Vermont to take pictures of the colorful maples? How much color will there be in the leaves this year, which has been touted as the hottest year on record?

Because of the weather, even apples did not get a full blush to their skins. Folks may notice more green patches on McIntosh and other apples like Empire and Cortland.

FYI - Typically, the ever-shorter daylight hours conspire with cooler temperatures to doom chlorophyll in our tree leaves and expose the underlying yellow/orange pigments. Technically, when the chlorophyll in the leaves breaks down from the cold, the green color disappears and the yellow, red and orange colors become visible. This is what gives the leaves their fall splendor; without those cool temperatures, the usual brilliance of Autumn is much subdued.

Other organisms bask in the season's extended warmth. Cyanobacteria flourished in September in the warmer-than-normal surface waters in the region's lakes and ponds. Often called blue-green algae, these organisms, like leaves, photosynthesize their sugars. Like maple leaves, cyanobacteria are visually striking as they wither, although the latter's remnants are slimy, sometimes stinky, and occasionally toxic. Swimmers and dog-owners are cautioned against contact with bacterial concentrations - commonly referred to as "algae blooms."

Canoe Can You? Part I

I canoed on Goshen Pond on my birthday in late September some 5 miles from Robert Frost's cabin in Ripton, Vermont - with my friend, Richard, few years ago. With the warm weather, I was surprised that the red maples shone bright in all their glory at the far end of the pond where a lively mountain brook heads down from the high peaks. The brilliant colors were due to the moisture, dew and coolness of the water.

By the way, Richard came up with the word, "kvetchtables." Kvetch is the Yiddish word for a complaint. It's one way to deal with all the "tsuris," another Yiddish word meaning trouble, in the garden patch or anywhere in the world for that matter. The "Chuckster' just shook his head again and said, "Enough already."

Back home, I transplanted a Jackmanii clematis vine in my front yard. Jackmanii has rich purple flowers that appear in profusion in early summer. This fine garden addition is best grown on a trellis. Jackmanii is possibly the best-known clematis in the world!

I moved a non-invasive climbing hydrangea to a sunnier spot in my garden. I transplanted an aggressive trumpet vine from my home garden to my community garden because it wanted to take over the wood siding on my house. It dug into the wood with its claws and wouldn't let go. When it comes to this pernicious vine with orange flowers, I don't share the Spanish words, "Me Casa, Su Casa." The "Chuckster" actually agreed with me on this one as he knows how much I've fretted over its rampant growth and destruction.

In late October of 2015, my snapdragons flowered along with snippets of dandelions and forsythia. I've heard from other gardeners that a few daffodils and crocuses are blooming as well. I'm worried about the swelling of the buds in the fruit trees. We're messing with nature.

In my cold frames I'm still growing lettuce, arugula, chard, and Chinese mustard greens, rebuilding garden beds, adding compost, and turning in annual rye and oats as cover crops. Normally it would be too late for these activities as the ground would have begun to be freeze, but again, there is no "normal" anymore.

Don't get me wrong: I mean it's great to be able to extend the growing season and play and dig in my garden longer than usual, but I'm worried about what's happening beyond my garden: the warming of the planet is responsible for the loss of insects, birds and animals worldwide, not to mention wildfires, droughts, floods, and rising seas from melting polar caps.

>EARLY FALL
>wind and rain pick up
>sky darkens
>the cold will come
>I recall
>and walk my famous dog Hercules
>his step picks up after a hot, humid summer
>colored maple leaves on green grass
>lie flat on earth
>brightening the morn
>along with red sumac and Virginia creeper and yellow locust
>a bellwether beckoning others to follow
>looking across Lake Champlain
>to the mountains of the Adirondacks
>dense morning mist hovers above the water
>valley fog descends
>over the land
>like a grey-white blanket
>
>*-The Woodchuck Gardener*

Fall Persists
Now is the time to bring in my rosemary plants. I re-pot them and the smells enliven my home. Herbs like parsley, chives, thyme, oregano, and sage can handle some cold, though I find it best to mulch around them. Soon, I'll harvest and dry these herbs for garnishes, soups, and casseroles. Earlier, I dried comfrey, mint, raspberry leaves, and lemon balm for my famous, Bonzo Punch tea.

Canoe - Can You? Part II
What could be lovelier than canoeing on a pond while watching the reflections of sugar and red maples in the water, and listening to the haunting sounds of loons and loud honkers (Canadian Geese) as they swoop down to the water? For many years on my birthday, I've gone to Green River Reservoir in Morrisville for my annual overnight camping trip with my dog and perhaps a companion, along with the loons and honkers of course. One year it got down to 15 degrees Fahrenheit, but I had my canine companion, Kaily Girl, a Chesapeake Bay Retriever, to keep me warm. The "Chuckster" just said, "please don't mention your birthday again."

Of course, you can decorate your yard with scarecrows, cornstalks, and pumpkins, but to me the greatest gift comes with the changing hues of the maples and later on, the yellows and golds of tamaracks alongside the greens of the conifers. And who can forget the deep purples of wild New England asters along the side of roads and in the fields. They are more colorful than Michaelmass daisies, which have a lighter purple/white hue. Or how about the sedums like Autumn Joy in gorgeous pink, a staple in many fall gardens.

Fall northern landscapes may be best known for the brilliant displays of maples, but many other trees like ash in golden brown color the hills as well. They all lift my spirits. In September, sumac changes from green to a strong red. Cloudy, rainy days reflect muted colors and clear days showcase reds, oranges, and purples. Sometimes, I prefer a gray sky as a backdrop for viewing color versus a bright blue sky. It all depends on my mood. Since I tend towards a melancholy temperament, I love the not-so-bright days now and then.

> Autumn is the mellower season, and what we lose in flowers we more than gain in fruits.
>
> -*Samuel Butler 1835-1902*

ALL PERENNIALS IN MANY HUES

Over the years, I've noticed the many colors of fall perennials. Here are my favorites:

Yellow and Gold - Hostas turn shades of yellow and ferns turn gold. Other yellow and gold perennials include daylilies, coneflowers (Echinacea) and Siberian Iris. Ornamental grasses provide yellow, gold and blue. Some examples are moor grass, Japanese silver grass, bluish switchgrass, and blue fescue.

Goldenrod is another possibility. There are many cultivars, including 'Golden Fleece,' which grows to a low, uniform height of two feet. Contrary to popular belief, goldenrod doesn't cause allergies. Rather it's the ragweed, which is out at the same time.

Solomon's Seal - Although the dangling, tubular white flowers and black seed pods that follow are charming, it's the arching stems and foliage that make Solomon's Seal (Polygonatum) such a favorite in shade gardens and woodland settings. Once established, Polygonatum slowly spreads out and creates a nodding blanket of foliage that turns a golden yellow in autumn.

Red and Burgundy - Red fall plants include geraniums, euphorbias (spurge), and peonies. Ornamental grasses have really come into their own of late, including Japanese blood grass (Zone 5) and some of the switchgrasses. Flame grass turns to tones of red and burgundy in the sun, softer pinks and peach colors in part shade.

Purple - Purple leaves stand in contrast to plants with red and yellow colors. These include sedums, coral bells, and black snakeroot. New England asters are later-blooming perennial choices. My favorites are the purple ones plus they are hardy. How 'bout New York asters (one to two feet high) and the taller New England asters. Flowering kale and cabbage make nice fall plants to replace dying annual flowers. Both will turn into beautiful purple colors with the cold and will last until covered with snow.

Silver - Perennials with silvery leaves include artemisia and lamb's ears.

Multi-colors - How could one not include the many colors of chrysanthemums? Snapdragons hold out for one last breath of colors in late fall. They are my favorite fall biennials. Sometimes, they drop seeds and reappear in summer, as they've done in my front yard garden for years.

If your soil is moist in a sunny spot, try out Helenium, Helen's Flower cultivars, with fall colors of reds, oranges, and yellows. Helen's Flower is a genus that is believed to be named by Linnaeus for Helen of Troy. As the legend goes, the flowers grew up from the ground wherever her tears fell. Another common name, sneezeweed, is based on the story that the flowers and dried leaves were used in making snuff. When it was inhaled, it caused sneezing. Other names for Helen's Flower are bitterweed, autumn sneezeweed, and false sunflower. Producing an abundance of blooms, Helen's Flower is a perennial plant that belongs to the daisy or aster family (Asteraceae).

Vermont/US Climate Report 2020 & 2021

2020 was very hot and dry with little rain, even hotter than 2019. Back then, 2020 was listed as the hottest year on record. This dubious distinction resulted in changes in rainfall and in more extreme weather. The East is wetter and the West dryer. Almost every place in the U.S. has warmed, including Vermont. Out west, reports of record-breaking heat has led to young birds fleeing their nests, dying or injuring themselves, and terrible wildfires destroying habitat.

In 2020, I found it hard to germinate carrot, parsnip and beet seeds in my community garden due to dry soil. The flowering crabapple tree in my front yard had fewer pinkish red blossoms. It usually develops scab on its leaves which causes them to drop to the ground early. This is because it's an older crab and doesn't have resistance to scab like the newer varieties. I had planned to spray sulphur for fungus on the leaves, but this year, it was drier, and the leaves looked healthier than previous years because we didn't have cool wet weather in spring and early summer, which is ideal for scab. Sulphur is an organic spray used to control scab.

2020 in Vermont featured a wacko late fall and early winter with lots of swinging temperatures. One day it snows and rains and then drops down to low temperatures. And then, it's fifty-five degrees and then back to the 30s. With drought, temperature swings and a little rain, perennials are showing a little wear and tear, but no worries as their roots are growing quickly. And roots are truly the most important part of your perennials!

It used to be that if a perennial was planted in the wrong hardiness zone it wouldn't survive. Our Vermont winters have become unpredictable with less snow cover, freezing and thawing cycles and dry winter winds. Add to this our higher winter temperatures. Even the Lenten rose (Hellebore) began to bloom in the display garden at Full Circle Garden in Vermont in November when it should be blooming in late March. This is because the rose sensed it had gone through winter dormancy and then warm spring temps arrived.

In 2021, it was hotter in Vermont than 2020. Hercules was panting endlessly, and I was endlessly changing my t-shirts. The summer began with a prolonged drought and then we had torrential rains. Hurricane Ida caused devastating flooding from Louisiana to New York.

California and the Pacific Northwest have been on fire all summer.

The Golden state recorded the driest year in a century. It was a time of both extreme heat and extreme drought. California reported its driest water year in terms of precipitation and experts fear the coming 12 months could be even worse. A total of only 11.87 inches of rain and snow fell in California in the 2021 water year, according to the Western Regional Climate Center. The last time the state reported so little rain and snowfall was in 1924.

WHAT ARE REASONS NOT TO CLEAN UP YOUR GARDEN?

In times past it was conventional wisdom to prepare your garden for winter by cutting everything down to the ground. That may be neat and tidy (and a whole lot of work) but there are now compelling reasons to leave parts of your garden intact through winter.

In other words, fall meant that every leaf was raked and burned, every shred of dead plant material cut down and hauled off to make your yard clean and devoid of life... ready for winter! But "the times, they are a' changin." While many still approach the garden as they would a room in the house - with an annual scrubbing - the job of "preparing the garden for winter" is not what it used to be.

So if you haven't cut your perennial garden back, it's a good thing! In the past, when snow cover was a given, gardeners were taught to cut everything back for neatness. The benefits to not cutting perennials back are not just for the plants but for our pollinators as well. Our local pollinator bees need have a place to spend the winter, and birds have more grass seed. The "Chuckster" just said, "You made your point. Enough already."

More and more, with native-plant gardeners leading the charge, the yard and garden are seen as havens that support a host of pollinators and other inhabitants. Our actions in the garden can either enhance or inhibit their lives.

You may want to remove your spent annuals from the garden as well plants showing signs of disease. But for the rest - put the tools away and enjoy the sunny days of fall.

Habitat for Pollinators - Many vital pollinators such as bees, butterflies and ladybugs will find a place to burrow in the remnants of a summer garden. Hollow plant stems, a light layer of fallen leaves and tree bark can all offer shelter to these beneficial critters.

Food and shelter for the birds and bees - The seed heads of many perennials including rudbeckia, echinacea, and asters will feed your local birds throughout the year. Sarah Salatino of Full Circle Garden in Vermont told me that she leaves the seed heads of rudbeckias, echinaceas and asters for food for the birds in the winter and not cut back the foliage until spring.

A yard scraped clean and bare gives the birds good reason to fly on by. A highly textured landscape signals a diversity of plants and better opportunity for food. The spent plants also offer a screen and a safe place for birds to forage. In spring, the extra plant material means that there are more insects, and insects are a critical food source for nesting birds as they feed their young. All bird babies need these insects. The seed heads offer food in the fall and winter. Your native plants provide the right material, the right environment, and the right nutrition, just when the birds need them.

Bees, Butterflies & Predatory Insects - Native bees hibernate in a variety of ways in your garden. They may overwinter under bark, in a rock crevice or in a burrow. Queen bumble bees create underground burrows. In spring they wake up and start constructing a new nest, and never return to the old ones. Piling heavy mulch on the ground in fall inhibits the queen from building her nest. Leafcutter bees, mason bees and yellow-faced bees will nest in the hollow stems of many native plants. Leave your native plants standing over winter, and in the spring instead of cutting them all the way down, leave 12 - 15 inches of stalk stubble standing for pollinator nesting sites.

FYI - Interesting factoid! Bees eat "meat"! Soil microbes would be the equivalent to a steak for a bee. Microbes are a big portion of their diet for the needed protein levels! This knowledge needs to become more mainstream.

*Despite all the current lawsuits glyphosate is still being used quite heavily. There are hundreds of studies done on the adverse effects of glyphosate (aka Roundup) on the soil biota.

FYI - Soil Biodiversity is especially important to plants and animals. However, less attention is being paid to the biodiversity beneath our feet. Soil biodiversity drives many processes that produce food or purify soil and water. Soil scientists are raising awareness of the importance of soil biodiversity.

Butterflies - Declining butterfly populations are one of the best reasons not to clean up the garden. Swallowtails, the cabbage whites, and the Sulphur's form chrysalis in late summer and use dead plants' leaves and stalks for hibernation. Mourning Cloak and Eastern Comma butterflies hibernate as adults in the plant litter. The Red-Spotted Purple, Baltimore Checkerspot, and Meadow Fritillary spend the winter as caterpillars rolled into a fallen leaf, or inside the seed pod of a host plant. When we cut down and clean up our gardens, we remove overwintering sites for butterflies.

Predatory Insects - Native ladybugs (not the invasive Asian ones) enter hibernation soon after the temperatures drop and spend the winter under a pile of leaves or hidden under a rock. Native ladybugs are known pest-eaters, each one consuming dozens of soft-bodied pest insects and insect eggs every day. Other predatory insects including assassin bugs, lacewings, damsel bugs, and ground beetles spend the winter hibernating as either adults, eggs, or pupae. Predatory insects help control and maintain a balanced insect population. If you have a vegetable garden, predatory insects are your best friends.

Toads and Salamanders - It's all making sense now. Where do critters overwinter? In spent plant material or in the ground, protected by the plants. What do they eat when they emerge?

Insects and Protection - The spent plants, and the snow they gather, add a layer of insulation that protects the plant root from harsh winter winds and sub-zero temps. The plants offer protection for themselves, the soil, the critters that harbor there, and the birds that feed there. Wait until spring to cut down the plants and lay them on the ground as a mulch layer. For supporting life in the garden, and protecting the health of soil, your available leaves and spent plant material beat wood mulch or bark chips. No more store-bought mulch!

Free Plants - When plants self-seed you have several options. You can let 'em grow - some plants have shorter lives than others, and the self-seeded plants will replace the old ones. You can remove some seedlings, and leave others to grow and fill in as needed. Or you can move the new seedlings to a different location entirely or share them with friends.

Beauty - There is so much beauty to experience in a winter garden. Seedheads, leaves and stems in brown, black and gold. Snow resting on dried seed pods and berries clinging to bare branches. Frosted leaves and glittering grasses. Beauty makes us fall in love with our world, and that's what gardening is all about.

There are hundreds of varieties that remain upright while dormant that will add structure and winter interest, often holding dried flowerheads and stems that will create a dramatic flair when dusted with snow.

So if you want to support life in your garden, leave your natives standing. Instead of pruning, raking, and scrubbing it clean, think about the critters living there that depend upon those plants! Next spring, when we all emerge from our winter hibernations, we can greet the garden with even more anticipation for the life that is harbored there. Clean the house, but nurture the garden.

Jessica Walliser provided some material in - *"Not Cleaning Up Your Garden."* Walliser wrote *The Savvy Gardener.*

ON THE OTHER HAND, & THERE'S ALWAYS ANOTHER HAND!

- THERE ARE REASONS TO "CLEAN UP" PARTS OF YOUR GARDEN. LIFE PRESENTS US WITH THIS PARADOX. SO WITH THAT BEING SAID, "HERE IS THE OTHER HAND."

Fall is the good time to get a jump on spring. Without proper precautions - cold temperatures, drying winds and snow cover can all cause problems in the landscape. Plants can get wind-burned and tree branches can be broken from snow load.

Cleanup - A moderate fall cleanup helps eliminate places for insect pests to overwinter. Yard waste help diseases and insects survive the cold weather, removing some yard debris means fewer pest problems next spring. Just don't be anal-retentive. "Hmm! I'm confused," said the "Chuckster." "This stuff is complicated."

While some of the plants you cut back in fall can go in your compost pile, you'll want to avoid putting any plants with diseased foliage in the pile. That's because most compost piles don't heat up enough to kill diseases, and you don't want to risk spreading them back into your garden next year. Gather as much of the diseased foliage as you can, bag and seal it, then dispose of it in the trash. Fungi can remain in the diseased foliage and recur the following spring if not removed.

Perennials - Once your perennials have gone dormant, it's a good idea to cut down some of their foliage but not all the way to the ground. This is especially important around plants like hostas that have received slug damage during the growing season. Slugs lay their eggs in the dormant foliage, and removing it in fall will cut down on slug issues the following year. In most cases,

DO NOT cut these perennials back in fall: Evergreen or semi-evergreen perennials like pinks (Dianthus), coral bells (Heuchera), creeping phlox (Phlox subulata) and bugleweed (Ajuga). Don't cut back perennials with woody stems like rose mallow (Hibiscus), Russian sage, lavender, and butterfly bush.

Others include perennials with winter interest like false indigo (Baptisia), coneflowers (Echinacea), Prairie Winds ornamental grasses, Rock 'n Grow autumn stonecrop (Sedum), ornamental onion (Allium) and Lenten roses (Helleborus). Little pruning is necessary other than old flowers.

Weeds - One final weeding done late in the season can help eliminate hundreds of overwintering seeds that will just be waiting to sprout in spring.

Chelone - Full Circle Gardens

THE FALL BLOOMERS

We begin the next glorious season of flowers. As the leaves start to change colors, the temperature drops, and the daylight shortens. The pollinators, birds and plants sense the change.

Remarkably, there are flowers that are yet to bloom! We have many late season perennials for you to help feed pollinators going into hibernation, or migrating birds. Coreopsis tripteris will be blooming through October for butterflies. Chelone flowers require bees to vibrate off their pollen with loud buzzing. Grass florets and echinacea seed heads feed birds.

New England asters, non-invasive goldenrod, veronica, hardy ageratum and rudbeckia all provide late season food through October into November to a wide variety of pollinators.

But isn't it getting to be too late to plant perennials? Not at all! In fact this is the best time to plant them. Like all organisms, perennials have a balanced amount of energy to put into growing vegetation in the spring, budding flowers, making seed and preparing for winter dormancy. While folks tend to plant perennials when they are flowering, it takes a while for the roots to set in because perennial energy is taken by flowering. Right now, perennials are putting all their energy into root growth to store food for winter dormancy and spring bud break.

See below on How to Care for Herbaceous Perennials.

FALL GARDEN CHORES

Soil Tests - Test your soil in fall before the ground freezes, especially if you're planning a new garden. The test indicates the amendments you need to add to your soil to ensure healthier plants in spring.

I add compost every fall and seed down winter rye and oats as green manure crops in late summer.

For more info on Cover Crops, go to My Woodchuck Garden Website.

Mulch - Every summer, I scrounge around for hay mulch and fresh grass clippings. Saving mulch for the next growing season gives you a jump on next spring's landscape chores. For the past three years, I found a stash of mulch in an open undeveloped field which is cut once a year and not fertilized with chemicals. The "Chuckster" just said, "I don't want to say anything, but I bet he won't tell you where that field is located."

By the way, if your neighbor offers you grass clippings in the fall, find out if they've used any chemical weed killers or pesticides on their lawn. You wouldn't want to use these clippings for mulch as they are filled with poisons.

Wait until the ground begins to freeze and then use old mulch hay, evergreen branches, leaves, straw, or any other organic material that won't mat down or smother your overwintering plants. Prop mulch around the foliage of perennials so the plant leaves are protected

Mulch the base of the shrubs and trees with bark mulch or seasoned wood chips. Collect pine needles from under red and white pine trees. I use them for the oval path in my front yard. They are soft and brighten up my garden with their golden colors.

Compost - Fall is a good time to mix in any extra unshredded and shredded leaves to the compost pile. That's one good thing about living in the Green Mountains: there are plenty of leaves.

I turn my five compost piles -- four at my community garden and one behind my house -- once in summer. I wait two years to let the compost break down before spreading the compost on my garden.

Compost or what I call "black gold" is the top contender in the organic gardening world. Everyone loves to make compost, including my nearby gardener, Fred Schmidt, at the Tommy Thompson Community Garden. He mixes leaves with soil and water in large plastic bags at the end of the growing season and come spring it's ready to spread.

Compost helps sandy soil retain water, helps clay soil drain better, makes nutrients more available to plants, and supports soil microbial activity that defends your plants against disease.

Starting a compost pile is as easy as following a cooking recipe. Just get the right ingredients together, mix them well, and let it cook. In a matter of months, you'll have finished "black gold" to mix into the soil of your flower, herb, and vegetable gardens.

Compost is decomposed or well-rotted organic material. It can be made from a variety of organic materials, such as vegetable waste, leaves, grass clippings and animal manures. You can create brown and green layers. The brown materials include leaves, old grass clippings, shredded paper, peat moss, hay, and straw. The green materials include fresh grass clippings, vegetable kitchen wastes including coffee grounds and egg shells, and animal manures. The brown layers are high in carbon -and the green layers are high in nitrogen. Add water between each layer and then let it cook until done.

If you are low on green materials, you also can use high-nitrogen organic fertilizers, such as blood meal and cottonseed meal. I spread wood ashes from the woodstove into my backyard compost pile plus on my icy walkway so as not to fly high in the sky. I also use with my urine mixed with water at a 5 to 1 ratio - five gallons of water to one gallon of urine. That's right, urine.

Avoid using meat and bones, large amounts of wood chips or sawdust, pet manure, herbicide-treated grass clippings, and diseased plants. For more information on compost and building a pile, see my first book, The Woodchuck's Guide to Gardening.

In the fall, I spread compost on the garden beds and work it into the soil. I spray the Biodynamic (BD) cow manure preparation (500) over the entire garden, including the compost piles. This homeopathic dilution helps to stimulate the microbiological activity in the soil and compost and also to sequester carbon.

See a further explanation of Biodynamics in my first book, The Woodchuck's Guide to Gardening.

Antibiotics in the Soil - Streptomyces is a common soil and compost bacteria that grows in threads like a fungus! Over 500 species of Streptomyces bacteria have been described. They produce the majority of antibiotics used medicinally. Streptomyces is the largest antibiotic-producing genus, producing antibacterial, antifungal, and antiparasitic drugs, plus a wide range of other bioactive compounds, such as immune-suppressants. Its shape resembles filamentous fungi.

Leaves - I rake up lots of leaves shredded by a lawn mower and loosely place them in perennial beds to protect the plants. These leaves act as a mulch, conserve moisture and provide insulation against the cold. Fallen leaves provide cover for overwintering beneficial insects, such as lacewings and ground beetles.

It's good to shred tree leaves and leave some of them on your lawn. The other shredded leaves can be placed on your perennial beds to protect your plants as just mentioned. They will conserve moisture and provide insulation against the cold. Fall mulching also gives you a jump on next spring's landscape chores.

I pick-up large paper bags of leaves along the streets. Run your mower back and forth over the leaves to crush and shred them. Shredding the leaves prevents them from packing together in layers, and allows for better air circulation and water to flow through.

Autumn leaves are like a big load of free organic fertilizer. If you pile up the leaves - in a couple of years, they will break down into low-nutrient compost. While you're at it, why not build a big pile of leaves and let the neighbor kids jump on top. Or use them to make a scarecrow by stuffing leaves into my old clothes, of which I have many? Some of my friends including the "Chuckster" would like me to get rid of them, the clothes that is. He suggested I set up a scarecrow with my old clothes filled with leaves in an old rocking chair in my front yard.

I pile shredded leaves in the paths between my raspberry rows. They'll provide a dry walking surface, and next spring you can rake the decomposed leaves into compost piles or just leave them there. Why not add leaves to indoor worm composting bins. They introduce key decomposers, such as springtails and microbes, to the worm bin ecosystem that help the worms do their jobs better.

Leaving the leaves provides habitat for animals as they search for a place to hibernate. Frogs, snakes, salamanders, and many other animals rely on fallen leaves to provide cover in the winter months. Many caterpillars and pupae of moth and butterfly species overwinter in fallen leaves as well. Insects roll up in leaves on the ground, emerging in the spring as perennial plants begin to break dormancy.

Leaf litter is also a vital food source for decomposers, like millipedes, snails, and worms, which not only help create soil, but are also important food for songbirds. Leaf litter is a great natural fertilizer, helping bring nutrients back to the soil as it breaks down.

Many cavity-nesting bees make their homes in standing stems of native plants. Solitary bees will burrow through the pithy stems of wild hydrangea, shining blue star, and many other native plant stems to overwinter.

The Grow Native! program offers a "Leave the Leaves" garden sign, which homeowners can install to help inform neighbors about the purpose of leaving leaves and stems in yards and gardens through the fall and winter. A "Leave the Leaves" sign is available at the MPF/Grow Native! online gift shop.

Native Plants - Autumn is a great time to plant native plants. As cooler weather approaches, perennial native plants begin to go dormant and cease above-ground growth. Planting in fall gives roots time to set in and develop a foundation before the next season. In the spring, perennial plants have a head-start as they emerge naturally with a strong base beneath them.

Lawns - Early fall is the best time to winterize your lawn. Rake the thatch and matted grass to provide room for new growth and to allow air and moisture to reach the earth. Aerate means to poke a hole in the ground to allow air and water to penetrate the surface of the soil. I use a fork with tines.

In early fall on bare spots, you'll need to scratch the soil with a rake, seed it down, add compost and soil, and tamp the newly reseeded area. Spread a light mulch over the area. Then water for a few days until the seed has germinated.

Apply compost to lawns in fall. Fall fertilization with compost helps lawns recover from the stresses of a hot summer by encouraging deep roots and denser growth which will compete better with weeds. Add horticultural lime or wood ashes to make the soil more alkaline if indicated by soil testing or if the grass is not growing well. The freeze-thaw cycle of winter helps breakdown the lime pellets so it can work into the soil more fully.

You can cut the grass using a lawn mower one last time in October. Make sure and set your mower at its highest setting. My front yard is so small that I only use an electric weed whacker when necessary. I know folks that are taking out their lawns and putting in perennial beds ad infinitum plus fruit trees, berries, and shrubs.

The wastefulness of lawns populated with alien grasses demand high-nitrogen fertilizers, broad-leaf herbicides, and pollution-belching mowers. If you are going to replace the lawn with ornamental grasses, try little bluestem, switchgrass, and prairie grasses. Let them mature as they support bees and other wildlife in our lawns.

Containers - Tender perennials and tropical plants in containers can be moved indoors. If you're bringing containers indoors or burying them, be sure to protect them. Wrap terra cotta pots with layers of bubble wrap and burlap. Cover with plastic wrap to prevent further absorption of moisture. Turn empty pots over to keep water from collecting and freezing, and cover those that are too large to flip or relocate.

Protect your container plants outside: Huddle them together, placing the most cold-sensitive ones in the center. Locate the grouping in a sheltered area against a building or structure. Provide protection from wind with a windbreak or screen. Cover with leaves.

Other Chores - Clear water from hose connections. Shut off the water at the source, then run the faucet to drain all water from the pipe. Drain outside water faucets, spigots, hoses, and lines and clean and store tools in garden shed. Sharpen metal blades and clean them off with oil to prevent rust and apply boiled linseed oil to your wooden tool handles.

Relocate half-hardy perennials to a basement or garage where they will go dormant. Plants that need a chilling period in order to bloom or set fruit should be left outside and protected and then brought inside.

THE RELATIONSHIP BETWEEN PHOTOSYNTHESIS, MYCELIUM & CARBON

During photosynthesis, plants use solar energy to extract carbon molecules from carbon dioxide in the air to make carbohydrates or sugars. Ten to twenty percent of the carbon-based sugars are later exuded from the plant's roots, feeding bacterial and fungal mycelium in the nearby soil. In turn, these microorganisms symbiotically transform soil minerals into nutrients that feed plants and help them fight disease, increase drought resistance and trap carbon in the soil for decades, even centuries.

Fungi help trees and other plants to grow. Because the fine threads that make fungal mycelium can spread over long distances, fungi can capture water and nutrients from far away and bring them back along the fine threads and close to plant roots. The roots take up the water and nutrients that the fungi offer and in return the trees and other plants give the fungi sugars that they made during photosynthesis.

Mycelium is a vast underground network of fungus that holds soil together. It forms a network under the soil that captures the carbon. Certain types of mycelium form symbiotic relationships with plants extending the plants' root system a thousand-fold and receiving up to 70 percent of the plant's carbon in exchange.

THE CARBON CYCLE

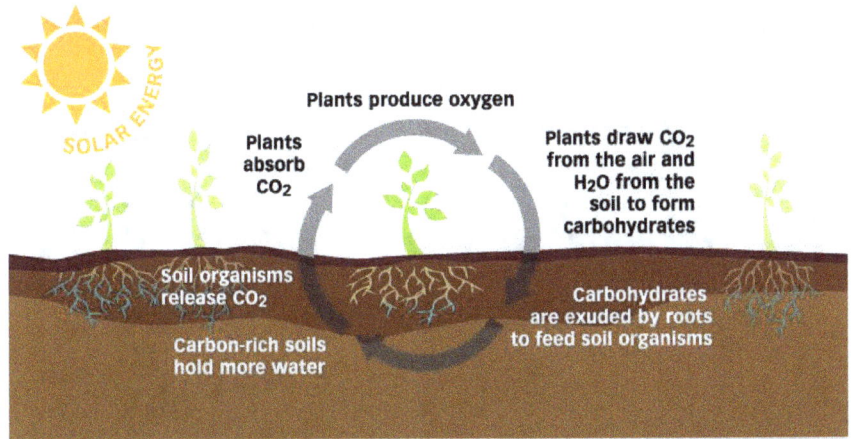

Research has shown that mycorrhizal fungi hold 50 to 70 percent of the total carbon stored in leaf litter and soil on forested islands in Sweden. Scientists claim it could absorb carbon dioxide to slow climate change if we used regenerative/organic farming practices. Synthetic pesticides and herbicides destroy the mycorrhizal relationship.

Mycologist Paul Stamets says, mycelium offers the best solutions for carbon sequestration, for preserving biodiversity, for reducing pollutants, and for offering us many of the medicines that we need today, both human and ecological.'

He refers to mycelium as 'nature's internet' because if part of a fungus is harmed, the rest of the network can respond quickly to disruptions. For example, if one branch of the thread-like mycelium is broken, the organism finds alternative pathways to carry nutrients and information, much like how packets of data can be transported across the internet.

Stamets goes as far as saying that complex chemistry of mycelium has been shown to produce antibiotics powerful enough to prevent many diseases and stop pandemics.

> "The soil is the great connector of lives, the source and destination of all. It is the healer and restorer and resurrector, by which disease passes into health, age into youth, death into life. Without proper care for it we can have no community, because without proper care for it we can have no life."
>
> ~Wendell Berry

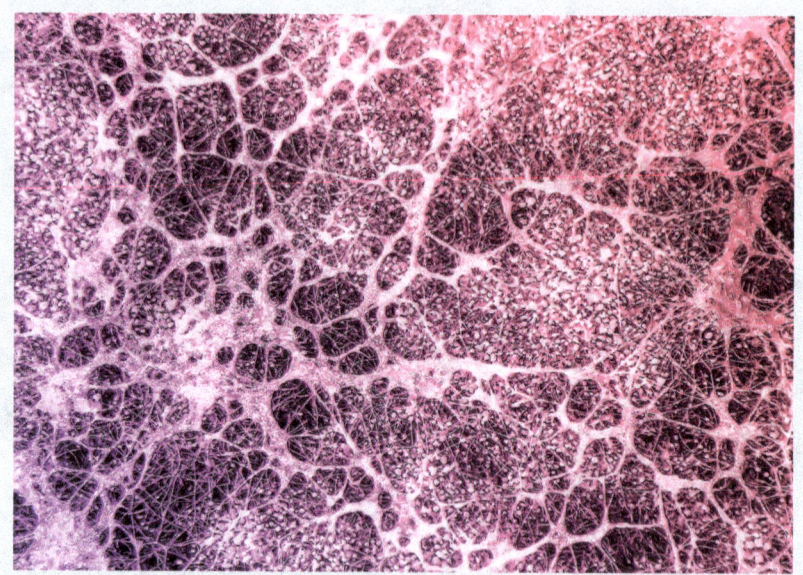

MYCELIUM & THE MOTHER TREE

"Forests are communities, a rich mixture of organisms engaged in relationships and interactions with each other, built around the living architecture of trees. These communities parallel healthy human communities in many ways, not because they are simple and uniform but because they are messy, dynamic, diverse and interconnected, engaged in a complex process of renewal and change that will never be completed." Ethan Tapper, the Chittenden County forester

Trees are part of a large, interconnected community interacting with their own and other species, including forming kin relationships with their genetic relatives. In mapping the mycorrhizal (fungal) network, research has shown that the biggest and oldest trees are the most connected nodes in the forest. These highly-connected hub trees, also known as Mother Trees, share their excess carbon and nitrogen through the fungal network with the understory seedlings, which can increase seedling survival. The carbon moves along a source-sink gradient, where the larger tree is the source of carbon, and the seedling is the sink.

These Mother Trees in this way act as central hubs, communicating with the young seedlings around them. In a single forest, a Mother Tree can be connected to hundreds of other trees. These connections have been known for a long time by Aboriginal peoples.

Trees can also form complex relationships with other species, similar to partnerships or friendships. Birch can compete with young neighboring conifer trees for light and reduce their growth. However, in contrast to conventional thought, birch can also help Douglas-fir by sharing carbon through mycorrhizal networks. The more birch shades Douglas-fir, the more carbon it delivers through the mycorrhizal networks. As well, cutting out birch trees stimulates infection of neighboring Douglas-fir with root disease. The trees also trade resources seasonally - Douglas-firs shares excess sugars with the leafless birches in the spring and fall, and in return the birches provide the Douglas-firs with sugars in the summer.

Ethan Tapper went onto say, "the forests of Vermont are infused with the legacies of the past. Nearly all of them were cleared in the 1800s, while about 75 percent of Vermont is now forested. Most of our forests are still in recovery, dramatically shaped by this clearing. Today, Vermont's forests are generally much younger, less diverse and less complex than the forests that covered our state just a few centuries ago. Being responsible stewards of our forests forces us to take the long view, as the life span of a single generation of trees may exceed ours by centuries."

When I take my dog Hercules for a walk in Red Rocks Park near my home, we pass the Mother Day. As I look up at this tall and wide white pine, I bow my head in reverence. Some call it the "Wolf Tree."

See more on Mycelium and Trees in My Woodchuck Garden Website #8

ACORNS ABOUND
acorns went wild in 2019
dropping by the millions
like a war movie
on metal roofs and cars
called by botanists a "mast year"
happens every two to five years
even the squirrels were overwhelmed
I slipped and fell on a few
but not on my head
-*The Woodchuck Gardener*

The Red Burning Bush 2015

This is one of the fieriest fall plants I've ever seen. When I visited my good friend, Richard Foye, in South Newfane, Vermont, on October 22, 2015, the invasive burning bushes were taking over his yard. Richard was none too happy about their wanderings as he was constantly cutting them down. He said it was those dammed birds that loved to eat the seeds, and with their droppings, spread the flaming bush just as they do the sweet-smelling invasive honeysuckle.

The sound of the word, Euonymus, flows off my tongue. Euonymus alatus, known variously as winged spindle, winged euonymus, and yes, burning bush, is a species of flowering plant in the family Celastraceae, native to central and northern China, Japan, and Korea. It is often wider than it is tall. The stems are notable for their four corky ridges or "wings". The word alatus (or alata, used formerly) is Latin for "winged", in reference to the winged branches.

Euonymus spreads into natural areas, invading and crowding out native plants close to woodlands and other landscapes. At one time, it was often used as a landscape plant. It was easily planted into hedges, or planted in masses. Left unpruned, it can reach 10 to 14 feet high and wide. Today, its importation and sale is prohibited in most New England states. Yet, I still see euonymus in many yards as single shrubs in Burlington they are so attractive.

People use the leaves and roots of burning bush to make medicines. It is used in traditional Chinese medicine for digestive tract disorders including cramps, stomach problems, and worms in the intestines. It is also used for urinary tract and genital tract disorders. Women take burning bush to start menstruation, as birth control, and to help force out the placenta after childbirth.

In England, this popular ornamental plant can be seen in gardens and parks due to its bright pink or orange fruit and attractive fall red color. The cultivar 'Compactus' has gained the Royal Horticultural Society's Award of Garden Merit.

Question - Why did God speak to Moses out of the burning bush?

Answer - The story of God speaking to Moses out of the burning bush is found in Exodus. Through this remarkable event, Moses encounters God and God reveals Himself. The burning bush is described in Exodus as the appearance of God in a form that is visible to man. The bush itself was most likely some kind of bramble or thorn bush, and the fire burning the bush was in the form of the angel of the Lord who appeared to Moses as flames of fire. Or so the story goes.

Euonymous Alternatives

There are several shrubs you can grow instead of burning bush. *Highbush blueberry is a good native alternative, not quite as tall but also with red fall color. This plant has edible berries for both people and wildlife. Even though it is self-pollinating, you may get more fruit from using at least two different cultivars. It can tolerate damp soils. Good choices for red fall color are the hardy 'Friendship', which reaches only 2 to 3 feet high and wide; 'Tophat,' which grows only 1 to 2 feet high and 2 to 3 feet wide (hardy to Zone 5); and the hardy 'Toro' (Zone 4), the biggest of the three at 4 to 6 feet high and wide.

*Fothergilla has species that can be used both for foundation plantings and for naturalistic settings, reaching 3 to 4 feet high, or 6 to 10 feet high, respectively. Their habit is dense and rounded. They have fall leaves mixed in colors of red, yellow, and orange for an attractive effect. Fothergilla is hardy in the warmer parts of the north (Zones 5 and warmer).

*Redvein Enkianthus has good red fall color on plants that can get 6 to 12 feet high, and a bit less wide, giving it an upright appearance. The yellowish-pink, hanging bell-shaped flowers have red veins and are attractive in spring. The bright young red stems during the summer usually persist through the winter, giving it year-round appeal. Enkianthus is hardy to Zone 5.

Enkianthus and Fothergilla prefer acidic soils (lower pH of 5.5-6.5) in comparison to highbush blueberries, which prefer quite acidic soils (pH 4.0 to 5.0).

*Red Chokeberry (Aronia) is a slow grower, eventually reaching from 4 to 10 feet high, depending on the cultivar and half that wide. They don't grow that tall in Vermont. The berries are delicious and healthy. This native plant has an open and upright habit in landscapes, but will produce suckers that will eventually form a broad mound. I planted one in my community garden 2018 and now have dark nutritious berries to munch on.

Another alternative to the burning bush is *American Cranberrybush. 'Alfredo' and 'Redwing.' The more brightly fall-colored cultivars of this native species can be used where the viburnum leaf beetle isn't a problem. The beetle does not cause the damage it once did.

*Winterberry (Ilex verticillata) is a deciduous type of holly that can grow wild. The shrub adapts easily to the home landscape. Our native Vermont winterberry provides brilliant red fall color from its berries on female plants. Keep in mind if planting these that you'll need a male plant or two for pollination. This species of winterberry is often seen in natural areas in wet, boggy soils, although this plant tolerates dry soils as well, where it will grow less quickly. It can reach heights and widths of 4 to 8 feet, depending on the variety. The attractive bright red fruit of winterberry is eaten by small mammals and more than 48 species of birds.

OTHER COLORFUL FALL SHRUBS:
DOGWOOD, CORAL BARK WILLOW, ROSA RUGOSA,
VIBURNAMS, HYDRANGEA & WITCH HAZEL

*Dogwood - Some of the other brightest red colors in fall appear on year-old dogwood stems. Cut back the old stems in spring to encourage new stems to grow from the base. Overgrown dogwood shrubs can be renewed by pruning all the stems down to within a few inches of the base. I don't cut down the Red Osier dogwood in my community garden. I just do a little trimming.

*Coral bark willow, with its golden stems and red-orange twigs, rivals the red dogwood stems for winter color.

*Rosa Rugosa might just be the perfect rose as it doesn't have any special requirements. This pink and red rose with dark green foliage gives gardeners the pleasure of recurrent and fragrant blossoms in the fall, though not as prolific as in the summer. And you don't have to fiddle and diddle with them like the hybrid tea roses as they are very hardy. Rosa Rugoses have been providing a hedge in my front yard for many years. They turn into burnished red in October. In fall, I harvest the rose hips for a vitamin C tea and prune out the old canes.

*Viburnum and some of the hardy *hollies are quite spectacular with their showy fruit and leaves in summer.

*Hydrangea blossoms come in late summer and fall with white, blue and red flowers fading to pink. Even in October, the paniculata types, such as 'PeeGee,' have lovely blooms. They are easy to cut and dry the flowers.

You can try growing an indoor hydrangea called Hortensia, which has purple blooms, in a container. It won't survive too long unless kept in a cool space. It needs bright light, out of direct sunlight. You could try to grow it outside in a protected area but it's an iffy proposition as Hortensia is sensitive to cold.

*Witch hazel (Hamamelis virginiana) with its long-lasting fragrant yellow and orange blossoms stands out in all its glory if planted against a backdrop of evergreens or a red barn. The native species is the hardiest.

This very common shrub in our region is often overlooked. Witch hazel is one of the only woody plants to bloom late in fall. Its slightly aromatic flowers consists of 4 slender twisted yellow petals. It is usually the last shrub to bloom, giving it one of its alternate names of "Winterbloom."

Since there are few pollinators available so late in the season, the flowers can self-pollinate and are not picky as to which pollinators make use of them. Often, they are gnats or Noctuid moths. Each flower lasts quite a long-time giving potential pollinators ample time to find them.

Witch Hazel can reach 30' in height, but rarely does where I live. It is usually an understory shrub, twisted in form. The seeds take a year to mature, with last years seed pods often still unopened next to the following year's blossoms. It has an interesting seed dispersal mechanism, popping audibly and shooting the dark seeds up to 30' feet away. This has led to such additional common names as Snapping Alder or Snapping Hazel. Once the seeds have been expelled, they commonly take two years to then germinate.

Witch hazel has some interesting natural history and folklore associated with it. Although many magical qualities are associated with this plant, its common name of Witch Hazel is actually derived for different reasons. The "witch" part comes from older English word "wych" meaning "bendable" or "bending." It looked similar enough to the European Wych Elm that the name was applied to the New World plants. This was later corrupted to "witch" but possibly because so many magical properties were also attributed to it. Hmm!

For many years, an astringent was made from the leaves, stems, and bark of witch-hazel. Native Americans produced an extract by boiling the stems. It was used to treat swelling, inflammation, and tumors. Early Puritan settlers in New England adopted this remedy from the native peoples. I use a bottle of witch-hazel elixir for mosquito and bug bites during the summer.

HOW TO CARE FOR HERBACEOUS PERENNIALS, VINES & BULBS IN FALL

Fall is the right time to divide and plant perennials because most perennials have flowered, and seed production is over for the season. As plants prepare for winter dormancy, root production and food storage increase transplant success. Make sure and water the perennials and plant them in the soil with compost and mulch.

Dividing perennials is a great way to add plants to your garden in the fall. It will rejuvenate the plants to be stronger and produce more blooms the following year. The general rule is to "divide summer-blooming perennials in the fall and fall blooming perennials in the spring." Some examples in fall are peonies, irises, daylilies, and creeping phlox.

When dividing in fall, do it early enough (mid- September to mid-October) to allow new roots to develop in the soil before the colder weather of late fall sets in. Mulch newly planted perennials to reduce the amount of frost heaving. Frost heaves occur when the soil freezes and thaws, pushing the roots out of the ground.

In late September of 2013, I dug up irises in a friend's garden and transplanted them into a large bed, which I then covered with lots of mulch. I also transplanted some peonies by digging down through the roots with a square spade and moving the clumps to sunny locations.

Successive frosts will kill back the greenery in perennials in late November. So it's good to cut them back - leaving four to six inches of stubble.

Perennials benefit from cutting the top third in late October and November, while others don't want to be messed with. Here are a few examples:

Butterfly Bush - They are slow to break dormancy in spring. They do not need to be pruned except to control size. On the other hand, pruning will get them going earlier in the spring.

Snow in the Summer - This evergreen ground cover can be cut back severely after flowering has finished. This invasive has to be kept away from other perennials as its very invasive.

Russian Sage - Cut back plants to about a foot in the fall or leave standing for winter interest. Cut back to six inches in the spring before new growth emerges.

Pinks - They are slow to break dormancy. Remove the messy foliage from them along with the seed heads. Cut back six inches from ground in late winter. It's better to make a cut flat or parallel to the ground than to make a rounded c.

Lavender (Lavandula) - It's slow to break dormancy in spring. Prune established plants, removing up to one-third of foliage after flowering. However, don't prune back the old woody growth or it may set back the bush. Some hardy lavender varieties grow in Zone 4.

Lavender has a rich history. This Mediterranean herb has been found in Egyptian tombs and was used extensively by the ancient Greeks and Romans for a variety of purposes. It has healing properties, including use as a remedy for headaches, fatigue and tension. Its sweet scent was favored to clean the air of unpleasant odors and provide a perfume for clothing and bodies.

By the way, lavender is sensitive to the changes that take place in November and will rot if not covered. I cover lavender with evergreen boughs and place over each lavender plant for a little shade and protection from the wind. The boughs also keep the sensitive crown from the freeze-thaw temps. Lavender is hardy to Zone 4. Finding conifer boughs this time of year is easy.

Daylilies - It's been so hot and dry during the fall of 2016 that the colors of daylilies look washed out. Normally, the late bloomers have good color but not this year, because of the stress of multiple 90-degree days. Despite that, it's still time to begin removing the dried leaves and trimming back the daylilies to about 3 to 4 inches. It's critical to remove the spent flower scapes and pull out the debris at the base of the clumps. This reduces the possible carry-over of fungal issues or insects that hide from this year to the next.

You can also spray the plants with horticultural oil for fungi such as powdery mildew. The oil is also effective against many soft bodied pests including aphids, adelgids, spider mites, scale insects, greenhouse whiteflies, mealybugs, plant bugs, lace bugs and some caterpillars.

Late September and October is the time to begin trimming, dividing, and transplanting daylilies. Make sure to pull off the old, dried leaves. This will help to eliminate the places where insects or fungus can hide over the winter.

Trimming back the foliage makes digging and dividing the daylilies that much easier and they weigh less. The absence of leaves makes it easier to see how the plant has been growing and where to make your divisions once it is divided.

Hostas - I don't do anything with hostas. If you cut them back, you can spread a virus from one plant to the next. They will die back naturally over the winter, and in the spring, new vegetation will begin to come forth. Fall is the time to clean up around the plants.

Peonies - Mid-to-late August is when peonies set buds on their root stocks. In order to insure good blooms next season, make sure that your peonies are well watered. They need water below the surface so that the buds can grow.

Peonies like a good chill in the winter. In order to set their flower buds, peony roots should be planted relatively close to the soil surface - only about 2 inches deep. It may feel odd to leave roots so exposed, but peonies actually need this chilling to attain dormancy and set buds. Planting deeper will encourage lots of foliage but not much in the way of blooms.

Late August and September is a good time to plant peonies. They should be settled in place before the first hard frosts. Peonies generally don't like to be messed with, but if you must move an established plant, this is the time. Spring-planted peonies just don't do as well; they generally lag about a year behind those planted in the fall.

To move a peony, first dig a generous sized hole, about two feet deep and two feet across in well-drained soil, in a sunny spot. Dig down through the roots of the peony with a square spade and move the plant to a sunny location. Set the root so that the eyes face upward on top of the firmed soil, placing the eyes two inches below the soil surface. If the soil is heavy or sandy, add compost and one cup of bone meal to the soil in the hole before planting, and mix it in well. Backfill the surface after planting the peonies, water thoroughly and add a little mulch on top. Peonies take time to develop - usually a few years to establish themselves, and to bloom and grow. You don't need to fertilize every year.

Two Vines: Clematis - You can cut clematis to your desired height if it's taller than you'd like, but it's not necessary. Some varieties may not bloom as well the following year, but the plant will thrive in the long run. I don't cut mine back. Native Honeysuckle - It's best to cut honeysuckle back in fall to maintain desired height. The "Chuckster" just added, "Here he goes again with more tips. Will it ever End?"

Preparing Bulbs for Winter: Gladioli (Glads), Dahlias and Cannas

After a couple hard frosts in late fall, it's time for me to dig up my dahlias, gladiolus and cannas. Always dig them up rather than pulling them out. I dry them in the sun for a couple days before storing in paper bags in a cool dry spot in my damp cellar. I add a little dry germinating mix to the bags. Spray water on dahlias every couple of months, but not on the glads. I just started growing cannas.

I've been growing glads and dahlias for more than 20 years. I give many away as they keep growing and my stash gets larger. The glads and dahlias that grown in containers never reach the size of the bulbs I plant in the soil.

BULBS PLANTED IN FALL TOO LIVE FOR IN SPRING

The way I see it is that Vermont winters are too long, and our cool, wet spring season are also longer than we wish for, but what are you going to do. I've lived in Vermont since the fall of 1965, and this is where I'll head to heaven one day.

Spring bulbs are the bright spots, the color-rich buoys of hope in a sea of mud and snow squalls. 'Yellow Winter' aconite and bobbing white snowdrops yield to pastel crocuses. Then comes the show of narcissus and early tulips, reminding us it won't be long before we'll plant peas.

Let's not forget the dwarf irises. A native of Turkey and the Caucasian Mountains, dwarf Iris (Iris reticulata) is a four-inch-tall beauty (10 cm) with grass-like leaves and a violet-blue or purple flower with yellow markings that bursts into bloom in late winter to early spring. They create an effect reminiscent of butterflies hovering low to the ground.

Bulbs are planted in mid-to-late fall. October is the ideal time, with soil temperatures in the 40-to-50-degree range, but bulbs can be planted as long as the ground is not frozen, well into November. Of course, it all depends on the weather as it's much warmer than when I was a young hippie in the 1970s.

While it may seem odd to plant bulbs in fall, the reason is that spring-flowering bulbs need time to develop a root system before winter sets in. Four to six weeks of time is optimal for bulbs to set roots and establish themselves before going dormant until spring.

The term "bulb" has come to include a variety of plants with a large, swollen storage root or stem section from which a flowering plant grows each year. Some are true bulbs; others are corms or tubers. In New England, most bulbs are planted in fall, but there are tender summer bulbs like gladiolus and dahlia that are planted in early summer and dug in fall for over-wintering in cool storage. I store mine in my damp basement.

Bulbs prefer full sun. Planting early spring bulbs under a deciduous tree works, because the bulbs get light and are able to bloom before the tree fully leaf's out. Planting in full sun works better for mid-to-late spring flowers. Southern slopes warm earlier and promote earlier bloom than north-facing ground. A heat sink such as foundation promotes very early blooming like with my crocuses in my front yard.

Bulbs do not like to "get their feet wet" and will grow poorly or rot in poorly drained soil. Avoid low-lying areas or beds that catch rain and snow melt off the roof. Crocus bulbs tolerate water far better than narcissus.

You can plan your bulb garden for an ongoing show of color. When you purchase bulbs, the catalog and package will denote whether they are early-, mid-or-late season (spring) bloomers. Bulbs like crocus, snowdrops, aconite, and scilla come up earlier than daffodils, tulips and grape hyacinth. They bring color to the spring landscape and to our diminished lives after a long winter.

I reach my limits in March wondering if "Spring" will ever arrive? The "Chuckster" just said, "You don't need to remind us again."

You can buy bulbs at most garden centers or order them through catalogs. By choosing different varieties, you can enjoy flowers from spring to early summer.

When purchasing bulbs, buy only top-quality bulbs - ones that are large, firm, and of good color. Cheap bulbs will perform poorly, or sometimes not at all. Plant the bulbs at a depth of two to three times their height. It's a good idea to add some bone meal and compost when planting. These additives will promote rooting. Cover the bulbs with soil. Some folks put down chicken wire over the bulbs on top of the ground, so the squirrels won't harvest them.

Crocus - Let's face it, crocus are probably the most popular small bulbs, with colors ranging from yellow, such as 'Orange Monarch,' to deep blue like 'Blue Moon.' Instead of planting a dozen corms of crocus, consider planting drifts of 50 to 100 corms throughout the garden. The mass of color, when everything else is brown, is magical! The first to bloom are the whites called "Snow Crocus" and then come the yellows and purples. Plant crocus in tightly packed clumps under trees, roses, and perennial flowers for the biggest impact in spring. The only drawback to crocus are the rodents that like to snack on them, although I've never had a problem with them in my garden. *See more on crocuses in Spring.

Scilla - Perhaps you're looking for something different from the usual early spring blooms of crocus. Why not try the lovely bright blue star-like blooms of Scilla sardensis? Easily grown from tiny bulbs in the fall, scillas do best when massed together in the flower garden. 'Turkish Glory of the Sun' is a favorite. Scilla are known to spread rampantly, so they are great for carpeting an orchard floor, planting in a lawn or among tall deciduous trees.

These small, or so-called minor bulbs are fun to grow because not only do they spread, filling in an area over time when planted in groups, they can also be visually stunning. So when you're planting tulips and daffodils don't forget to include some of the small bulbs in the mix.

Snowdrops- Snowdrops, or Galanthus, are one of the first bulbs to flower in late winter, often popping up through the snow. Like crocus, they are best planted in groups and in sunny spots that lose snow fast in spring so you can enjoy the fragrant blooms.

Winter Aconite - The flowers from this bulb come early. They push up out of the hard, cold soil with bright yellow blooms encircled by a green foliage ruff. Plant a few now and in a few years, you'll have a nice, naturalized patch that you can count on to get you through the end of winter with electric color and a promise. Rodents do not generally bother these bulbs.

> Daffodowndilly has come to town.
> In a yellow petticoat and a green gown.
>
> ~Traditional Old English Rhyme

Daffodils - Narcissus and daffodil are both correct common names for all species. Jonquils are daffodils with several small, fragrant yellow flowers growing on a stem. Most species have long, narrow leaves, either rush-like or flat. These vigorous, long-lived flower bulbs thrive in sunny, well-drained places, are shunned by hungry deer and voles, and will prosper and multiply with little care on your part.

Tulips - If you love to plant tulip bulbs in the fall, why not include a mix of tall tulips, the ones we're most familiar with, along with species tulips, which come in varying heights but are mostly shorter and smaller. Species tulips are more closely related to wild tulips and are hardier. They look like the "tulips of old." One lavender-colored cultivar is `Lilac Wonder.' `Persian Pearl' has petals of deep magenta tinged with rose, and a yellow center. They originally came from the Mediterranean, Asia Minor and the Caucasus and were referred to as "Jewels of the Garden."

Tulips add grace to the spring garden. These classic, elegant blooms provide a broad spectrum of colors - from traditional reds and yellows to oranges, purples, and pinks. When they arrive after Snowdrops, Crocus, and Daffodil flowers, they usher the garden into the height of spring. Tulips in their native habitats tend to be perennial meaning they return year after year. Gardeners have the considerable pleasure of planting in fall new Tulip varieties each year.

Grape Hyacinth- Grape hyacinth, or Muscari, produce small hyacinth-like flowers. While blue is the most popular color, pink varieties such as 'Pink Sunrise' and white varieties such as 'Album' are also good to try. `Christmas Pearl' is a lovely cultivar of Grape Hyacinth. Muscari offer some of the truest shades of blue among flowers, blue being the most elusive color in the garden. As with the Winter Aconites, rodents do not bother them.

Dutch Iris and Flowering Onion Bulbs

Dutch Iris (Low and High) are also known as Iris hollandica and Iris reticulata, which have orchid-like flowers with silky petals. Unlike other types of iris that grow from thickened roots called rhizomes, Dutch iris grow from teardrop-shaped bulbs that are planted in fall.

Low - These are sweet, small bulbs that grow into dainty flowers.

The dwarf iris or Iris reticulata only stands 6 inches tall, but when planted en masse, is a beauty in a perennial border or rock garden. Blue varieties are the most common but there are other colors available as well. Iris reticulata can also spread over time if naturalized in your yard.

High - Dutch iris (Iris hollandica) is hardy to Zone 5 with protection. It can be planted in fall. These bulbs grow up to 2 feet tall, have grass-like leaves, bloom in early summer, and are great for cutting. Two nice selections are 'Yellow Queen,' with bright golden-colored flowers, and 'Lion King,' with light maroon- and orange-colored petals.

When planting these small bulbs remember to only plant them a few inches deep like tulips. If you want to naturalize them and let them spread, plant in a meadow or other area that won't be mowed until June. If you mow too soon, you will cut off the seed pods and green foliage, which will eventually kill the bulb. Plant where you can let the foliage naturally yellow before mowing it down.

Like all bulbs, these irises grow best in full sun in well-drained soil. If you're naturalizing the bulbs make sure you don't cut the foliage in spring until it starts to yellow. Iris reticulata will probably naturalize best in a perennial garden.

Flowering Onions (Alliums) - They add personality and style to gardens. Their globe-like flowers bridge the gap between spring bulbs and early summer perennials. Alliums can look regal yet playful, and they are magnets for honeybees and other pollinators.

Alliums can be planted in the fall, are low-maintenance, and aren't bothered by moles or deer. Some varieties are `Red Mohican,' a small bright, red-colored flower with a sweet scent, and `Globemaster,' with a large purple ball. These are rather common like the ones you see in yards in spring like in my community garden. `Drumlike' alliums have smaller-sized flowers in white and purple. Plant the bulbs in well-drained soil in full sun and make sure to mark them so you can see them come up in the spring as they hidden in winter.

Bulb Tips - Don't use fresh wood chips as a mulch for the bulbs and other perennials as they draw out lots of nitrogen. It's best to let the chips sit for a couple of years. You can then mix them with shredded leaves in a compost pile. It's good to protect newly planted tulips and other spring-flowering bulbs by covering them with mulch, which will both keep the soil warmer in the fall and prevent it from warming up too quickly in the spring. By the way, blueberries also like two-year seasoned wood chips for a mulch, not fresh chips.

Bulbs are planted at a depth of two to three times the height of the bulb: tulips 6 to 8 inches deep; smaller bulbs, 4 to 6 inches. (See the planting chart at (fedcoseeds.com/bulbs/bulb_chart.htm)

> The tree which moves some to tears of joy is in the eyes of others only a green thing that stands in the way. Some see nature all ridicule and deformity ... and some scarce see nature at all. But to the man of imagination, nature is imagination itself.
>
> *- William Blake (1799)*

PLANTING & CARING FOR TREES, SHRUBS & EVERGREENS IN FALL

Fall is a good time to plant trees and shrubs since their roots will continue to grow into November, giving them plenty of time to get well-established before winter. The soil is still warm and the air cooler, so the plants are less stressed. You might find some good clearance sales this time of year, but don't let price dictate what you buy. Leftovers at the end of the season can often be just that. Poor quality means they might require more help to survive.

Potted Plants - I have found that nurseries sell rootbound plants at the end of season. Make sure and check out the trees and shrubs before you purchase them. What happens it that the roots have grown tightly around each other and unless they are loosened up, the tree or shrub may not survive. The term "rootbound" means that the roots of a plant have completely taken up space within the pot that contains it, often circling and creating a dense web of roots. It takes a lot of work to root-prune a potted plant, but it truly is a kindness when a plant has outgrown its pot. Use scissors, pruning shears, or a sharp gardening knife to cut around the edge and along the bottom of the root ball. You can cut away large and small roots, and don't be afraid to be a bit forceful. You won't harm the plant, and it'll be encouraged to spread its roots out and grow stronger.

Choose varieties that do well in the hardiness zone where you live and make sure they fit into the space you have available. Allow ample room for growth as when trees and shrubs mature, they widen and grow taller. Providing enough room for young plants to grow into mature plants is a common problem of gardeners including myself. The "Chuckster" said, "It takes using your noggin projecting out into the future.'

Fruit Trees - Mow grass around fruit trees to deter deer and moles. Place tree guards around young trees. You can also spray red pepper as a deterrent. It's good time to remove any dead branches from the trees in your garden. Dead wood is not only hazardous and unattractive, but it's also a host for insects and fungal diseases. February is a good time to prune your fruit trees.

Tender Trees and Shrubs - The first step is to protect tender trees and shrubs. For young trees, cover the trunks with tree wrap. This can be a plastic, mesh, or wire material wrapped around the trunk up as high as possible and sunk 1 to 2 inches below the ground level. Tree wraps will protect the bark from nibbling by voles, mice, and rabbits. If your tree gets girdled in winter (all the bark is chewed off all the way around the tree), then your tree may not survive.

Knock snow off the branches of trees and shrubs to protect them from being damaged, especially if it's a heavy wet snow.

Roses - Fall is the time to condition your more delicate roses for the winter. Some folks prepare them for the cold months too early. You need to wait till after Thanksgiving because they need to harden up. Mound dirt around the crowns, wrap burlap around the roses and then stuff leaves into the burlap so air can get through. Also, mulch around delicate perennials and shrubs, especially roses, which aren't that hardy.

Broadleaf Evergreens - Rhododendrons, azaleas, pieris and mountain laurel need protection from the cold wind and bright winter sun. They do better in protected settings and in north-facing slopes. Other evergreens include holly and boxwood, introduced to North America from Europe in the 1600s.

Dr. Norman Pellett, Emeritus Horticulturist of the University of Vermont told me that many gardeners aren't aware that broadleaf evergreens continue to need to transpire moisture during the coldest days of winter in order to stay alive. If the ground is too dry or their roots aren't firmly established, then the leaves may not get enough moisture. That's why it's best to plant evergreens in the spring when the soil is wetter, not in the fall.

Winter injury is caused when water is transpired or lost through plant tissue more quickly than it can be absorbed through the roots. This happens when there are long dry periods of cold along with strong winds. If these conditions persist, evergreens will become stressed and may die.

For exposed evergreens in your home garden, wrap with a burlap wrap. Drive stakes in around the shrubs and wrap chicken wire around the stakes making an enclosure. Wrap burlap around the chicken wire and fasten in place. This will block cold winds from drying out the leaves. Don't let the burlap touch the leaves or it will wick away moisture and add to the injury. Protect plants under eaves with wooden teepee structures that will shed falling snow and ice from off the roof.

I've noticed winter injury from the bitter cold on many evergreens. You'll notice the browning of the needles and in some cases, the dying of the trees and shrubs. A January thaw certainly helps in providing moisture to the needles of the evergreens.

Anti-desiccant sprays add a protective waxy coating to the leaves of broadleaf evergreens to help slow the process of transpiration. It reduces the amount of drying. The spray needs to be applied before the temperature goes below freezing - somewhere around 40 to 50 degrees Fahrenheit. It can be used more than once, but it's hard to know what the winter will be like. If it's a snowy cold winter and the plants are healthy, there is no need to apply the spray. Foliage needs to be dry when applied, and the spray needs time to dry afterward.

Always follow the label instructions carefully! Don't spray too early: Wait until December to spray conifers, because these plants must be completely dormant (which involves moving water down to the roots) before applying, or else the spray will trap water in the leaves that will freeze and cause cellular rupturing.

Spray thoroughly: Evergreens and rhododendrons lose water from both the upper side and under side of the leaves. Be sure to spray the entire plant! Don't spray conifers such as blue spruce as they already have a natural coating that you don't want to damage.

Winter injury to evergreens close to roads can be caused from salt spray from salt trucks. You'll notice the brown and golds on the needles, but this is only on evergreens that grow close to roads, especially along the Interstate highways. My neighbor asked me what she should do with the damaged parts of her evergreen shrub. I said to cut out the damaged part of the shrub and hope it will fill in over the summer. The "Chuckster" just said, "Why don't you tell her to spray the dead needles with green paint." That sounds like the "Chuckster.

Winter Injury 2015

I can't remember a winter of such severity to plants. Plus my wood pile went down from the severe cold. I noticed injury on many plants and shrubs including azaleas and rhododendrons (broadleaf evergreen shrubs) and perennials like bleeding hearts, butterfly bush, coral bells, pinks, and two vining plants in my front yard - clematis and climbing roses, which were damaged but not lost. Pine and spruces don't need any help as they're real tough customers.

LATE OCTOBER

The American Tamarack

One of my favorite activities is to travel to the Northeast Kingdom of Vermont in late October after the maples have lost their color. And lo, I behold the brilliant yellow/gold of the native tamaracks against the greens of the tall conifers. I call this my second fall. The American tamarack is also called larch; folks in Nova Scotia called them hackmatack. Wild groves of them make quite a statement in the forest. Years ago, when I traveled to Scotland, many of the mountains were planted with larch and pine.

This native, eastern North American tree is unique. It's one of the few needled trees that is not evergreen: It has needles like spruce and pine, but it's a deciduous tree. American tamarack is one of the last trees to turn color in autumn. Its bluish-green needles are attractive in summer. It loses its needles later in fall close to winter.

Tamaracks are best grown in groves for the most dramatic effect. They produce cones that are small and egg-shaped -- not particularly ornamental. Purchase trees from a local nursery and plant in spring or summer in well-drained, acidic, moist soils. American tamarack also grows well in wet sites. Space trees 20 to 30 feet apart.

American tamarack needs cool soils to thrive. Plant trees near streams or in wet areas. It is most suited to a naturalized setting with acidic soils. Add a little compost when planting. Tamaracks also do well in lawn settings or in shade. Plant dwarf versions of these trees in the garden as an unusual specimen tree. Weeping tamarack has a cascading growth pattern that creates a unique small tree in a garden. They can even be trained to cascade over walls and down rock gardens, almost like a ground cover.

Besides tamaracks, the lovely honey locusts turn yellow and produce stunning colors as do the willows in the fall. Honey locust, also called locust, is a genus of 12 species of thorny trees or shrubs in the pea family (Fabaceae). Honey locusts are native to North and South America. Other stunning trees are crabapples with their colorful fruit in red and yellow. Hawthorns have red and orange fruits and Mountain Ash has clusters of pumpkin orange fruit. Sumac has amazing tones of red leaves and fruit.

Rhubarb Leaf on Garden Floor

For The Birds

One of my favorite late autumn activities is to set out my bird feeders with seeds and suet and birds flitting and fluttering about. There is much delight in watching chickadees, goldfinches, robins, cardinals and nuthatches arrive at the feeder. It's amazing how quickly the word spreads among the avian species. Within an hour of putting up a feeder I had a steady stream of customers.

Birds are happiest when they have places to hide as well as eat and drink. I have many shrubs and a large crabapple in my front yard in which the birds hang out, waiting for their turn at the feeder in the protective shelter of the twigs and brush. There are many websites with information on bird-feeding such as *www.duncraft.com*. Go to your local garden center for supplies.

LATE FALL AND BEYOND

maple leaves
rest on forest floors
with crunch of feet
as cinnamon perfumes the air
so much to behold
such amazing grace of color
golden beech and dark brown oak leaves
blanket hillsides below
green haloes of conifers above
blueberries turn amber
as does brilliant burning bush
with red foliage and berries
the fields of barberries
birds love to eat
seeds drop to earth
and persist not to our liking
suddenly sunlight breaks through clouds
in late October light
high mountain peaks come aglow in myriads of color
like impressionistic paintings
fluttering leaves of the golden honey locust
fall in spirals covering the cold earth
a corkscrew willow sits out my window
keeping me company
soon thin curling yellow leaves
layer the ground
its large weeping cousin with wide, thick trunks
and overhanging delicate limbs
dance in the wind
children hide under its boughs
nature is almost bare
one can see in distant morning light
her yellow willow brightness
golden tamaracks
stand lonely in groves
near conifers
fall hasn't passed

greens of moss and ferns
light up cool, damp forests
brown hydrangea bouquets hang
as do red foliage of linden and sumac
and purple kale
and crab apples in red
bird's sing and eat fruits and berries
winterberry shrubs
surprise eyes in bright red
soon turn black with winter cold
looking out my window
gazing up at mountains
a green cast shelters the tops
with brown shades below
at eventide on lake of Champlain
sun drops over Adirondack high peaks
waves of water saturated with
shimmering colors
as I dip my quiet paddle in the bay
sky illumined in red, magenta and purple
darkness arrives
fall fades snow comes
winter ice enters
limbs crack white birch bends
high mountains awash with
greens of fir and spruce
purple buds of maples below
cast plum hues at eventide
stars gaze down
her wide-open eyes
reddish limbs of dogwoods
brown/yellows of wild grasses
in frozen wetlands crunch to feet
whale pings soon on frozen bay
keep me company
and I wait

-The Woodchuck Gardener

WINTER

DECEMBER

You've got two choices when surviving the time of ice, snow and cold. You can hang out in the confines of your home on cold gray days and watch the flames emanating from your wood stove. Or after warming up, you can go out and meet nature in all its wonderment. Just have a warm winter coat, scarf and wool cap and a great dog like mine for long walks.

Yet, winter must be endured, but not all the time. If Shelburne Bay freezes over close to my home, it's an opportunity to walk or ski out on the frozen snow-covered bay where I experience expansiveness. With each breath, I get revived with new life.

Or I can walk through snowy fields amongst brown and yellow grasses and watch the deep blue sky with purple shadows cast by the trees and plants. What a feast winter can be.

The "Chuckster" just said, "please don't romanticize winter as it's not so much fun." I need to remember that in summer when I can take my canoe out on the water, but it's not summer anymore.

TWO CROWS
Last night
I heard haunting cries
of south-bound geese
crossing the veiled light
of October's half hidden moon.
In the icy morning hours
I walk among blackened leaves
of tomato plants and pumpkin vines.
I pound frozen water buckets
and hear the cattle bawl for hay.
The orange gold
of yesterday's Indian summer
lies dull and matted
under bare limbs
of our backyard maples.
Two crows
cross a rising pale sun
and slide silently into
Fog that hugs the river
in the valley below.

-Ann Day, Fayston, Vermont

NIGHTS COLD
snowflakes fly
winds blow
first signs of winter
on my doorstep
perusing winter coats, gloves, and hats
sewing and knitting
around wood stove
I wonder
where animals go
which ones' leave
others asleep
some not

-The Woodchuck Gardener

Late November 2018 brought frigid temperatures, with the coldest day of the year occurring, believe it or not, on Thanksgiving. I still had carrots, beets, and turnips in my community garden beds, covered with mulch, and greens in my cold frames covered by wood/plexiglass covers.

The "Chuckster" just said, "I've been tellin' you winter would come, and you just kept enjoyin' the warmer fall-like temperatures with little concern for the onslaught." Now, sleet, snow and rain came along with their sister companion - cold temperatures and I became a snow-shovelin' man. Down in my garden, I picked kale and Brussels sprouts. It won't be long before the deer will browse the plants amongst the crusted snow and leave me their droppings in place of sprouts.

On December 27th in 2019, winter flew through with a vengeance.

In early winter I bundled up. My dog Herk and I walked through the woods of Red Rocks Park down to Shelburne Bay, where grasses grow in the water, mallards swim and hundreds of crows screech as they come back home late in the day to the tall white pines in the woods above the bay. They roost close together at night to protect themselves from the owls.

I love to close my eyes and listen as cold waves lap on the shore. There's always something happening. I might notice a mackerel sky, a cloud formation of high-altitude cirrus clouds resembling the scale pattern of the Atlantic Ocean's mackerel fish. This indicates a change in the weather as it typically precedes or follows stormy weather.

The winter sky is more illuminated because sunset and sunrise are closer together at this time of the year. It is particularly beautiful at sunset as the sun goes down over the Adirondacks with glows in red and yellow into my home. That's when I feel most warmed.

Shelburne Beach Winter - Pat Jackson

JANUARY AND FEBRUARY

I cross-country skied through the woods along with my old chocolate lab, Autumn Girl in 2013. Shelburne Bay on Lake Champlain froze in 2014 and 2015 in February and now again in 2019. In those years, I skied out on the frozen snow-covered lake with Autumn Girl. Sadly, she took off to heaven in the summer in 2014. I miss my old, fine brown lab. In 2018, I was rewarded with my fourth dog, Hercules. Perhaps you've heard of him? Hmm!

January 30, 2019 - January brought frigid cold and heaps of snow.

Hercules doesn't mind the wintry weather - with his black, newfie/lab - long-haired coat. I walk him every day in the late afternoon through the woods near my home where I sometimes can hear the cracking sounds of the trees. We continue down to the Lake of Champlain as the sun just begins to hide behind the snowy purple peaks of the Adirondack Mountains.

For the first time in years, Shelburne Bay froze over in February. Hercules and I walked gingerly out on the frozen bay. The white snow and Herk's black coat create quite a contrast. I just heard whale pings emanating under the frozen water as the "Chuckster" said, "Just how many times are you going to mention your dog?"

Writing of ice, I remember years ago, I took my young friend, Lilliana Bright, age 9, over to Shelburne Pond to ice skate on the Sunday before the New Year. It was a lovely chilly day as kids played hockey and Lilliana twirled around me as wind-sailors flew past.

The landscape is now black and white with little sun. Inside, I pop Vitamin D and C pills and have broad-spectrum lights in my study where I write - to help mitigate the effects of SAD - Seasonal Affective Disorder.

The creatures seem to have vanished, yet even on the coldest days the woods and fields are full of life if you know where to find them. That's never true with the squirrels of course, which continue to be everywhere, especially toppling my bird feeder.

It's too early to start seeds, though my seed catalogs have been studied until they're dog-eared. In the dead of winter, when gardeners are dying to get their hands in the dirt, you can get your fix by playing with avocados, carrots, ginger and pineapples. Take an avocado pit and make a small hole through the pit, place a pencil through the hole and drop it into a small glass filled with water. Leave half of the pit above the water.

Or try sprouting some carrot tops placing the top of the carrot in water. Or you can place a piece of ginger in potting soil with the buds facing up, and in a couple of weeks, it will begin to grow. The top of a pineapple that would otherwise end up in the compost - can be planted and grown into an ornamental new pineapple tree - by simply placing half of it in a cup of water. The "Chuckster" said, "I don't want to say anything, but this guy can't help himself as his growing compulsion just won't quit."

FYI - The Canadian North is unrelenting in sending bitter air down south the last couple of years. Forecasters say millions of people in the Midwest, Great Lakes and Northeast have experienced record-shattering wind chills and temperatures near or below zero. This phenomenon is called the Polar Vortex. This large pocket of very frigid air, typically the coldest air in the Northern Hemisphere, normally sits over the polar region during the winter season. But that's changing as the North pole is warming.

The cold air finds its way into the northern tiers when the polar vortex is pushed farther south due to "Global Warming" at the poles. The warmth pushes the cold air south. A growing body of research has proposed ways in which rapid Arctic warming can lead to harsh winters, summer heatwaves and even floods and droughts across the mid-latitudes. Scientists say that climate change and Arctic sea ice loss are the root cause of these events, but others are more circumspect.

January 2021 - We've had a long stretch of cold cloudy weather, so the grays, browns, and whites are leaving me in a color deficit. There's been about half the normal snow cover. With so much time on hand due to the COVID epidemic, I'm planning my garden and preparing seeds for germination and working on my next garden book. That's this one. I should be receiving my first vaccine injection in February.

Can you find the bird in front of my house?

My Colorful Winter Garden

I don't want to forget the world of intriguing shrubs in winter with their unusual branch structures and color. The red berries of winterberries stand out if the birds don't get them first. These bushes cast amazing silhouettes against the snow. The berries blacken with the cold.

I recall from a friend how, much earlier in the year, a voracious crowd of cedar waxwings discovered the bright red fruits. They swooped down from perches in maple trees to a feast. Cedar Waxwings are well known for devouring strawberries in summer. I cover my berries with floating row covers and it works - sort of.

Again, let's not forget how our winter garden takes place in the dormant landscape. A well-kept lawn has little to offer when covered in snow, but a winter garden is a wonder to behold with tufted grasses, stalks, and seed clusters in many shapes, textures, and colors - all covered in white and brown when the snow falls.

Few plants have more colorful winter bark than red-stemmed dogwood (Cornus sericea), a large shrub with a wide range in the U.S. and Canada that grows six to eight feet tall if left unpruned.

Winterberries   Tufted Perrenial

Yellow-stemmed dogwood varieties like Cornus alba also add a bright highlight to the winter landscape.

To create your winter garden, imagine planting conifers in spring and grasses next to a stone wall in summer or building a gazebo where you can sip hot herb tea in winter. Let your creative juices run wild. As the English poet, Alexander Pope, once said, "All gardening is landscape painting. And winter can be the same."

> I love the winter, with its imprisonment
> and its cold, for it compels the prisoner
> to try new fields and resources."
>
> -*The Writings of Henry David Thoreau, The Journal,*

(December 5, 1856) Walden Pond

FYI - Did you know that Walden Pond and its surroundings in Concord, Massachusetts, doesn't look like it did in Thoreau's day? Too many folks walk on its paths and attempt to commune with nature, even though the town of Concord is trying to spruce it up. My friend, Heather Skilling, who now lives in Richford, Vermont, used to ride her horse around Walden Pond when she was a young girl. When I walked around the pond ten years ago, I was not inspired. Instead, I would suggest reading the book "Walden" by Thoreau, especially the chapters, "Where I lived and what I lived for."

NATURE SPIRITS & TEMPERAMENTS - A LITTLE HELP FROM OUR FRIENDS

While we endure the long winter nights, lets listen to the thoughts of Rudolf Steiner, the Austrian philosopher and scientist who brought us Waldorf Education and Biodynamic Farming and Gardening. He wrote of Nature Spirits and how they help us in the garden. Steiner said they are the offsprings of the angelic beings.

You may encounter a variety of nature spirits working in your garden. Each one is comprised of an element: gnomes are earth spirits, mermaids are water spirits, sylphs are air spirits, and salamanders are fire spirits.

For example, during winter, the gnomes live deep in the earth shining crystals and preparing the soil for seed planting. They cut crystal from the rock, develop grains of ore, and work with precious stones, gems, and metals. Their name means "earth dwellers." Gnomes absorb energy from the ethers and release the energy into matter giving it life.

Earth, Water, Air, and Fire

Earth - Gnomes are an example of spirits related to the element of Earth: they work in solids; in relation to plants they are especially associated with the roots. Blue is the color associated with the Earth element.

Water - Water spirits work with fluids and in moisture - permeated air; in plants they work in connection with leaves and sprouting. Undines are an example of water spirits, and the color green is associated with them.

Air - Sylphs exemplify air spirits, those who work through air and light. The flowering stage of plants is their domain; yellow is their color.

Fire - Fire spirits work with warmth, as when seeds develop, and fruits ripen. They are associated with red.

Human beings, in contrast to the elemental spirits, are considered in many traditions to comprise five elements - water, air, earth, fire, and a fifth element called akasha or spirit. *Source: Excerpted from Mermaids, Sylphs, Gnomes, Salamanders, by William R. Mistele (North Atlantic Books, 2012). The author is William R. Mistele.*

The "Chuckster" just said, "I don't want to say anything, but do you really believe in them, the gnomes and all?" And I said, "We always need a little help from our friends."

Biodynamics - Biodynamics was the first modern organic agricultural movement. Its development began in 1924 with a series of eight lectures to farmers on agriculture given by philosopher and scientist Rudolf Steiner at Koberwitz in Silesia, East Germany. In them, Steiner said we have been living in a Garden of Eden, where whatever we needed was given to us. Now, he said, we need to help. He said it was up to us to heal the planet.

See more on Biodynamics in my first book, The Woodchuck's Guide to Gardening - where I focus on Companion Planting and Planting By The Stars.

"There is no spirit without matter and no matter without spirit."

~Rudolf Steiner," 1924

INDOOR WINTER BULBS

I try and keep the joys of gardening alive in my home in winter by forcing bulbs like amaryllis and paper whites.

Amaryllis is a small genus of flowering bulbs, with two species. The one we're most familiar with is the genus Hippeastrum, widely sold in the winter months for their ability to bloom indoors.

I was given a Red Lion amaryllis bulb for Christmas along with a light growing medium. I'm told that the larger bulbs produce larger flowers and more of them, and that one should look for bulbs that still have roots at the base. To plant Amaryllis, make sure the pot is large enough for the bulb. A five- to seven-inch pot will do. The bulb needs to feel a little crowded to bloom. Partially fill the pot with potting soil, then place the bulb in the soil so that the top third of it will be exposed when you fill in potting soil around the sides of the pot. Place a bamboo or wooden stake along the side of the bulb because the flowers can get top heavy. Inserting the stake when you plant will help you avoid damaging the bulb and roots later. Feed the bulb with compost tea.

Keep the bulb in a warm place but not in direct sunlight. Keep the soil moist but not soggy. Then place the bulb in direct sunlight. Within six weeks, the bulb will blossom.

After it blooms, remove the flower stem just above the bulb and continue to water. The idea is to let the long green leaves die back completely, so they release their energy into the bulbs for its next bloom. When the leaves have withered, clip them off.

Plant the bulb outdoors in the spring and add compost. Stop feeding it in August. After the first frosts, dig the bulb and store in a cool dark place for two months in order for it to go through a dormant period. Then you can re-pot the bulb, and a new cycle will begin.

I've found that my amaryllis bulbs don't always flower. From what I've read, that's because either they didn't get enough of a dormant period, they had insufficient light while actively growing, or the soil was lacking nutrients. Any other suggestions? When successfully replanted, the Amaryllis will produce bigger and better blooms, so it's worth the effort.

Paperwhites - I've been forcing paperwhites for years. It's easy. They need only 3" of root room in shallow containers. Pretty glass or ceramic bowls are ideal. Plant your paperwhites in soil, or use pebbles, chips, or marbles in a clear vase for added visual interest. The planting medium just needs to provide support for the plants and allow roots to grow through; it doesn't need to supply nutrients.

Plant the bulbs with their wide bottoms down and the top inch of each bulb above the soil/pebble line. Plant close together, almost touching, for the most floriferous display.

Add water so the soil is moist. If planted in pebbles, chips, or marbles, add enough water to come within three-fourths of the top of the growing objects. This will keep the base of the paperwhite bulb moist without soaking the entire bulb. The goal is to have the very bottom of the bulbs just touching the water as this will encourage root growth.

Place the pot or bowl in a sunny, bright location. Lots of light will keep stems from growing too tall and becoming floppy. In a week or two, roots will appear, with top sprouts following shortly thereafter. Bud and blooms develop quickly; it's fun to watch the daily progress. You'll be enjoying blooms and fragrance in a few short weeks.

Icy branches in winter at Shelburne Bay Beach

A CONTINUANCE OF WINTER'S PATH
a surprise storm
brought heavy snow and ice
frozen limbs cracked
power lines downed
sparks flew
poplars and white birches hard hit
nuthatches, chickadees, and redpolls
to the feeders came
the quiet of winter returned
emerged in stark beauty
in a myriad of hues
red berries of winterberries darkened
conifer greens held
a full moon light
shadows in white and black
as I wandered the woods
the pallet change
around each corner
truth is found in silence
the natural world greets me
this longest of seasons
slowed down in darkness
with grace

-*The Woodchuck Gardener*

Andrew Wyeth, born 1917, once said,

"I prefer winter and fall, when you feel the bone structure of the landscape - the loneliness of it, the dead feeling of winter. Something waits beneath it, the whole story doesn't show."

Them Bones - A Continuance of Winter's Path

While the land lies asleep in winter, I'd like to take a step back and spend time in planning my spring garden. While plants go dormant in winter, we don't have to. In fact, certain landscaping projects are actually better suited to the off-months.

I've found that one of the keys to landscape design isn't just the greenery that catches your eye. It's the unchanging structural framework that organizes and supports those flowers and shrubs. These are known as the "bones" or skeletons of a garden. Some of these may be trees, stone outcroppings, or a pond. As well, the constructed, architectural elements - such as walls, fences, patios, benches, bird baths, pathways, and arbors - add definition to an outdoor space and make it useful for everyday activities. Winter is an ideal time to see how bones add character to the landscape.

And even though the smells, the sounds, the movement of wildlife, and butterflies have vanished, what's left behind is the structure of the gardenscape. You may have noticed a neighbor's old stone wall. Behind my house, a tall green classic water tower once stood. I loved looking up at it.

Judith Irven of Goshen, Vermont accentuated her garden with vertical elements including a gazebo and an arbor; stone walls; plus, shrubs and small trees. Together these vertical elements became the skeletons of her garden.

And even though the trees are bare, and the perennials are below the snow, Judith loves to gaze out her window looking at all the shapes - like abstract pieces of art. And if they are not to her liking, she may use the winter months to do pruning exposing their exfoliating bark and curved branches. But please don't prune spring flowering shrubs as they have already formed their flower buds for next season.

Judith Irven and Dick Conrad live in Goshen where together they nurture a large garden. Judith is a Vermont Certified Horticulturist and teaches Sustainable Home Landscaping for the Vermont Master Gardener program. You can subscribe to her blog about her Vermont gardening life at *northcountryreflections.com*. Dick is a landscape and garden photographer; you can see more of his photographs at *northcountryimpressions.com*.

I love the solitary shapes of fruit trees in winter. I can't wait to get out my pruning shears. I first like to observe the way the limbs unfold from the trunk. I call this the quiet time before I start pruning. We have twenty fruit trees at the Tommy Thompson Community Garden in the Intervale in Burlington.

Winter Alternatives - I've traveled in winter to the Montreal Botanical Gardens for an indoor flower show in the greenhouses with lovely tropical plants and their perfumes. There is also the Boston Arboretum where you can see the textures of tree bark. Of course, there are the forests around my home with the oak, pine, cherry, maple and basswood trees with amazing bark. I especially love the bark of old maple trees. There is also a climax forest close to Potash brook close to my home. I've heard Smith College in Northampton, Massachusetts has a great winter greenhouse. Check it out.

> COLD
> I trek to the barnyard
> in the icy pre light,
> the frozen air stings
> and pulls my skin tight.
> Boots squeak on the path
> where footsteps have gone
> into sharp crystals
> of a January dawn.
> The cattle stand close
> in rigid regime,
> their breath surrounds them
> with frigid white steam.
> Frost etches their eyelids
> and backs as they wait,
> while smoke from the valley
> rises thin and straight.
> The sky in the east
> shows a yellow haze
> where winter's sun
> begins to glow.
> Yet in the gleam
> of those feeble rays,
> the temperature stays
> at Twenty Below!
>
> -*Ann Day, Fayston, Vermont*

In January, I read my two favorite ornamental garden magazines, Fine Gardening and Horticulture, plus my other favorite seed catalogs. Johnny's Selected Seeds and Fedco Seeds of Maine. Prairie Nursery also has a great perennial catalog. I just began the process of planning my gardens for the year. What new pollinator plants would I like to try, and which plants do I need to give away as they love to take over?

FEBRUARY BRINGS LIGHT AND HOPE 2018

While there has been much wintry weather with below zero temperatures of late in Vermont, the return of the light is full of cheer as the days grow longer. This afternoon, I skipped rocks across the frozen water on Shelburne Bay. I did not dare walk out on it until I saw the ice fishermen doing their business.

I began gathering seed-starting supplies of seeds, flats, pots, germination mixes and a heating pad. Soon, I'll plant flower seeds like impatiens, geraniums and snapdragons in the confines of my home. Snaps are one of my favorite fall flowers with their many colors. Sometimes, the seeds will drop from the seed pods in your garden soil and reappear as young seedlings the next summer. If you start them from their tiny black seeds inside your home, they take a while to germinate. Just manage them carefully when transplanting. It won't be too long before these flower seeds rise up and germinate. It's always a miracle when they do.

Therefore, every gardener ought to be careful
and diligently to foresee, that the seeds committed to the
earth be neither too old, thin, withered nor
counterfeited, but rather ful, new and having juyce

-From the Gardener's Labyrinth by Thomas Hill Born 1529

METAMORPHOSIS: FROM SEED TO SEED
let's begin with the seed
with inner life and least form
the seed so small
will soon grow into a plant
as the plant grows
life enters into form
and form begins to expand
from flower into seed

-*The Woodchuck Gardener*

*If you want to plant seeds by the stars and moon during the growing season, check out the Stella Natura Biodynamic Planting Calendar. It's a reliable source of information and a way of connecting in a more intimate way with the cosmos through the Earth (roots), water (leaves), fire (fruits), and air (flowers).

This Calendar has many aspects: a basic introduction to astronomy, a simple ephemeris, a planting guide, a star map, aid for following the movement of the planets in the night sky, and articles by ten different authors.

E-mail: info@stellanatura.com.

Mail: Stella Natura, PO Box 783, Kimberton PA 19442

Snowflakes

How can one fathom the hexagonal miracle of snowflakes as they float down on my dark wool coat like white melting stars?

I love to look at snow crystals and snowflakes. They shine and glow in every color of the rainbow. Snowflakes are so tiny that you can't really see the details with your eyes unless you photograph them as did Snowflake Bentley, the famous snowflake photographer from Jericho Center, Vermont. I simply enjoy looking up as they fall quietly to the earth and tickle my nose.

The Snow Storm
Announced by all the trumpets of the sky,
Arrives the snow, and, driving o'er the fields,
Seems nowhere to alight: the whited air
Hides hills and woods, the river and the heaven,
And veils the farmhouse at the garden's end.
The steed and traveler stopped, the courier's feet
Delayed, all friends shut out, the housemates sit
Around the radiant fireplace, enclosed
In a tumultuous privacy of storm.

-Ralph Waldo Emerson (1803-1882)

I frequently tramped eight or ten miles through the deepest snow
to keep my appointment with a Beech Tree, or a
Yellow Birch or an old acquaintance among the Pines.

-Henry David Thoreau Quote (1817-1862)

FEBRUARY

The Thin Time

We are halfway between the winter solstice and spring equinox - called the "thin time" of the year. It's been cold in 2014-15 with little snow and my wood supply is getting low. In early February we had bare grass on cross country and snowmobile trails. In mid-February Shelburne Bay on Lake Champlain froze over. The "Chuckster" just said, "I hope Ron will getting out on his ski's soon and heading out in the fields, so that I can have some peace and quiet."

Candlemas, better known as Groundhog's Day, is almost upon us (February 2nd). By the way, groundhogs have colorful names, including "whistle-pig" for their tendency to emit short, high-pitched whistles. They're also known as land beavers, but of course, their most famous nickname is "woodchuck," of course!

Candlemas in old times represented the end of the Christmas holidays. The time of Candlemas tells us that like the "thin time" we are halfway between the winter solstice when the day is shortest and the spring equinox when day and night are of equal duration. Candlemas is commemorated as a religious occasion when the Virgin Mary, in obedience to Jewish law, went to the Temple in Jerusalem both to be purified 40 days after the birth of her son, Jesus, and to present him to God as her firstborn.

The perennials are suffering with little snow on the ground and in places, there is bare ground. The freezing and thawing can harm plants causing them to heave, especially young ones planted this past fall. Check out your yard for plants with exposed roots that can dry out and die. Cover them with mulch to protect them. Perennial herbs like thyme and oregano can also suffer from exposure in colder climes. It's not too late to protect your outdoor plants from winter's harm. This will help them stand a better chance of survival.

The birds are feeding heavily, trying to warm up their bodies with fluffed up feathers as the blue jay's pound away on the suet and peck at sunflower seed and cracked corn in the feeder in my front yard.

I've started to long for spring and the wet warmth and breezes of summer. In a few months, I'll hear the morning sounds of the mourning doves, one of the most familiar bird sounds in spring. They consume seeds, which make up over 90 percent of their diet. They love the seeds from plants such as ragweed, sunflower, wheat, millet, corn and pokeweed.

Many people see winter as the season that must be endured. Others go to the ski slopes while others take off for warmer climes. A beautiful place to stroll in winter is the Missisquoi National Wildlife Reserve in Swanton, Vermont where you can learn about the diversity of hardy plants during the long, winter months. The reserve is located in northwestern Vermont close to Canada. The bogs at Charcoal Creek in the reserve are home to unique plants and animal communities in winter. There you can find thin, shin-high patches of wild rice protruding from the snow, wool grass, a type of sedge and the emptied fruit heads of meadowsweet. Take a botanist along for even a better trip. And please don't slip on the ice. It's best to wear snowshoes or traction cleats over your winter boots.

*See more on the Missisquoi Reserve in My Woodchuck's Garden Website.

I've lived with winter and snow and ice for a long time and like everyone else, I have touches of melancholy. I often wonder how the earth could once be so soft and damp and green in summer and then turn so hard and white in winter except for the soft snow. Lately, I've been using hot water bottles to warm my low back and bum. "Here he goes again kvetching ad infinitum," said the "Chuckster."

FYI - Truck Day, the annual event foreshadowing the start of spring training for the Boston Red Sox - set for February 8. This is when the truck leaves for Florida.

ICE WILL SUFFICE 2019
a cold winter indeed
Shelburne Bay froze over
first time in years
Herk and I traverse the wide
open plain of snow
and ice below
hearing whale pings
I ski across
to the west
where Adirondack white peaks loom
I turn to the east
and the Green Mountains
as they cast their shadows
years ago as the ice melted
there were pools of turquoise water
close to shore
as though I was sunning
in the Caribbean
and home along the bluffs
water ran down
in icicles of green blue
can't wait to hear the sounds
of Red Wing Blackbirds
in the wetlands
with their spring calls

-The Woodchuck Gardener

SPRING

EARLY MARCH

On March 9, 2019, while walking out on frozen Shelburne Bay with Herk, I ran into my neighbors, Brenda Patoine and her friend, John. They asked me if I had seen any peregrine falcons and I told them no, even though I had seen them in the summer. Brenda and John and Herk headed out further on the bay to the rocky cliffs of Red Rocks Park where they sighted peregrine falcons, perched high and swooping down past them. My spirits were lifted when I heard the story later that day.

March always tests my patience as I'm ready to "get down" in the garden. It's a tough month for all occupants of earth who live in northern climes. If you're a woodchuck gardener, you're tempted to put seeds in the ground in late March and early April. Just make sure the soil is crumbly and not wet. If it stays together in heavy damp clumps, it's still too wet and cold for planting seeds. Once the soil warms up, I'll plant seeds in my cold frames, which are covered with wooden/plexiglass frames. This covering allows the soil to warm up and protects the young plants once they emerge. A cold frame with a cover warms up the soil an added twenty degrees.

A late spring indeed. In early March, I cut the lower stems of forsythias. Then I pounded the stems and placed them in a vase of water, and they flowered in 2 weeks. That's when I say, "Wow, spring is a comin." I also cut pussy willows and placed in water. I hope it won't be too long before the first blooms of crocus will emerge followed by hyacinths, daffodils and tulips.

> POUND THE RUGS
> shake the curtains
> dust the corners
> mop the floor
> take off long underwear
> and jump in pond
>
> -*The Woodchuck Gardener*

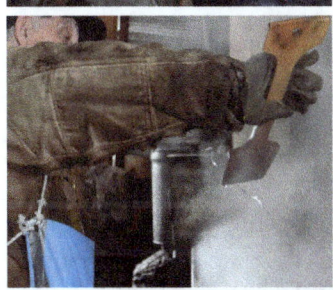

Maple sugaring with Clem Patoine taken by his daughter Brenda.

SAP RUNS

purple blue sky gives way
to cold nights and warm days
sugar snows abound
tree limbs heavy
sun shines
maple sap runs hard
sugar shacks spill out steam clouds
sap flows into sweet amber syrup
pancakes float and songbirds sing
spring comes quickly
as a fly
bringing joy and maple pie
saw a bald eagle and whiffed a skunk
yet spring is slow to arrive.
snow mountains melting
dormant roots arising
snowdrops appear
melancholy drifts
daffodils unfold
days grow longer
chill in the air
daffodils sulk
sun springs forth
blinding me
earth oozes
smells permeate
back roads give way
spotted salamanders emerge from mud
to their vernal mating pools
crossing backroads
as peepers
start their soundings at eventide
grass sprouts forth
the celebration of leaf tones begins
in bright lime greens and yellow
my body warms, my soul aches
puddles in forests emerge

along with ephemerals
hepaticas, hepaticas
in three-lobed leaves
in white and lavender
air filled with honey
dizziness pervades
fever consumes
a time of mating
weather ever changing
hither and dither
fragrances arrive
petals dance
in the wind

-*The Woodchuck Gardener*

SPROUTING
seeds soon sprout
we as well
with sun and warmth
and dripping rain
the thrust of crocus
rise from wintry rest

-*The Woodchuck Gardener*

Crocus is a genus of flowering plants in the iris family comprising 90 species of perennials growing from corms. Many are cultivated for their flowers appearing in autumn, winter, or spring. The spice saffron is obtained from the stigmas of Crocus sativus, an autumn-blooming species. Crocuses are native to woodland, scrub, and meadows from sea level to alpine tundra in North Africa and the Middle East, central and southern Europe, in particular Krokos, Greece, on the islands of the Aegean, and across Central Asia to Xinjiang Province in western China.

Early season crocuses in my front yard next to the foundation

CROCUS 2012-2019

2012 - A late spring indeed. In early March, I cut two inches off the lower stems of forsythia and pussy willow. Then I pounded the stem with a hammer and put it in water in a vase and soon it will flower. That's when I say, "Wow, spring is a comin." I hope it won't be too long before the first blooms of crocus will emerge followed by hyacinths, daffodils and tulips.

Each year is different in these days of climate disruption. I use the crocus as a barometer of what's happening out there. It's amazing how individual years can be characterized by the blooming of the crocus.

By mid-March, the sun was getting stronger, and the soil was heating up. Warm, weird weather began to take hold on March 18th when I saw my first crocus. Every day after, more blooms arose.

On March 20th, the first day of the Spring Equinox, the crocus spread its beauty, hugging the foundation of my home. The southeastern exposure of the sun warmed the earth close to my home. The daffodils shot up and began to bloom and then it got cold again, making me worry that the buds on the fruits trees would freeze.

FYI - The Spring Equinox, or the Vernal Equinox as it's more formally known, marks the astronomical start of spring when the vertical ray of the Sun passes north through the Earth's equator. After March 20 the days will begin to get longer and the nights shorter as the Earth wakes up from its winter hibernation.

I celebrated the first day of spring by raking dead leaves and debris and putting them in my compost pile. The snowdrops began to come out from their tight buds slowly as the cold weather persisted. By March 27th, the crocus went wild with joy and color.

The sun rose higher, and I went wild as well.

CROCUS 2013 - The crocus began to bloom on March 12th and the green shoots of the daffodils rose rapidly and then it began to turn cold again. The early bulbs do well close to the warmth of the foundation of my home where it is protected from the wind. That certainly wasn't true the last two years of 2014 and 2015 with the cold, brutal weather. The snowdrops came out of their tight buds rather slowly as the cold weather persists. By mid-March, I noticed that the snapdragons barely pushed from the snap seeds that dropped to the earth last fall.

CROCUS 2014 - On March 11, I barely noticed the little green shoots of crocus that came up in the garden bed next to my home. We'll see what happens in 2015.

CROCUS 2015 - On March 21, it was bitter cold and there was a nary a sign of the crocus. The only thing I saw was 2 inches of a little green daffodil stalk close to the foundation of my home. A week earlier, I covered my cold frame with a large piece of clear plastic to warm up the soil so I could turn the earth and plant seeds. The bulbs and everything else in my life is very late in coming out. 2014 was cold and gray and 2015 was even colder.

Sugar Making is late this. Shelburne Bay close to my home is still frozen over. I couldn't get warm this morning. At least the sun is out. I didn't see my first white crocus until March 26th, the latest I can remember. By now, I should have been planting seeds in my cold frame in front of my house. When I removed the clear plastic from the cold frame the soil had warmed enough to be turned. I'll plant seeds within a week, fourteen days late.

CROCUS 2016 - This is one of the warmest winters on record. Sugar-making is starting very early. On March 7th, 2016, my crocus pushed out through the soil. I can't remember what happened in 2017 and 2018.

CROCUS 2019 - A cold, cold winter. My first crocus didn't come up until March 29th.

MARCH MARCHES ON WITH THE VERMONT FLOWER SHOWS: 2015, 2017, 2019

I like most folks are happy to get out of the cold and blowing snow. And for just three days in early March, the Vermont Flower Show invites us to do just that every two years.

The common thread in the 2015 flower show was "Water and its Reflections in Nature." Water sprung from the ground, tumbled over rocky streams adding sparkle to the indoor garden landscape. The Grand Design Garden featured many water elements, like a pond made from a 12-foot diameter satellite dish, a wetland where the observer could hear the sounds of birds, and a Persian garden oasis and mill pond. Plus, the colorful beauty of thousands of blooming bulbs, shrubs and trees.

In 2017, the theme of the Vermont Garden Show was "The Road Not Taken" in which "The Yellow Wood" was represented by an entrance filled with daffodils, where there was a replica of the Robert Frost Cabin in Ripton, Vermont. It reminded me of the time when I got lost years ago on the back roads in Ripton and ended up next to the Frost cabin. Hmm!

The 2019 Vermont Show was entitled "Wonder - A Garden Adventure for All Ages." Children have a remarkable sense of wonder about living things like a butterfly or a single blossom. The Flower Show shared an Urban Courtyard, A Walk in the Woods, a Breathing Room with an indoor space filled with plants that oxygenate the air and promote relaxation, a Mandala and Standing Stone Glen like Stonehenge and so much more - all filled with thousands of colorful bulbs, perennials, shrubs and trees.

GEORGE AND GAIL AFRICA - 2016

George and Gail live near Peacham Pond (Zone 4) in West-Central Vermont, a colder zone that where I live in (Zone 5) close to Lake Champlain. George said, "Crows call loudly from the compost pile as blue jays complain at my office window about a lack of seed in the feeders. There is an average of 20-25 jays a day at the feeders as well as 10-15 mourning doves so regardless of what other birds arrive to feed, the food supply quickly runs on "low".

The first grackles appeared, and Canadian geese are flying high in V formations. This is the last day we will have the feeders out as the birds are actively taking down all the remaining suet. You don't want the bears making a visit.

George went on to add that the 2016 winter has been on track as the warmest conditions since 1912. He said, "The back-gravel roads are filled with mud. I just watched a neighbor say a prayer and gun his engine and power through the mud. If you're coming to see me today, park at the top of the hill and walk. A tow truck operator I do not aspire to be."

George owns and manages the Vermont Flower Farm in Marshfield with his wife Gail. It's warmer there than their home in Peacham. He said, "This spring we are planning more riverside plantings of willows in hopes of stemming the erosion that is ready to take out our fences in the southwest corner of the farm. Over ten feet of the Winooski river bank on each side of the river has eroded in the nine years we've owned the property."

George and Gail will plant along the riparian way with a variety of trees and shrubs that will not only help to stabilize the bank but provide refuge for wildlife and help to cool the river water temperatures which have gotten so warm that the fish population is almost nonexistent.

George Africa's Blog - The Vermont Gardener - Vermont Flower Farm

(The Africas have been cultivating and selling blooming beauties since 1983, first at the Burlington Farmers Market and then on their five-acre nursery in Marshfield. They expanded the business in 1992 and today have more than 500 varieties of daylilies and almost as many types of hostas, with display gardens and fields surrounding their small office emblazoned with the company sign.)

FROST HEAVES

In March, frost heaves are nature's speed bumps, especially when you're driving down back country roads in Peacham like where George Africa lives. He feels those painful washboard sounds and bumps along with spilled coffee just like I did when I lived in the hinterlands of rural Vermont.

When the temperature goes through fluctuations during the cold months, previously fallen snow will melt and trickle down into the soil on gravel roads. Light soil handles this well but soil that has a denser structure like clay, tends to capture water and hold it under the pavement.

When the temperature drops again and water in the soil refreezes, this raises ice crystal formations, which are called, "Jack Frost." These formations are just like the frost typically seen on your windowpanes. Water creates a negative pressure in the soil as it freezes, sucking up moisture from the warmer soil by capillary action. Eventually, this pressure raises up the soil on back roads.

Frost heaves in garden soils push up plants and expose their roots to winter temperatures, damaging or even killing shrubs and perennials in very cold winters. Repeated frost heaves have traditionally given us in New England a bumper crop of rocks, which have provided many rocks for stone walls.

MARCH PRUNING TIPS

This is a good time to prune dead portions of roses, fruit trees, grapes and the dead portions of blueberries - if you haven't already. But do it soon like in early March. Make sure and prune the grapes heavily. Look at pruning pictures as a guide. You'd be surprised how much you need to cut out. I prune my grapes earlier in February.

Don't prune spring flowering trees like dogwoods, crabapples, smoke trees or flowering shrubs like lilac, azalea, pussy willow and forsythia. This isn't done until summer.

Eradicate woody invasives like buckthorn. Uncontrolled buckthorn (both common and glossy) can grow up to 20 feet tall and wide and kill forests by growing up under their canopies and outcompeting the native plants for resources. This is happening in Red Rocks Park near my home. It's very troubling.

Meadows, too, can be better managed when grasses and annuals have died back, revealing trees overlooked the previous spring. The exposed invasive trees can be removed by cutting them down along with rubbing branches and damaged limbs.

FYI - There are few herbaceous plants that flower in March and April like the *Christmas Rose (Zone 3) and *Lenten Rose (Zone 4), two of the Hellebores. Both have dark evergreen leaves and flower for six to eight weeks. They prefer well-drained soil in shade or partial shade. It is rare the Christmas Rose ever blooms in Vermont, especially in the colder spots.

APRIL

April 2013 - A cold spring indeed, much colder than 2012. I know because I'm burning more wood. What else is new? I need to transplant the small flower seedlings of hollyhocks and snapdragons started from seeds in my home into individual pots. For the young seedlings, I mix a soil-less germination mix with added compost for the potting soil: 5 parts soilless germination mix and 1-part compost. The germination mix is a commercial product of peat moss, vermiculite and perlite. My home-produced compost provides nutrients to the germination mix.

> *See more on germination mixes and potting soils in my first garden book, The Woodchuck's Guide to Gardening.*

I've been giving away bouquets of crocuses to friends. My first daffodil bloomed on Sunday, the 7th of April.

April 2015 - We had a blinding snow storm on the evening of April 8th as I was driving back from the Champlain Islands after doing a garden talk at the South Hero Community Library on my newest book, The Woodchuck Returns to Gardening. By the next day, the snow on the trees and shrubs had melted.

George Returns - 2015

George Africa said that on April 9th, the earth was covered in snow in Marshfield. Their hosta garden and all the potted hostas they sell remain under an insulating blanket or a blanket of snow.

He said that the winter of 2015, January through March, set a record as the coldest of 121 years. George said, "There is so much frost in the ground that it may still be frozen come May. Sometimes it feels as though winter stays in our bones, but with the sun and warmth, the soil warms up and so do we."

George went on to add that the best thing you can do for hostas is to save your coffee grounds during the winter months. Slugs and snails are often a problem with hostas but the caffeine in coffee kills these critters and make for much better-looking plants. Perhaps that's why roses also love coffee grounds. Why not secure spent coffee grounds at your local restaurants and gourmet coffee processors.

FYI - I pick up coffee grounds at Speeder and Earl's coffee shop on Pine Street in Burlington and mix them with compost in the soil around my blueberry plants. I'm given burlap bags from the Vermont Coffee Company in Middlebury. I use them on the paths between my garden beds plus I love their coffee.

> WALKING
> I walk Herk in the morn
> my feet crunch heavy snow
> as billions of sparkling-colored lights
> shine like stars in the universe
> I look across the wide lake
> behold the mountains of the Adirondacks
> glowing purple
> White Face mountain stares at me
> cardinals sing again and again
> will they ever stop
> hundreds of crows fly above
> honking geese in formations
> I walk Herk in the afternoon
> through forests and brown grass
> pine cones lay in abundance
> down to Shelburne Bay
> where ice floes fall apart
> jingling close to shore
> shimmering in rhythms
> ducks swim
> no polar bears to be seen
>
> *-The Woodchuck Gardener*

As noted, earlier, I describe plants in the order in which they bloom in spring and onto summer and fall. I place a *next to the name of the plant.

APRIL'S WOODLAND EPHEMERALS 2018

In mid-April, the woodland plants began to rise from the forest floor near my home in Red Rocks Park. I saw *yellow coltsfoot, *white snowdrops, *whitish Dutchman's breeches, *white and purple hepaticas, *light purple spring beauties, *yellow trout lilies, *white bloodroot, and others like *white and blue wood anemones and *white lily of the valley. Later came *white and red trilliums and *pink and red bleeding hearts.

In The Woodchuck's Guide to Gardening, I have a chapter on The Woodland Plants, often called ephemerals, a word with such a pleasant sound off your tongue. Just take a walk with friend who has knowledge of these plants, and you will begin to learn of spring beauties. And then every year, you will walk with the ephemerals again and again.

Here are my favorites;

*Coltsfoot - I want to mention one of my favorites spring plants. The small yellow coltsfoot is found along rural country gravel roads, muddy banks and open forest floors. It is one of the first spring plants to bloom in Vermont. Small flowers that look similar to tiny dandelion blooms appear and die before leaves are produced, leading to the name Filius ante patrem (the son before the father).

The seeds of the plant are soft, hair-like tufts often used by birds to build nests, and the leaves are broad and hoof-shaped, with hairs on upper and lower surfaces. The leaves and flowering buds are mainly used for medicinal purposes. I had never seen coltsfoot on the edge of the woods near my home until 2020. I was rather surprised as I had only noticed them on the damp banks of back-country roads.

Please note: The leaves will stick around for most of the summer, so the life-cycle for coltsfoot is too long for it to be considered a true Spring ephemeral, but it does bloom in early Spring, when the ephemeral flowers are blooming. Coltsfoot is a perennial that will return year after year.

*Snowdrops These are the earliest of the spring-blooming bulbs, often poking out above the snow as early as late March. Common snowdrops are tiny plants (3 to 6 inches tall) that produce one small (1 inch or less) white flower, which hangs down off its stalk like a "drop" prior to opening. The leaves are shaped like narrow blades, growing about 4 inches long.

*Dutchman's Breeches - One of the first ephemerals to arrive is Dutchman's breeches. This herbaceous perennial has many common names depending on which part of the country you come from. One is Little Blue Staggers, derived from its ability to induce drunken staggering if cattle graze on it, due to the narcotic and toxic substances in the poppy-related genus. This native wildflower is common throughout the eastern United States. Dutchman's Breeches blooms in early spring from April and into May. Flowers are white to pink and resemble a pair of pantaloons hanging upside down. You can't miss them. They're cute.

*Hepatica - This spring woodland ephemeral has three-lobed heart-shaped leaves in delicate flowers. In eastern North America, one of the most delightful early blooming species is hepatica (Hepatica nobilis). Its bright blue, white, or pink flowers warm the hearts of us humans.

*Spring Beauty - Perhaps no other wildflower announces the new season as fervently as spring beauty (Claytonia virginica). This is one of the most common native perennial wildflowers in eastern North America with its low-growing sweet small delicate flowers in star-like clusters of five white to light pink flowers. These woodland plants die back when the leaves of trees emerge in late spring.

*Trout Lily - A beloved spring ephemeral, Trout Lily is named for its maroon-mottled leaves, which appear in early spring in woodlands and shade gardens. The mottled leaves give rise to slender stalks with lovely nodding yellow flowers. I find them everywhere in the woods close to my home.

*Bloodroot (Sanguinaria canadensis) - This beautiful native wildflower of the eastern woodlands, blooming before the tree leaf canopy develops like the other ephemerals. It is considered to be endangered. This popular flower for shade gardens is one of the first plants to appear in spring, with delicate white flowers and a distinctive wrap around leaf. Bloodroot is often found along the banks of rivers where soil tends to be moist and alluvial with a seasonal replenishment of organic material thanks to the high waters.

Bloodroot pokes its white blossoms up from the soil with its leaves following below. Its flowers are self-pollinating. They form a seed pod ripening around July. Ants are important allies in spreading the seeds, and eating the rich lipid coating on the seeds, aiding in germination.

Indians used the root juice as body paint. Its curious name comes from its blood-red sap emitted from rhizomes, which was once used as a dye for wool and fabrics by Native Americans. It was also used for medicinal properties in the past. The red juice comes from the compound sanguinarine in the rhizome. While sanguinarine has anti-bacterial and anti-fungal characteristics, it can be toxic, so do not ingest it.

Bloodroot has other names including Red Indian Paint, Red Puccoon. It is one of about 60-65 species in the Poppy family (Papaveraceae) in North America. It is found only in North America and is most closely related to a plant native to China which has the common name of Snow Poppy or Dawn Poppy.

*Wood Anemone -(Anemone nemorosa) - This early-spring flowering plant is in the buttercup family Ranunculaceae and is native to Europe. Other common names include windflower, thimbleweed, and smell fox, an allusion to the musky smell of the leaves. It is a perennial herbaceous plant growing two to six inches tall. Other names are Lady's Nightcap, Moonflower, Nightcaps, Old Woman's Nest, Wood Crowfoot, and Wood Windflower. Flowers may be white, greenish-yellow, red, or purple, depending on the variety. I'm familiar with the white flowered ones.

Anemones, also known as windflowers, offer pretty blooms to bridge the seasons in spring and fall. Spring blooming anemones such as Grecian windflower (Anemone blanda) and poppy anemone (Anemone coronaria), are low growing plants that are perfect for woodland and shaded rock gardens.

The Japanese windflower (Anemone hupehensi var. japonica) blooms in mid-summer to early fall and reaches a height of 24 to 36 inches. Plant windflowers in the fall, from late October through November. I grow them in my community garden.

*Lily of the Valley - The delicate, fragrant flowers of lily of the valley typically appear in late spring and early summer where I live, and the plants bloom for three to four weeks. Lily Of The Valley is a delightful spring bloom with tiny, bell-shaped white flowers that do well in shadier, damp areas of the garden. The delicate white blooms brighten even the gloomiest corners of your garden. Once established, this springtime favorite forms a lush green carpet of foliage that makes excellent ground cover. And for a grand finale, this tiny flower packs a real punch when it comes to perfume. It is not considered a woodland plant. "So why did Ron mention it," said the "Chuckster."

*Bleeding Hearts - One of the most well-known and well-loved of the spring ephemerals is the old-fashioned bleeding heart, a graceful ornamental with rose-pink, nodding, heart-shaped flowers hanging off of arching stems.

Bleeding Heart's unique blooms delight children, and the plant's elegant appearance enhances cottage gardens and shady retreats. I grow in a shady spot in my community garden near the blueberries.

Dicentra spectabilis is the Latin name for bleeding hearts. This easy-care, heirloom favorite deserves a place in every shady garden. Its distinctive, heart-shaped blossoms open in late spring, dangling from slender, arching stems. Lacy, fern-like foliage creates an elegant backdrop for the flowers.

Generations of gardeners have lost their hearts to this lovely and reliable plant. The flowers of Dicentra spectabilis are a marvel. Each plump blossom has a little white teardrop that protrudes from the bottom of the heart. There can be 10 to 20 flowers on each stem and dozens of stems per plant.

Old fashioned bleeding heart can survive Zone 3 winters. The plants are very long-lived and seldom need dividing. They are also not troubled by insects, disease, deer or rabbits.

Bleeding heart is a woodland plant, and it should be grown in full to partial shade and moist, humus-rich soil. Mature plants can grow to be quite large, reaching 3 feet tall and 2½ feet wide.

As with many other spring ephemerals, it dies back to the ground after it has bloomed. When the foliage begins to yellow, the leaves can be cut back, or you can just let them gradually wither away.

Bleeding Hearts are native to northern China and Japan, and were discovered and brought to England by a plant explorer of the Royal Horticultural Society in 1846. The name Dicentra was derived from the Greek dis ("twice") and kentron (a "spur"), in reference to the two hooks on each bloom, and spectabilis refers to the plant's "showy" or "spectacular" appearance.

*Trillium - Trillium (trillium, wakerobin, tri flower, birthroot, birthwort) is a genus of about fifty flowering plant species in the family Melanthiaceae. Trillium species are native to temperate regions of North America and Asia, with the greatest diversity of species found in the southern Appalachian Mountains in the southeastern United States.

Plants of this genus are perennial herbs growing from rhizomes. There are three large leaf-like bracts arranged in a whorl about a scape that rises directly from the rhizome. The bracts are photosynthetic and are sometimes called leaves. The inflorescence is a single flower with three green or reddish sepals and three petals in shades of red, purple, pink, white, yellow, or green. Most of the petals are white. These amazing plants grow in the woods close to my home. To see hundreds of white trilliums is a wonder to behold. You almost can't catch your breath.

The red ones are called, "Stinking Benjamin", Trillium Erectum. I remember this one well. Years ago, I was teaching reading to elementary students in Jamaica, Vermont and the boys loved to take long sticks and pretend they were up at the plate and swing at the red trilliums. I asked them to wait until we were out on the ballfield.

Oops, I forgot to mention *Marsh marigolds, which are not related to common garden marigolds. They are in the Ranunculaceae family and are actually succulents. As their common name suggests, these wild yellow and green plants need damp soil, such as the boggy area around a pond or marsh. They require little in the way of care besides monitoring to make sure their soil doesn't dry out. They flower best with a little sun and shade. I call them, "Woodchuck spinach," as I love to steam the leaves a couple times and partake of the nutritious minerals in their greens, which you can literally taste.

skunk cabbage flower

P.S. - Oops, I forgot to mention skunk cabbage as well, where the flowers appear before the leaves just above the mud.

P.P.S. - If you want to grow woodland plants, purchase them from a reputable company and plant them in the right shaded locations. Just don't dig them up in the wild and replant them in your yard. That's not kosher.

> The kiss of the sun for pardon,
> The song of the birds for mirth.
> One is nearer God's heart in a garden
> Than anywhere else on earth.
>
> *-Dorothy Francis Gurney 1913 English Poet and Hymn writer*

> Everything is blooming most recklessly;
> if it were voices instead of colors,
> There would be unbelievable shrieking
> into the heart of the night.
>
> *-Rainer Maria Rilke, Letters of Rainer Maria Rilke 1910-1926*

Earth Day

Earth Day is celebrated on April 22, in which community events take place to demonstrate support for environmental causes. Earth Day began on April 22, 1970, and has been an important day for me ever since. It's a day to reflect on our planet and what we can do to help keep earth healthy. I describe the event in detail in the section The Unsettling Ecology of the New World in My Woodchuck Garden Blog.

Earth Day supports environmental protection and includes a wide range of events coordinated globally including 1 billion people in more than 193 countries. Check out *EarthDay.org*.

Two Old Trees

A New Jersey tree that survived the Revolutionary War was chopped down on Earth Day in 2015. This swamp white oak at 29 Ocean Street was believed to be 200 years old. A developer needed to have the tree chopped down in order to build on the property. The courts sided in his favor. "When will we ever learn." From the song of Peter, Paul and Mary, "Where Have All the Flowers Gone."

The oldest tree

The Oldest Tree in the Nation

It was believed to be among the oldest in the nation - took its final bow in the church graveyard that it's called home for 600 years. Crews began removing the relic outside the Basking Ridge Presbyterian Church in New Jersey. A huge yellow crane was seen towering over the tree as a helmet-clad worker moved about its centuries-old limbs. It took two or three days to remove the entire tree from the bedroom community about 30 miles west of New York, which has long celebrated its white oak. According to legend, it was a picnic site for George Washington.

Well before Columbus sailed to the New World and even before Gutenberg invented the printing press, there grew a great oak tree in a land that would one day be called New Jersey. The oak was already old when farmers built a church beside it in 1717. And when the people came and kept coming, a town called Basking Ridge was built around the church that was built beside the tree. I'm sure it was a "Mother Tree."

These highly-connected hub trees, also known as Mother Trees, share their excess carbon and nitrogen through the mycorrhizal network with the understory seedlings, which can increase seedling survival. In a single forest, a Mother Tree can be connected to hundreds of other trees.

Arbor Day

Arbor Day is celebrated on the last Friday in April to encourage individuals and groups to plant trees. Today, many countries observe such a holiday. Though usually observed in the spring, the date varies, depending on climate and suitable planting season. For more information, contact the Arbor Day Foundation. Millions of trees have been planted by members. I've been a member for years and have planted many of their trees including Hawthorns with those sharp thorns.

> EARLY APRIL
> as sap flows
> and sugar snows abound
> limbs bend
> mud slips
>
> *-The Woodchuck Gardener*

MID-APRIL
Herk's lilt picks up
wisps of grass in green
morning sun smarts my eyes
crocus abounds
here come the daffodils
the nearby bay floods
streams and rivers overflow
piles of logs and sticks
float to shore
no place to walk
my reliable harbingers of spring
will soon be here
shad in bloom
and peepers singing
the earth awakens
full of vigor
bird feeder comes down
hummingbird feeder goes up
with sugar and water

-The Woodchuck Gardener

Sunrise Over Camel's Hump - Joanne Denee

APRIL - 2019

This has been quite a spring. I don't know of anyone who isn't kvetching unless they're a snowbird who flew to Florida in early January and hasn't returned. The snow totals this winter were exceptional. The highest Vermont mountain, Mt. Mansfield, still has over 100 inches of snow at the top in late April. And Lake Champlain surpassed it's 100-foot flood stage and the main rivers that flow into it - including Otter Creek, the Winooski, Lamoille and Missisquoi rivers - along with flooded roads and fields - providing waterfowl habitat for ducks, Canada geese, and great blue herons.

I keep on praying for sunny, dry conditions but then it started to rain again and stay cool. This is getting old and I'm kvetching. I'm ready to plant flower seeds in the earth. The "Chuckster" just shook his head and said, "Maybe you should move to California, except for the wildfires."

EARLY FLOWERING BULBS, SHRUBS, TREES & PERENNIALS SPRING 2019

Please remember the plants you are familiar with and when they bloom and how they compare with my list. Sometimes I describe a plant one rarely hears about like hobblebush, which I find on Camel's Hump, the third highest Vermont mountain. Camel's Hump is an icon of Vermont. Its image is found on the Vermont coat-of-arms and on Vermont's contribution to the United States series of twenty-five cent coins.

The "Chuckster" just said, "Why not 'Play the Game' with Ron by identifying plants as they come into flower?"

*Pussy willows is the name given to many of the smaller species of the genus Salix (willows and sallows) when their furry catkins in early spring come out. My favorite pussy willow is black pussy willows! Much like the standard (and lovable) gray variety, (Salix gracilistylus) black pussy willows burst forth with bunny-like blooms or catkins, in velvety, jet black. This dark specimen is bewitching. They are not too common.

*Crocus - You may have noticed how earlier how I described croci from (2013-2019) and the different times when they bloomed.

*Daffodils - Daffodils are a hardy and easy perennial that grow in most regions of North America. They are a fall-planted bulb, so plant them in autumn and they will bloom in spring.

The traditional daffodil flower may be a showy yellow or white, with six petals and a trumpet-shape central corona, but many cultivated varieties ("cultivars") exist today. Leafless stems bear between 1 and 20 flowers; sometimes the flowers need to be staked so that they don't weigh down the stems.

Daffodils are suitable for planting between shrubs or in a border, or for forcing blooms indoors. They look wonderful in a woodland garden and in large groves. You'll find that many gardeners plant the bulbs not just by the dozens but by the hundreds! Daffodil flowers also make for great springtime cut flowers.

After my first crocus bloomed at the end of March in 2019, daffodils slowly emerged in varying shades of white with soft, pale yellows and yellows with orange trumpets.

By the way, daffodils are known botanically by the name Narcissus. They are poisonous to cats and are toxic not only to felines but also other animals including horses and dogs. The whole plant is toxic, especially the bulb.

Oftentimes a gardener will blame moles for eating their daffodils, but moles do not eat the bulbs or roots of plants. And voles don't eat all types of flower bulbs including daffodils. On the other hand, they love to eat my beets, carrots and sweet potatoes.

Animals such as squirrels, rats, mice, moles and skunks may dig up the daffodil bulbs in your flower bed. There is no proof that any animal will eat a daffodil bulb even though it is a standard assumption. There is a possibility that a skunk will dig into an infested bulb to get the grubs.

***Cornelian Cherry** - One of earliest shrub-like dogwood trees in spring has the name cherry, but is not a cherry at all. Cornelian cherry or Cornus mas, grows up to 20 feet tall and features bright yellow flowers that bloom early in spring, even before the forsythia open. Native to Europe where the bright red fruits produced later in the season are used for preserves and syrups, if you can beat the birds to harvest them.

A first cousin to the American Dogwood - Cornelian cherry is amazingly versatile. Left to itself, it will form a thick dense shrub that is perfect for screening and hedges. Apply just a little trimming and you have one of the most beautiful small trees around. Either way, the Cornelian cherry will provide a year-round show of beauty! I planted one in a friend's yard five years ago as part of a plan to replace her lawn with trees, shrubs and perennials.

This dogwood has clusters of fuzzy yellow star-like flowers followed by dark shiny green leaves and then accented by beautiful bright red olive-like berries, which ripen in late summer. In the fall, it provides a jazzy mahogany red display, as the leaves begin to turn and. Just when you think the show is over, Cornelian cherry comes back with an encore, as its bark begins to exfoliate and curl, revealing shades from gray too brown, in a visually pleasing display of texture and color.

*Shad - The snowy white blossoms of the native serviceberries (Amelanchier) are a familiar sight in spring. Also known as shadberries, shadblow, juneberrie and shadbush, these trees and shrubs are members of the rose family. A source of beauty year-round, they've earned a place in the bee garden. You may recognize it as that large shrub or small tree blooming in natural areas.

The shadberry is one of the earliest trees to blossom. Here is a fine poem by Ann Day of Fayston, Vermont, an old friend.

> TREE OF MANY NAMES
> Shadberry, you are the first too come
> with delicate blossoms of snow white.
> We see you by the roads and streams
> dancing in the April light.
> May brings the cherry blossoms out
> and then the apples show their flowers.
> But when we remember you were first
> to brighten early springtime hours.
> You delight the tastes of many birds
> when you ripen with June berry fruit.
> Squaws ground flour from your seeds
> and named you Serviceberry to suit.
> During the chilling frosts of fall
> your roundish leaves turn brilliant red.
> But I like you as the shadow of spring
> when flowers wave gently overhead.
> ~Ann Day Fayston

The fruits of the shadberry were important to the Native Americans and the settlers. They both used it dried much as we used raisins and prunes and as an ingredient in pemmican. Pemmican is a mixture of dried meat and fruit, corn, and or nuts. Different fruits were used, but shadberries were preferred. The early colonists used the shadberries in puddings, wines, pies, and as dried fruits.

You've heard me exclaim the "Woodchuck" Vermont principle of "It Depends." Well, the shadberry bloomed profusely in parts of Vermont in the higher elevations in 2018, but did poorly where I live in the warmer Champlain Valley. "It All Depends" said the "Chuckster." Thanks for saying what I just said.

*Forsythia - My forsythia shrubs began to flower on April 25th in 2019 - later than normal. These plants with their intense yellow flowers pop out in strong color in our yards. There is nothing subtle about forsythia as it's loud and screaming after months of greys and browns. We need this passion in spring.

Tulips and forsythias in my front yard

*Magnolias - And then came the magnolias. When it comes to spectacular spring blooms, nothing can compete with them. First is the star magnolia, (Magnolia stellata), with its white star-like flowers. Any winds will move the tepals, and if you squint hard enough, look like twinkling stars. Star magnolia is native to Japan and is a common specimen tree here in the U.S. What's amazing is that you only see the blooms with no leaves. They come later.

Magnolias, in general, have fleshy roots and few root hairs. They do not transplant well, once established. So find the proper place before digging the hole. As with any tree, do not plant them too deep.

Saucer magnolia (Magnolia x soulangiana) blooms a week or two later with its cup shaped flowers in various shades of pink depending on variety. Its parents come from China. Once the leaves drop in winter, the bark is an attractive smooth gray. They are commonly planted in Boston, probably because the heat of the buildings protects them against frost damage.

Dr. Norman Pellett planted Magnolia 'Leonard Messel' on his land in Charlotte, Vermont. Noted for its frost resistance, this award-winning variety is a vigorous medium-sized deciduous shrub or small tree of remarkable beauty when in full bloom. Opening from purple buds, the fragrant flowers, 4 in across, are deep pink with a delicate white tinge inside their 12 narrow tepals.

I was surprised when I saw a magnolia in the yard of Margaret Daniel high on the mountain above the town of Bethel on Christian Hill. The best feature of this magnolia are the bright whitish pink star-shaped blooms. While visiting Margaret in late January in 2019 on a bitter cold and snowy eve, I was amazed when I saw what looked like furry catkins flitting about in the air like birds on the Star magnolia. They reminded me of pussy willow catkins you see in spring. Any ideas?

I mention Margaret in my first book, The Woodchuck's Guide to Gardening. I call her "The Good Witch on the Hill," as she collects herbs and makes up tinctures and remedies.

Merrill Magnolia - According to Henry Homeyer, the author of 4 gardening books, one of yearly high points occurs when his Merrill magnolia blooms. This year, and most years, his blooms around his birthday, April 23. Only once in 25 years has it failed to put on a great show, when there was a hard frost just before the buds were to open. (Homeyer lives in Cornish New Hampshire, close to the Connecticut River.)

The Merrill magnolia is a "Loebner" hybrid, created by crossing the star magnolia (Magnolia stellata) with a Kobus magnolia. Most are hardy from Zone 4 or 5 to 7 - fine for all of New England. Homeyer's are white, with a soft light pink stripe on the outside of the petals (though technically they are tepals, not petals). And the blossoms are large - 4 inches or so - and fragrant. What more could you want? Other Loebner hybrids are pink or dark pink.

It really is a 4-season tree. The leaves are handsome all summer, turning a nice yellow in fall, and the flower buds are large and furry all winter, like pussy willows on steroids.

Star Magnolia - The star magnolia is a species magnolia, not a hybrid. It stays smaller than the larger Merrill - perhaps to 15 or 20 feet tall and nearly as wide. So for smaller landscapes, it is a good choice. It is rated at hardy to Zone 4, but some grow in Zone 3. The blossoms are white, and come earlier than the Merrill - so they can be damaged by late frosts. There are single blossoms and double blossoms with extra petals.

The southern magnolia is only hardy to Zone 6 or 7, so I can't grow one here. Too bad. The flowers are 8 to 12 inches across, creamy white and superbly fragrant. But the trees grow to be 50 to 80 feet tall - and live forever, it would seem. They bloom in May or June.

*Ornamental Apples (Malus) is a genus of about 30-55 species of small deciduous trees or shrubs in the family Rosaceae, including the domesticated orchard apple. The other species are commonly known as crabapples, crabtrees or wild apples. The genus is native to the temperate zone of the Northern Hemisphere.

Crabapples lost favor as landscape trees due to chronic disease problems, but newer varieties are disease resistant. The red-flowered crabapple Malus 'Prairifire', 15-20 feet high, is a perfect example. High disease resistance, colorful spring flowers, and persistent red crabapples now make a top-notch landscape tree.

Two more remarkably compact and disease resistant crabapples include the white-flowered, orange-fruited 'Adirondack' Malus 'Adirondack', 12 feet high, and dwarf, spreading 'Tina' Malus sargentii' 'Tina', 5 feet high, which offers fragrant white flowers and red fall fruits.

*Redbud - What could be lovelier that the brilliant light lavender pink flowers that line the bare branches of redbud (Cercis canadensis, 15-20 feet) in late spring. They have an elegant branching structure and heart-shaped leaves that look attractive through summer. I grew up in Kentucky and remember them.

A couple years ago, the redbud in the green across from my home was damaged by cold winter winds. It shouldn't have been planted there - in the open field with winds coming off the nearby bay, but in a more protected area. I pruned off the dead branches and it slowly recovered. Redbud trees can't take the cold weather of Vermont unless they are planted in Zone 5 and have some protection from the cold wind. They do best in full sun. In the hot summer of 2020, the tree grew to its greatest height and width.

This deciduous tree produces wood that is heavy and hard. They are known as the Judas tree. According to legend, Judas Iscariot hanged himself on a redbud species. The bark of the redbud has been used an astringent in the treatment of dysentery. Flowers of the redbud can be put into salads or fried and eaten. The seeds are eaten by wildlife such as cardinals, bobwhites, and deer.

*Japanese willow - I recently saw a small willow shrub with pink blossoms in late April. I wondered what it was. Known by many names, the colorful dappled willow continues to grow more popular in home-landscapes. 'Hakuro-nishiki' is synonymous with 'Albo-maculata', also commonly named 'Dappled Japanese Willow' or 'Variegated Willow'. It may also be marketed as 'Fuiji Koreangi', 'Fuiji Nishiki' or 'Albomarginata'. It is one of the smaller members of the willow family. The "Chuckster" just told me, "I don't want to say anything, but those names are fascinating."

*Lilac - I don't want to forget one of my favorite shrubs, the lilac. Consider planting them in a spot where you can enjoy their powerful fragrance in spring and early summer, especially with a breeze near a kitchen or upstairs like at my old farmhouse. I would awaken with their scent.

Dappled Japanese willow

Lilac

Lilacs (Syringa vulgaris) blooms in the northern states for 2 weeks in late May. However, there are early, mid, and late-season lilacs, which, when grown together, ensure a steady bloom for at least 6 weeks.

Lilacs come in many colors, but most are familiar with the common lighter purple lilac. It has dark gray-green to blue-green foliage (with no fall color change), and gray to gray-brown bark. However, there are officially 7 colors of lilac flowers: white, violet, blue, lavender, pink, magenta and purple with many shades within each color.

Lilacs need full sun to flower, and certain common varieties can spread aggressively, so it's best not to plant those types in a mixed border. Syringa vulgaris, the lilac or common lilac, is a species of flowering plant in the olive family Oleaceae, native to the Balkan Peninsula, where it grows on rocky hills. Grown for its scented flowers in spring, this large shrub or small tree is widely cultivated and has been naturalized in parts of Europe, Asia and North America. It is found in the wild in widely scattered sites, usually in the vicinity of past or present human habitations.

Lilacs are in the Genus, Syringa, one of 12 currently recognized species of flowering woody plants. It is commonly cultivated in temperate areas elsewhere. In Vermont, they bloom from mid to late May and early June in Zones: 3-7. Lilacs can be planted as a single bush or grouped together to form an informal, flowering hedge.

I have two common lilacs in my front yard, and they spread like crazy whereas my neighbor has a deep purple Canadian lilac, which has no desire to spread. I wish I had planted theirs. Sorry, but I don't know their variety. I grow common lilacs on both sides of my casa.

Lilac shrubs reproduce by seeds, but they also grow new plants from suckers. Shoots grow from the roots parallel with the surface of the soil. Each of these shoots can grow into a new bush. I snip off the suckers, but I never get all of them. Spring is a great time to do this as the soil is moist and easy to dig and the suckers are rapidly growing. If you want get a clone of your Grandma's lilacs, you can your propagate lilacs from suckers! Or you can install barriers that go down 6 inches or more into the ground that should keep the lilacs from spreading. The barrier could be a poly-based material with steel or metal edging.

Non-suckering lilacs will quite happily continue to grow for many years right where they were originally planted, without threatening to overwhelm neighboring plants. The creation of all these lilac varieties serves as a testament to the popularity of growing lilacs. The Miss Canada Lilac is by far the brightest pink of late flowering lilacs. It has a stunning and bright pop of color against the excellent dark-green foliage. This lilac shrub blooms around mid-June. This is definitely a vigorous grower and is a non-suckering shrub. Bloomerang Purple lilac is another non-suckering shrub.

Korean lilac (Syringa patula) has smaller flowers than the common lilac. This dwarf, spreading lilac with reddish purple buds that open to fragrant, pale lilac flowers. Blooms profusely in midseason, typically mid-May, and first flowers at an early age. Use in shrub borders with an evergreen background or plant in groups to form a low hedge. Their scent is intense and slightly spicy, with less sweetness than common lilacs. They bloom later than the common lilac. These are not the Japanese lilac tree, which come later than the common lilac.

Small Chinese hybrids (Syringa x chinensis) don't sucker as much as common lilacs, and they are more likely to stay within bounds.

Japanese lilac shrubs bloom later in June.

Dwarf Korean Lilac (5-6') is a small tree with spicy fragrant flowers. Several lilacs are actually trees instead of shrubs. Japanese tree lilac (20-25') is an elegant late-blooming specimen with enormous white blossoms.

When I have taken walks in the woods, I have sometimes found lilacs in scattered sites, usually in the vicinity of past human habitations, like near an old cellar hole along with a scattering of daffodils.

***Azalea** - Azaleas are flowering shrubs in the genus Rhododendron. They bloom in May and June in the temperate zones and their flowers often lasting several weeks.

A popular flowering shrub is Cornell pink azalea AKA Korean azalea, (Rhododendron mucronulatum). Blossoms come out before the leaves turning the multi-stemmed shrub into a mass of many clear pink flowers. It is native to Korea, Russia, Mongolia, and Northern China. Bees especially appreciate its rich nectar source and often can be seen visiting at all times of day.

Cornell pink azalea is one of the earliest blooming azaleas. Flowers bloom in clusters at the branch tips in spring. The flowers are a crisp, pure pink that fades to light pink. Shallow fibrous roots will benefit from mulching. It is exceptionally cold hardy and decorative as it is prized for its early blooms.

Most azaleas are smaller shrubs than rhododendrons, with thinner, more delicate leaves. They do best in filtered shade and moist, rich, well-drained and acidic soils.

Deciduous azaleas and evergreen azaleas generally live near or under trees; they are two of the eight types of the genus Rhododendron. Growing zones for azaleas depend on the variety.

All 17 species of azaleas native to North America are deciduous; they drop their leaves in the fall and are dormant in the winter. Their flowers bloom red, orange, pink/purple, yellow and white. Growing zones for azaleas depend on the variety.

See more on azaleas and rhododendrons later on book and in My Woodchuck Garden Website.

*Hobblebush - This Eastern native deciduous shrub abounds in rich, moist woods especially throughout the Adirondack Mountains. It is considered by many to be the best hardy native viburnum for New England and one of the earliest shrubs to bloom. The Latin name for hobblebush, Viburnum alnifolium, has been recently changed to Viburnum landtanoides. While it's hard to propagate conventionally and that may be why is so rare in the trade, it is a very hardy, care free plant in areas where it can be grown. The basic requirements are give it some filtered light shade, a damp soil and be patient. As it has a light root system it should not be moved once planted. While fairly widespread in its native range from Canada to high elevation areas of the Smokies, it's not really that common.

I have seen hobblebush when hiking on Camel's Hump, mentioned earlier. Where I saw it in the wild, it was always found near a stream or ravine and with hemlocks and or beech not far away. It was stunning.

The word Hobblebush comes from the fact that in nature, a low branch often "hobbles" along the ground, takes root and sends up a new plant. Often colonies seen in the woods that might be growing a hundred feet apart are actually the same plant. Don't let that image fool you, though, as this is a very attractive plant when grown correctly. Its overall form is a layered branch that looks kinda like a dogwood. When young it is very erratic with branches going everywhere (but not many of them!). Be patient, as it will mature into a fine shrub with tremendous branch appeal. It is very long lived - some which are 30 years old and still are going strong.

Nothing else has the distinctive copper-colored buds that hobblebush has. This winter feature that adds color to the landscape and is an easy way to "ID" the plant. Hobblebush's has naked' leaf buds, a term that refers to buds without protective scales. Where flower buds are present, they nestle between the two leaves in a pair. In this configuration, the flower buds resemble a moose head, with the leaf 'buds' playing the role of moose ears. That's why hobblebush is often called "Moosewood."

Since viburnums have leaves opposite each other along their branches and at branch tips, these leaf 'buds' are paired together, a perfect mimic of hands held in prayer.

The flowers: Like many viburnums the display is made of both fertile and sterile flowers. It is one of the first plants to bloom and leaf out, giving a cheery start to spring. More sun will increase the number of flowers, but in most climates, you want to give it partial shade.

A relatively flat flower cluster like those of hobblebush can accommodate lots of different pollinators, including many bee and fly species. As an insect moves from flower-to-flower foraging for food, its body brushes against and picks up pollen from the anthers at the tips of the stamens beneath it. This is an especially effective method of transporting pollen with insects that have hairy bodies to which the pollen can easily adhere. On the day I observed hobblebush flowers, flies were the most common visitors. Flies are important pollinators, especially when the weather is cool; many species are able to fly at lower temperatures than bees. If you look closely, you can see that the flies are actually eating the pollen.

Some butterflies and moths use hobblebush for food in a different way. The caterpillars of Spring Azure butterflies and Hummingbird Clearwing moths both eat the leaves or buds of this shrub.

In autumn, hobblebush leaves turn stunning shades of pink, red and maroon. At the same time the leaves are changing color, the fruit that results from pollinated flowers ripens from green to red, then deepens to a dark blue-black. The fruit is a drupe, a fleshy fruit with its seed encased inside in a hard coating. A peach is an example of a drupe. Many birds and mammals eat the fruit, and subsequently 'disperse' the seeds, complete with fertilizer.

In addition to reproducing through its flowers and fruit, hobblebush can reproduce vegetatively. Where its branches come in contact with the ground, roots can form, and a new shoot can sprout.

*Primula japonica - Commonly known as Japanese primrose, this perennial thrives in cool weather conditions. This charming herbaceous perennial has bright flowers and wrinkled, wavy cabbage green leaves. Japanese primrose makes an ideal plant for the wet shaded spots in a garden. Flowers first appear in May and continue into June. They come in a wide array of colors including pink, red, purple and white. The flowers open in tiers on a tall stalk. In order to succeed it needs moist, rich humus and neutral to acidic soil. If the site dries out the plants will not grow well. It has no insect pests or fungal problems.

Plants from the Primula Family, or Primroses, are famous perennials known for their bright flowers that grow in various shapes and colors. They are staples in cottage gardens as they can grow in various conditions. Primroses are bisexual flowers that are mostly yellow-colored but other varieties also produce white, red, pink and purple flowers.

Primrose flowers belong to the Primulaceae family and have a variety of 400-500 species. Primula plants will burn if planted in direct sunlight in hot areas and they need regular watering to keep their soil moist. Mulching around primula plants help keep the roots cool. This shade-loving plant is used in borders, mass plantings and containers.

They do well in a woodland garden or for planting among spring wildflowers in a shady spot of the garden - even without blooms the foliage is very lovely. In New England, it occasionally escapes gardens into forest fragments and the edges of brooks and streams. Given shade and moisture they will self-seed. Japanese primrose is native to Japan and is widely cultivated for its showy purple flowers.

Yellow evening primrose (Oenothera biennis L) is a sweet little wildflower that does well in almost any part of the United States. Though it's a wildflower, the evening primrose plant is as likely to be scorned as a weed as it is not to be welcomed into the flower bed.

Primula vulgaris, the common primrose, is a species of flowering plant in the family ... The primrose is distinguished from other species of Primula by its pale yellow (in the nominate subspecies) flowers produced singly on long flower stalks.

Primula veris, the cowslip, common cowslip, or cowslip primrose, is a herbaceous perennial flowering plant in the primrose family Primulaceae. The species is native throughout most of temperate Europe and western Asia. This species frequently hybridizes with other Primulas such as Primula vulgaris to form false oxlip, which is often confused with true oxlip (Primula elatior), a much rarer plant.

The common name cowslip may derive from the old English for cow dung, probably because the plant was often found growing amongst the manure in cow pastures. The species name veris (of spring) is the genitive case form of Latin "ver" (spring).

*Purple Leaved Plum - (Prunus cisterna) - It's not the fruit but the leaves that are purple. They are sometimes called Cherry Plum and is part of the rose family. This common Vermont shrub is planted most often because of its deep reddish-purple leaves and white to pale pink flowers, which are among the first to appear in spring. I see them everywhere. There is a Purple Weeping Plum.

*Purple Leaf Sand Cherry - (Prunus x cistena) is a hardy shrub that also belongs to the rose family. It is valued for its reddish-purple foliage and whitish-pink blooms. This widely planted deciduous small tree provides bright reddish-purple leaves that turn bronze-green in the fall.

The main difference between the two plants is their size and use. Purple sand cherries are generally grown as shrubs, and they rarely grow larger than 10 feet tall and 8 feet wide. In most cases, they stay much smaller. Purple-leaf plums, on the other hand, grow 15 to 20 feet tall.

Purple-leaf sand cherry, hardy in U.S. Department of Agriculture plant hardiness Zones 2 through 8, is a hybrid bred to have a smaller, more compact form. It's also known as the Bessey's cherry, American cherry or beach plum.

Native Americans consumed sand cherries ripe and fresh off the bush, but also dried them for later use. Early settlers also discovered the flavor of the sand cherries and featured them in many things such as pies, jellies, jams, syrups and wines. I planted two in my community garden.

This plant was first identified and given a Latin name by botanist Charles Edwin Bessey (1845-1915). Sand cherry pie was a pioneer favorite! In fact, it remains prized for consumption today. The y fruit is usually dark purple to black in color, indicating high anthocyanin levels, which suggest high antioxidant levels. Ripe sand cherries are also consumed by many wildlife species, so please don't take more than you can use. And don't eat the pits!

Many varieties of sand cherry are grown for their blossoms and will not produce fruit. You may have to do a little searching to find one that is bred for fruit production. The most commonly found one is the Purple-Leaved sand cherry and it is strictly an ornamental. The Nanking cherry - see-below is very popular as an edible bush cherry but it's actually a different species than sand cherry.

Purple-leaf plums are less winter-hardy than sand cherries, growing in USDA Zones 5 through 8. Although attractive in the landscape, both rarely live more than 10 to 20 years.

FYI - Identifying a flowering plum shrub is complicated because of a confusion of common names and the distinction between what is a shrub and what is a tree. In Vermont, it's a shrub.

*Purple Leaf-Nanking Cherry (Prunus tomentosa) is native to central Asia. It was introduced to North America in 1882. Other common names are Manchu cherry, downy cherry, and mountain cherry. I planted some at the Tommy Thompson Community Garden. It bears small red cherries. The tart, tangy fruit ripen in mid-to-late summer and can be eaten fresh or used in pies, jams, and jellies once you get the pits out.

Nanking Cherry is highly regarded as a shade tolerant fruit. We often see it planted as a hedge on the north side of a house where few other plants will survive, let alone thrive.

Nanking Cherry has fragrant white spring flowers, shiny reddish-brown bark and a favorite for mass plantings and borders. This is a vigorous, adaptable shrub is particularly suited to cold winters and hot summers. And the dense branching pattern means the shrub is also well-suited for use as a windbreak filler, hedge, or wildlife habitat.

APRIL GARDEN TIPS

Soil - As gardening season nears, I want to stress the importance of healthy soil. Please don't start working in your garden until the soil dries out. And please, don't treat it like dirt. Folks, dirt is a smudge or a stain. Soil is a living, breathing thing; it's a medium for growing plants and providing the nutrients they need for healthy growth.

The importance of soil is captured in the old garden adage that says, "you should put a $5 plant in a $10 hole." This advice is even more important when you're starting seeds indoors or growing plants in containers. When plant roots are confined to a pot, they need to get all their nutrients from a relatively small amount of soil. So it just makes sense to start plants off right.

Healthy garden soil contains a vibrant community of living organisms, including mycorrhizae, tiny microbes that form a partnership with roots to create healthy, resilient plants. (A mycorrhiza is a mutual symbiotic association between a fungus and a plant. The term mycorrhiza refers to the role of the fungus in the plant's rhizosphere, its root system.) Spreading compost and planting cover crops like annual rye, oats, buckwheat, peas and beans are key ingredients in supporting the mycorrhizae relationship.

Ron's Rube Goldberg Compost Tip - When I die, I would like to be laid out on an incline slab of wood. As my body decays, I would slide down the incline into a hole filled with soil and flower seeds. Soil would cover me with a little help from my friends and wildflowers seeds would bloom next spring. I just found out that folks in Vermont can be composted instead of being buried or burned into ashes, but it takes lots of paperwork. Hmm! The "Chuckster" just said, "I guess the old woodchuck gardener is ahead of the time." "When he dies, I'll let you know whether he was properly composted."

Hardening Off - Harden off annuals and perennials that you have been growing inside from seeds into seedlings before moving them into your garden. At first, leave them outside for about an hour or two each day and then increase the length of exposure to the cold, sun and wind. This is called "hardening off". Make sure not to put them in direct sun in the beginning. If it gets cold all of a sudden, bring them inside or cover the plants, which will protect them from the elements.

Dividing - Dig, divide and replant clumps of overgrown ornamental grasses, sedum, iris and daylilies. Spring is a good time to plant and transplant evergreens as there is plenty of water in the soil. Keep watering after planting. Fall is not the best time to transplant evergreens shrubs and trees because they dry out easily under stress.

Plant climbing hydrangea up a trellis or Boston ivy over a stone wall or chimney.

Lawn - Do not mow your lawn - if you still have one - until the grass is at least three inches tall. I haven't had a lawn for thirty years. When you leave grass clippings on your lawn, they are a good source of nitrogen for the soil, or use the clippings as mulch for your peas or in the compost pile.

Organic Controls - Use horticultural oil to manage mites, aphids and scale on trees and shrubs. Orchardists use the oil in spring to suffocate insects and any of their eggs that might be hiding on the bark of fruit trees such as apples, pears, plums, and cherries. It's commonly used and easy to apply. Mix the oil with water and a squirt of dish detergent to serve as an adherent, to help the oil stay on the plant. Go online for directions. Hort oil, available at agricultural, garden centers and hardware stores, is non-toxic and well worth the effort.

China - Over the years, I've noticed how some folks like to dig down to China in order to build raised beds. I've also seen the phenomenon of the "Bark Mulch Syndrome," that many gardeners and landscapers have embraced. It's like a rush to mulch everything from trees and shrubs in home gardens and onto college campuses and everywhere else. The problem is that when too much mulch is piled on, it leaves room for mice and other rodents to chew on the bark of the trunk, harming the tree.

Invasives - I've seen spreading poison ivy in the white pine forest near my home. And then there is garlic mustard, a very invasive weed. The roots exude a chemical that inhibit other plants from growing, and it can grow in full sun or full shade, making it a threat to a wide variety of our native plants and habitats. Each plant can produce up to 5000 seeds which remain viable in the soil for five years or more. Oy!

Favorite Flowers for Cutting - Highlighted here are some of my favorite blossoms for making bouquets - from springtime's fragrant sweet peas and peonies to the colorful summertime blooms of cosmos and zinnias. Annuals you plant this summer will offer an abundance of blooms, but the plants will not return next year as annuals only last one year. Take notes on which ones are your favorites.

Forget-Me-Nots

EARLY MORNING BLUES
I walk across
spring's soggy fields,
empty headed,
staring down.
seeing nothing but
old blue sneakers,
stepping on stalks
of last year's weeds.
Not hearing
Blue blacked swallows
swooping low
under gray skies.
Only my squashing.
slogging sneakers
with half a toe
sticking through,
heavy footed
in the wet of
morning.

-Ann Day Fayston, Vermont

DON'T LET THE BLUES GET YOU DOWN, LET THEM GET YOU UP

I want to share with you that most magical color of blue, so beloved in spring.

*Siberian Squills - Most folks don't know about the blue Siberian squills which begin as bulbs and are spread by seeds. They love to volunteer their services all over your garden and go well with yellow daffodils. Just wait a while before you mow the grass where the daffodils and squills bloom in yellow and blue. It's best to grow squills in a field or lawn, away from perennial beds.

*Bluets - One of the first spring flowers to show up are the native bluets (Houstonia caerulea). Most have four petals. Other common names are Azure Bluet and Quaker Ladies. Find them growing in moist areas near stream banks, rivers, and ponds. I see them in lawns where no herbicides were used. Cow fields are usually loaded with them in rural areas.

You may be pleasantly surprised to find thousands of bluets in a nearby woodland or popping up in other places in the landscape. If you look online to find out what they are, you may wonder, "Why are bluets called Quaker ladies?" Info on wildflower bluets says the petite little mounds of sky-blue flowers are so named because their shape is similar to that of the hats once worn regularly by women of the Quaker faith.

These tiny low-growing wildflowers appear in delicate clusters. Each flower in the cluster has four light blue and white pin wheel style petals, usually with a sunny yellow center. Popular in the May baskets of yesteryear, these beauties are one of the first wildflowers to show in spring.

*Forget-Me-Nots - These lovely blue flowers which spreads easily by self-seeding. You see them in May and June. These charming five-petaled, blue blooms with yellow center often grow well near brooks and streams which offer the high humidity and moisture desirable for this species. They don't look great after flowering.

*Lungwort (Pulmonaria) is a blue flower that receives its name from the spotted leaves silver-white splotches, which give people the impression of a diseased lung. They were actually used to treat people with pulmonary infections. Lungwort does best in the shade, but will tolerate some sun if the soil is moist. Pulmonaria is best grown in full to partial shade.

Keep in mind that most trees have not leafed out when lungwort blooms in spring and the weather is still cool and damp. Grow it in a spot that will eventually be shaded when the trees leaf out.

*Bluebells - Bluebell flowers are dainty bulbous perennials that provide a profusion of color ranging from deep purple to pinks, whites and blues. Although some confusion may occur from various English and Latin names, most bluebells are also known as wood hyacinths.

The native Virginia bluebells spread easily from self-seeding and look lovely with yellow English primroses. They will pop up everywhere. Virginia Bluebells features dainty nodding blue bell-shaped flowers at the ends of the stems. Its attractive pointy leaves remain bluish-green in color throughout the season.

They are one of the biggest favorites of shade gardeners and add a touch of real charm to any garden. Bluebells bloom in April and May - averaging about one to two feet in height. Their foliage tends to remain dense right to the ground. As this plant tends to go dormant in summer, it is best interplanted with late-season bloomers to hide the dying foliage. Bluebells do best in partial shade to shade. It prefers to grow in average to moist conditions, and shouldn't be allowed to dry out. It is not particular as to soil pH, but grows best in rich soils.

Creeping Phlox - Creeping phlox (Phlox stolonifera) is a low-growing, mat-forming plant that is often seen spreading as a ground cover, in rock gardens, and even in crevices of stone walls. It blooms in late April and May in Vermont with clusters of fragrant, five-petal blue, red, pink and white flowers that stretch almost an inch across. These flowers tend to attract butterflies and other pollinators to a garden. And after they're done blooming, the creeping phlox foliage still remains green and attractive for much of the year before dying back in the winter.

Creeping Phlox - Monica Marshall

Plant your creeping phlox in the spring after the danger of frost has passed.

***Wild Phlox** - At the end of May and beginning of June, the wild phlox came out. Phlox divaricata (Wild Blue Phlox) is also known as Woodland phlox and Blue Wood phlox. The colors range from pale blue to blue-violet to reddish purple, occasionally white. I love to see patches of wild phlox in open woodland settings. They jump out at you.

***Alliums** - My purple/blue ornamental onions (Alliums) bloomed in May late of 2019 in my community garden. They are one of the few perennials that come out early in perennial beds. I love to see them pop up in the garden. They really stand out.

They also bloom in other colors. Alliums are adored by bees, butterflies and pollinators, extending the spring flowering season with bold, dramatic colors.

FYI - Allium is a genus of flowering plants that includes hundreds of species, including the cultivated onion, garlic, scallion, shallot, leek, and chives. The generic name Allium is the Latin word for garlic, and the type species for the genus is Allium sativum which means "cultivated garlic".

*Borage - This biennial grows in the cold frame in my front yard. I can't wait for it to emerge at the end of May along with German chamomile with its small daisy like flowers. They make a lovely mix of color. Borage can be perpetuated by allowing the flowers to go to seed and self-sow. Pinching the terminal growth will force a bushier plant.

Borage and Chamomile in my front yard

Borage (Borago officinalis) is a common garden plant, alternately used as an ornamental flower, an attractor of beneficial insects and a culinary herb. It is native to the Middle East and has an ancient history in war as an enhancement for bravery and courage. Growing borage provides the gardener with cucumber-flavored leaves and flowers for tea and other beverages. This easy growing annual has vivid blue/purple flowers with the flavor and scent of cucumbers. It is considered a medicinal herb.

Borage is also known as starflower, bee bush, bee bread, and bugloss. It's not only a favorite plant of the honey bees, but also bumble bees. Borage adds trace minerals to the soil it is planted in, and is good for composting and mulching. Again, it readily self-seeds and thrives in full sun. It's so proficient in self-seeding that once a borage plant has established itself in your garden, you will likely never have to plant another one.

June and July are heralded by the presence of the borage flower in the cold frame in the front of my house along with chamomile. Its appealing, small, brilliant blue blooms should be included in your butterfly garden as it attracts pollinators.

The Blues Continue Down Summer's Road

***Blue Iris** - These perennial flowers spread fast and are easy to care for. Once planted, they will begin growing and multiplying each year, putting on a stunning show with their vivid hues. Dividing the blue iris bed every few years is recommended to maintain a healthy plot. Share your thinned out blue iris plants with your true-blue friends!

***Lobelia** - Great for window boxes and hanging planters, these small blue flowering plants will grow to spill out of baskets in charming disarray. Well-draining soil and partial sunlight will help these flowers to grow their best. They're also known to attract butterflies!

I jump for joy in spring when annual lobelias start showing up at my local nursery. Not only do many varieties have true blue flowers, a rarity in the garden world, but many also love cool weather and are in full splendor during spring and fall. They are a must-have for my spring containers, and anywhere else in my garden where I want to add a blast of blue.

***Veronica** - Everywhere I go in June; I notice the blue Veronica's which are also called Speedwell. The flowers are seen in the upper portion of their many stems. Veronica does well next to pink geraniums. You can cut them down once they've flowered. This carefree and easy-to-grow perennial has long spikes of small petals in purple, blue, pink, or white. Veronica grows in clusters from 1-to-3 feet tall, and blooms from spring to autumn. They bloom from June to August.

***Blue Hydrangea** - These large showy blooms come out in late summer. They make great floral arrangements and are a fun and easy flowers to dry. The color of the hydrangea flower is determined by the soil pH in which it grows. The pH scale is determined in terms of acidity or basicity (alkalinity). Aluminum needs to be present in the soil for it to be acidic enough to produce blue blooms. The white vinegar in your kitchen cupboard has a pH of about 2.4. A well-known base is sodium hydroxide, which will turn your hydrangea blossoms red. If the soil is naturally acidic, nothing needs to be added and the blue color will be maintained.

MAY

SUMER IS A ICUMIN IN
Spring has arrived,
Loudly sing, cuckoo!
The seed is growing
And the meadow is blooming,
And the wood is coming into leaf now,
Sing, cuckoo!
The ewe is bleating after her lamb,
The cow is lowing after her calf;
The bullock is prancing,
The billy-goat farting,
Sing merrily, cuckoo!
Cuckoo, cuckoo,
You sing well, cuckoo,
Never stop now.
Sing, cuckoo, now; sing, cuckoo;
Sing, cuckoo; sing, cuckoo, now!

-Anon Taken from an old medieval English song of the 1300s

May 2014

It's now the end of May and it's been warm and humid, but then, the cold blasted us right before Memorial Day and there were frosts in the higher elevations. I have notes going back to Memorial Day in 1997 when the temperature was 40 degrees, and the sky was overcast so I cranked up my woodstove and wondered why I live in the Green Mountains. The saving grace was that my lilacs were blooming, and I had my first fresh rhubarb pie from my friend, Antonia Messuri. I supplied the rhubarb. Such a deal!

The Old Woodchuck saying, "If it's not one thing, it's another" is quite appropriate for this time of the year. Just wait a minute and it might change. The "Chuckster" agreed with me on this one and mentioned another saying, "It Depends," which you can apply to anything in life.

The Grand Canyon of Lake Champlain - Brenda Patoine

MAY 2015

*Red Columbine & Canoe Can You - I took my first canoe outing of the year in mid-May of 2015 with a friend on Lake Champlain. We canoed from Shelburne Bay towards the open lake to an area close to the cliffs of Red Rocks Park. I call it the Grand Canyon of Lake Champlain as you can see a myriad of horizontal colors and striations on the high rock face. We saw the wild *eastern red columbine in bloom from the crevices on its rocky hillsides.

What I like about this beautiful woodland wildflower are its showy, drooping, bell-like flowers with distinctly backward pointing tubers. I'm referring to the red colored sepals and numerous yellow stamens hanging below the petals. The tubers contain nectar that attracts long tongued insects and hummingbirds adapted to it sweet secretions. Once started, columbine propagates for years, although this perennial increases as well by self-seeding.

Ear Wigs - My neighbor Marilyn Maddison called and said her house was being taken over by ear wigs. I suggested using diatomaceous earth as it kills many types of crawling insects. It's a naturally occurring, soft, siliceous sedimentary rock that is easily crumbled into white powder. This powder has an abrasive feel, similar to pumice powder. It consists of fossilized remains of diatoms, a type of hard-shelled algae. It's used in cat litter, a filler in plastics and rubber, a thermal insulator, and many other uses. And it worked on the ear wigs!

May in My Home Garden 2018

I was hoping for a May filled with perfect intervals of blue skies interspersed with soft rain, sun, and rainbows - an ideal scenario. So far, we've had mixed results with dryness and just enough rain. Every growing season has its quirks, but this year, the crabapples bloomed at the same time as the lilacs. Crabapples usually bloom before lilacs. That's weird, but what isn't in this time of climate disruption.

Unfortunately, my pink-red flowering crabapples got a fungus and many of the leaves dropped off. I need to spray them with an organic sulphur spray. Scab is a fungus that attacks crabapple and apple trees in cool, moist weather. It lives on the leaves throughout winter and begins to grow in the spring.

As a way to celebrate May, I gave my houseplants a party by moving them outside to a shady spot, providing them a good bath and feeding them with compost tea. I repotted the older ones. When it got cold, I covered them with blankets and floating row covers and watered when needed and left them out till late September.

When I bought annuals, I looked at the ones that were healthy and beginning to bud. Annuals look great in beds as well as mixed with perennials. If you don't have room in your garden, grow them in containers. Three favorite container varieties are `Pixie Sunshine' - zinnia, `Little Ladybird' - cosmos and `Junior' - sunflower.

I bought *purple petunias and *alyssum annuals on sale, which I transplanted into old clay and plastic pots in my front yard.

I've noticed that the soil was dry, so I began to do a rain dance, but just as I did, it started to rain. Hmm!

In May, I watered the three bird baths in my home garden. I keep the water fresh so those winged creatures will have a wonderful drink and dip. The bird baths lean over now and then from frost heaves, and I have to prop them up with wooden stakes.

My Crabapple In Bloom

Apple Blossoms On My Brick Walkway

In my front yard, I have yellow forsythias, a red/pink flowering crabapple for the birds to hang out on - plus light purple lilacs and a hedge of rosa rugosa's and a *snowball viburnum in that order.

May is the time to take down my bird feeder and put out my hummingbird feeder filled with sugar water. Most years, forsythias bloom out in early May and lilacs from mid to late May. *Rhododendrons and *azaleas bloom in May to early June. I cut *purple irises to lighten up my home with color. The buds kept on opening.

Magnolias - described earlier - began to flower from early to mid-May. Some are hardy in Zone 4, including the Star magnolia (Magnolia stellata), a shrub-like tree that comes from one of the most ancient flowering plant families.

Late May is a good time to transplant groundcovers of English ivy, myrtle, pachysandra and ajuga. *Myrtle has cheerful blue flowers and is also known as Vinca minor or periwinkle. It's a favorite of gardeners as it spreads rapidly and blocks out weeds and grasses. Plant it under a large shade tree along with hostas and astilbe.

I like to grow the annual, *Angel Trumpet (Brugmansia), a highly attractive and popular tropical flowering plant. It has trumpet shaped blooms, in a variety of colors including white, peach, yellow and orange. Hummingbirds are attracted to the bright blooms. Did you know Brugmansia was named after Sebald Justin Brugmans, a Natural History professor from Holland? It blooms in mid-summer.

Angel Trumpet is also called, Trumpet of Death, as it is a highly toxic plant, and a member of the Nightshade family as are tomatoes and potatoes. Historically, it has been used as a hallucinogenic drug. This dangerous plant has caused some deaths, especially from teenagers experimenting with it after hearing rumors about its hallucinogenic powers. It is most often ingested in the form of a tea. If you have children or pets, I highly recommend you consider the risks before growing this plant. Castor Oil plants are also dangerous to grow. They are large, lovely and toxic as well. I used to grow them in my community garden plots, but decided not to continue because of their hazards.

National Wildflower Week May 6-12, 2019

There are many wildflower mixes including: Deer Resistant, Drought Resistant, Regional Pollinator, Quick-blooming Spring into Summer Sun and Native Regional Wildflower Mixtures.

A Wildflower Meadow-like Lawn

I was asked to put in a back-lawn wildflower garden by a friend so here's the scoop. It wasn't that simple, and it took time. I began in early May.

I first used a lawn mower to mow and cut the existing vegetation very close to the ground and let it dry in the hot sun. I then tilled the sod with a rototiller, removing as much grass and weeds as I could. This was the hard part of the task. I tilled lightly again. I couldn't remove all of the sod or weed seeds, but I did the best I could.

I then watered and let some of the weed seeds germinate after a couple weeks. I raked up what was left of the sod and weeds. You're never going to get it all using this method, which by the way -isn't good for the health of the soil, but ...

I then added compost, watered, and raked the soil - creating a garden bed. I determined the right seed mixture and spread the wildflower seeds. I raked covering the seeds with a soil and watered lightly and guess what, it worked.

Now my friend has a back-lawn covered in wildflowers. There were still some weeds, but that's okay. Over the years, I've found that native wildflowers and grasses persevere.

FYI - Natural, low-maintenance wildflower meadows contain a mixture of native grasses with annual and perennial flowering plants. It's important to choose a mix that will thrive in your particular sun, soil, and climate conditions. Suppliers of wildflower seed mixes can advise you on the best mixes for your area. Perennials include Eastern red columbine, swamp milkweed, coreopsis, sunflower, blazing star, wild bergamot, common evening-primrose, lupines, goldenrod, black-eyed Susan, rudbeckia, and New England asters.

In subsequent years, plant additional perennials, annuals, and grasses to fill gaps. A meadow of mixed flowers and native grasses can replace your lawn, cover a slope, or enhance a roadside. Most meadows require much less water and fertilizer than lawns do, and they rarely need mowing. Many mixes contain common annual flowers, such as bachelor's buttons and cosmos because they self-sow.

May 2019 and 2020

I hope warm weather is a-comin. Well, in Mid-May in 2019, snow showered down. It continues to be cool and rainy in June. What else is new. And then May in 2020 was hot and dry with little rain, the hottest summer on record until 2021. Hercules did a lot of panting as I did as well. I kept the fans a-blowin.

May Festivals

May Day on May 1st is an ancient Northern Hemisphere festival to welcome spring and the world of flowers, green grass, and picnicking. When I attended Emerson College in Forest Row, England in 1980 to study Biodynamic Agriculture, we celebrated May Day with Maypole dancing. For some odd reason, I was chosen to lead my fellow dancers in costumes as we weaved around the Maypole. I led the group around the pole with no mishaps to my amazement.

May Day is also a day of solidarity and protest from labor groups. It dates back to May 4, 1886, when some 200,000 workmen engineered a nationwide strike for an eight-hour day. It was known as the Haymarket Affair in Chicago. It's now known as International Workers' Day throughout the world. The Haymarket Affair, sometimes called the Haymarket Massacre, was the aftermath of a bombing that took place at a labor demonstration. It began as a peaceful rally in support of workers striking for an eight-hour day and in reaction to the killing of several workers the previous day by the police.

Green-Up Day in Vermont is celebrated on the first Saturday in May. Its mission is to promote the stewardship of the state's natural landscape and waterways. You'll see thousands of people picking up litter with Green-Up bags plus old tires, parts of old rusty cars, appliances, metal and every kind of trash and plastic in the universe. I celebrate Green-Up day 365 days a year. How about you? The "Chuckster" said, "I don't want to say anything, but Ron loves to exaggerate."

The first official Green Up Day was held on April 18, 1970, after having been formalized by Governor Deane C. Davis. The State of Vermont cleans up the State Highways, and Green Up Day volunteers clean up all the town roads, waterways, ditches and other areas.

I described Earth Day earlier. It occurred on April 22, 2020, which marked its 50th anniversary.

Bird Day in the USA falls on May 4. It is one of the oldest observances - established by school superintendent Charles Babcock in Oil City, Pennsylvania, in 1894. Babcock intended to advance bird conservation as a moral value, that is why he introduced the holiday.

THREE ALTERNATIVE GARDENS: LASAGNA, RAISED BED & CONTAINER

Lasagna Gardens - In 2014, I built a lasagna garden bed - six feet long and four feet wide for a friend. This no-till/no-dig method is easy to construct. It was the craze a couple years back.

I simply created an oval using a hose for on outline and placed newspapers over the bed. I then layered browns (shredded leaves and old mulch) and greens (grass clippings and vegetable scraps) into the foot-tall bed. I continued to add whatever I could find to create a garden bed, including compost. The garden bed sat over the fall and winter and by mid-May, I added more compost and soil and began to dig down into the bed.

This lasagna garden got lots of sun. I decided to plant sun-loving perennials in the bed. The soil was dry, so I watered and dug holes for the perennials. I transplanted sun-loving yarrow, sunflowers, Shasta daisies, and daylilies, phlox, coneflowers, and comfrey. I know! I know comfrey spreads some, but it can be controlled, and it enriches the soil.

Raised Beds Gardens - I built a raised bed from wide boards of an old picnic table which had seen its last days. What's great about raised beds is that they're easy to grow plants in - even if the soil is clay. Just mix in lots of compost. They provide a great place to grow greens, vegetables and flowers with little maintenance.

The advantage of raised beds is that they warm up earlier with covers and drain water faster and you aren't standing on the soil plus they allow you to weed in a smaller space. You can start plants earlier and extend the growing season.

Raised bed gardening is a great way to break into your first garden. If you use wooden sides, raised beds work even better. Plus you can cover them to create a cold frame with wood and plastic like plexiglass. I describe them in my first garden book, The Woodchuck's Guide to Gardening. An ideal wood to use for the sides is hemlock as it can handle moisture, will not rot and last a long time. Hemlock has been used for making boats and bridges historically. You can go your local lumber yard for fresh cut heavy hemlock. Cedar is even better to use, but its pricey.

Go online for more on building lasagna and raised bed gardens.

Container Gardens - For many folks, container gardening is a practical way to have a garden on a balcony, deck, patio or rooftop. They are an easy way to add color to tight spots in your garden or on your porch. I use containers for growing dahlias in my small backyard as there is little room, even though they don't do as well as dahlias planted in my garden.

Here are some tips: Plants in containers need healthy soil, aeration, and drainage for root growth. Do not use soil from the garden. Use a potting mix with compost for the ingredients. You need a pot that is sturdy enough to hold the mix with drainage holes. The key is to water the pots thoroughly once a week.

You can use containers in sunny and shady spots. I've grown tomatoes, peppers, and basil in containers in my front yard garden, which has lots of sun.

Please understand, it's not as simple as throwing some impatiens in a pot and calling it a day. You need to pay attention to what plants you're pairing in a container. Some plants grow well in both sun and shade, while others are pickier in their preferred light exposure and water requirements. Aesthetically, it's important to vary the height, color, and texture of plants for an eye-catching display.

More practical gardeners tend to use three different types of pots; clay pot, ceramic pots, and plastic pots. Clay pots are great because they have a very old-fashioned look to them. You can grow plants that like dry conditions, like geraniums for example, because they tend to dry out. Ceramic pots are really nice because they're so beautiful and you can put so many different decorative plants in them. Make sure they have drainage holes in the bottom. You can insert a smaller plastic pot and it in your ceramic pot. This will provide enough drainage for your plant to survive. Then there are plastic containers. They are decorative, lightweight, and durable. The best ones are the self-watering pots. These have a water reservoir in the bottom. The dry soil in the plant will suck up the water. You can take a short trip without worrying about watering your plants. I have some of these self-watering containers.

You want to fill up your pot with your potting soil right up to the rim and then moisten it really well. You want to select plants that are going to fill out the whole container. This is called selecting a thriller, filler, and a spiller. For example, a thriller is a beautiful daisy. Place in the center of the container. Fillers go around the thriller like smaller ageratums. They fill out around the edges of the container and create a bushy effect right inside the container.

Finally, you want plants that will cascade over the edge of the pot. Lobelia is a plant for this purpose. They'll drape themselves providing color all around it. Add some compost to the pot and place in full sun and water and water.

The kiss of the sun for pardon,
The song of the birds for mirth.
One is nearer God's heart in a garden
Than anywhere else on earth.

-*Dorothy Francis Gurney 1913 English Poet and Hymn writer*

MY TOP GARDEN INVASIVES

There are many garden invasives weeds including goutweed, witchgrass and gallant soldiers (chickweed). They are at the top of my chart of undesirables, and mostly occur in vegetable and flower gardens. Other less problematic garden invasives include crabgrass, lamb's quarters, and pig weed (red root) - (amaranth), which can be controlled with persistent weeding.

*Snow-on-the-Mountain - The big one that gives folks the most trouble in their home perennial gardens is Goutweed or Bishop's Weed. The non-native invasive species Bishop's Weed (Aegopodium podgraria) is often called Snow-on-the-Mountain. I see it growing everywhere because it is so highly invasive. This perennial groundcover, which prefers shade and is part of the carrot family, loves to spread by way of rhizomes. It had been introduced around the world as an ornamental plant, but now is an invasive species. The trolls used goutweed as a cooking ingredient to make their stews more appetizing.

This variegated beauty is fast-growing and can even grow under maple trees. (Variegated foliage refers to any plant with leaves bearing more than one color.) It's hard to imagine a more difficult plant to control. This herbaceous ground cover is low-growing, creeping, very dense and mat-like, and 6 inches tall by 12 - 24 inches wide. It is covered with white flowers suggesting a snowfall along with silver and green foliage. It looks completely at home in hot, dry locations like in rock gardens, along the edges of retaining walls, and tucked into the cracks of stacked stone walls.

Prune plants and remove dead flowers after blooms have died. This has to be done time and time again. I use a weed-whacker.

Lynette Courtney of Greensboro Bend, Vermont torches goutweed. My friend of Wentworth, New Hampshire, Deborah Stuart, uses the "ring around the collar" approach. She digs a trench around the attack area and then digs up the gout weed as much as one can and covers it with black plastic. Deborah places thick newspapers in the trenches to keep the Gout weed from spreading. Her search and destroy method is somewhat effective, but it takes constant vigilance as the weed has a way of coming back to haunt the most ardent of serious anti-spreaders. After a year, Deborah pulls up the black plastic and digs up any remaining roots, being careful not to leave any rhizome sprouts, which is almost but impossible.

I use old cedar shingles that still had some life in them in the trenches as my "ring around the collar" approach to rid the "World of Gout Weed." In Marilyn Maddison's Children Garden across from my home, many folks have come to help to rid the garden of goutweed, but it persists more than the humans.

If Bishops weed takes over your perennial bed, you may need to carefully remove the perennials and create a new bed as you won't win the war against this pernicious weed even though you may be deceived into thinking you won the battle. Some folks give up on the garden path and allow the rather lovely weed to thrive. They practice the art of acceptance by starting other beds of perennials.

Another gardener took the dirt approach by digging Bishops weed up in the spring when the ground was moist. It took about him three years to remove but he still finds a sprout here or there popping up in unexpected places. He will admit it's a control issue. The little fellows just keep on coming but they can be controlled with tenacity and wit and an acceptance that one can never let down ones' guard. My neighbor at the community garden, Fred Schmidt, is now dealing with Gout Weed. He's working hard to eliminate this pernicious weed. "Lots of Ruck."

More on - Snow in the Summer (Zones 3-10) - Cerastium Tomentosum This easy-to-grow plant can be grown from seeds. This herbaceous ground cover is dense and low-growing. It is native to western Asia and Europe. It has naturalized across most of the United States, where again, it isn't welcome due to its extreme invasive tendencies.

Goutweed is covered with white flowers, but it also has striking silvery green foliage. It looks completely at home in hot, dry locations like in rock gardens, along the edges of retaining walls, and tucked into the cracks of stacked stone walls.

Since snow-in-summer is native to dry, rocky areas, keep drainage top of mind when growing this plant. If snow-in-summer's soil stays wet for long periods of time, the plant's roots may rot. Snow-in-summer does not handle high humidity and summer heat well, especially if the plant remains wet.

Snow-in-summer plants get their common name from their blooming habit. They flower profusely in the summer in a pristine white - suggesting a fresh snowfall.

*Witchgrass - (Panicum capillare) - Other names include old witchgrass, tickle-grass, witches-hair, tumble weed-grass and fool-hay. This common summer annual weed occurs in nursery crops, landscapes, roadsides, and gardens across a wide range of environmental conditions. Its most distinctive features are its dense coat of fine, soft hairs on stems and leaves and its large, feathery flowering heads. The root system has a taproot or rhizomes. I find that I have to dig out the rhizomes for a couple of years in my gardens and even then, they still come back, but there are fewer. Its hard to get rid of.

*Chickweed (Galinsoga parviflora) - Its common names include gallant soldier, yellow weed, joey hooker, potato weed, quickweed and small flower galinsoga. It has small yellow flowers.

Common chickweed is an invasive annual, low-growing herb native that occurs throughout vegetable and flower gardens. It prefers shady, moist locations. Common chickweed is able to create dense mats of shoots up to 12 inches long, shading young seedlings of other plants. It invades, spreads, and out-competes other summer annuals. Chickweed is easy to pull out.

Other Invasives - Deborah Stuart, mentioned earlier, has tended her gardens in Wentworth, New Hampshire in the foothills of the White Mountains for over forty years and is somewhat discouraged as many of her garden beds have been taken over by invasives other than gout weed. These include old phlox varieties even though the newer ones don't spread as much. Liatris spicata, whose common name is blazing star and gayfeather with its pink and purple flowers have also spread in Deborah's perennial beds. Other spreaders include Lily of the Valley and bee balm, though not as much.

Other invasive plants in our gardens, forests, fields and wetlands to pull out include purple loosestrife, which destroys wetlands. English ivy, which makes its way into forests where it climbs trees and carries diseases. Japanese honeysuckle vines can climb more than 80 feet, latching onto trees and forming a sense canopy that can shade out everything.

Oriental Bittersweet (Celastrus orbiculatus) is a deciduous, woody, perennial vine native to China, Japan and Korea, that was brought to this country in the mid-1800s as an ornamental plant. Oriental bittersweet has yellow capsules, while those of American bittersweet are orange. Both are now considered a serious invasive species because they pose a significant threat to native plants. There are no known biological controls of bittersweet. Small infestations can be hand-pulled but the entire plant should be removed including all the root portions. For climbing vines, first cut the vines near the ground at a comfortable height to kill upper portions and relieve the tree canopy.

Common and Glossy Buckthorn are two non-native, invasive buckthorn species. These trees were first brought here from Europe as a popular hedging material. They became a nuisance plant, forming dense thickets in forests, yards, parks and roadsides. They crowd out native plants and displace the native shrubs and small trees in the mid-layer of the forest where many species of birds nest. They are a serious invasive in Red Rocks Park close to my home.

Garlic mustard is a very invasive weed. The roots exude a chemical that is inhibit other plants from growing, and it can grow in full sun or full shade, making it a threat to a wide variety of our native plants and habitats. Each plant can produce up to 5000 seeds which remain viable in the soil for five years or more. All of these traits allow garlic mustard, once established in an area, to rapidly reproduce and spread, excluding native and landscaping plants while spreading quickly across the landscape.

Other serious invasives include burning bush, water hyacinth, Jerusalem artichokes, barberry, and Japanese knotweed. These terrestrial invasive plants disrupt our ecosystems and displace native plant species. However, management of these invasive species is possible with hard work and community involvement.

New Invasives In My Garden 2019 & 2020

These include the dangerous wild parsnip I found in my community garden for the first time. I dug out two of them wearing a long sleeve shirt and gloves. My neighbor, Fred, dug some out, but he wasn't as careful and got serious burns on his arms. You can see wild parsnip in the ditches along roadways.

The newest invasive to infiltrate my garden is Japanese hops (Humulus japonicas). This annual, climbing or trailing vine is native to eastern Asia. The plant was introduced to North America in the mid-to-late 1880s as an ornamental, and has become invasive in the eastern half of the United States. This vine has five-lobed leaves (generally), downward pointing prickles on the stem and bracts at the base of the petioles. It is real bitch to remove as it needs to be dug out.

Sign for identifying elmerald ash borers

Serious Tree Pests in Vermont include Emerald Ash Borer, Asian Longhorn Beetle, Hemlock Wooly Adelgid and the Southern Pine Beetle. This beetle is slowly making its way into Vermont. It is now in Massachusetts. The Emerald Ash Borer is the most serious of all the pests. Many ash trees are being removed. There is a chemical treatment, but its pricey. Some towns are planting trees between the ash as it won't be long before they are removed.

SUMMER

In summer, the song sings itself.
-*William Carlos Williams*

The Earth Laughs in Flowers
-*Ralph Waldo Emerson*

JUNE

National Pollinator Week June 17-23
Bees, butterflies, and other pollinators need our help. As gardeners, we have the ability to provide food, water and shelter - essentials they need to survive.

> EARLY SUMMER PICKING
> hot day
> picked strawberries and peas
> soaked tee-shirt
> dunked my head
> in barrel of water
> a mosquito heyday indeed
> legs and arms beckon for witchhazel
> my pants plastered in mud
> can't wait for home
> coolness on tree shadowed roads at eventide
> listen to the sounds of people walking
>
> -*The Woodchuck Gardener*

FLOWERS & THEIR SPIRITUAL MESSAGES

Red Poppies, Green Dill and Yellow Calendula In My Community Garden

When taking a rest from my community garden in June, I observed red poppies, green dill and yellow calendula, which drop seed and come back year after year. When watching them, I'm get a smile on my face along with quiet meditation. I've often wondered about the power of flowers and how they provide both beauty and practicality for insects, but it's much more than that.

Each flower in its color, form and fragrance embodies a particular spiritual quality. Flowers gives rise to a certain experiences. Perhaps, if you are able to identify your experience, you can perceive its quality.

In Shakespeare's time people were more aware of the language of flowers, and made use of this floral symbolism. "A rose by any other name would smell as sweet" is a popular reference to Shakespeare's play Romeo and Juliet. In A Midsummer Night's Dream, Shakespeare inspired the phrase 'gilding the lily.' Ophelia, the tragic heroine in Hamlet, drowned herself surrounded by garlands of wild flowers. That's odd as I just watched Ophelia on a DVD.

Shakespeare continues with the words, "I know a bank where the wild thyme blows, where oxlips and the nodding violet grows, quite over-canopied with luscious woodbine, with sweet musk-roses and with eglantine." Did you know that woodbine is an old name for honeysuckle, and oxlips are similar to cowslips, but larger? Cowslip is marsh marigold where I live, which I call "Woodchuck" spinach.

We all know that color is a significant aspect of a flower's consciousness. Each color represents a certain aspiration and can help us discover unknown parts of our own inner being. Yellow is the color of mental aspiration and thus, the yellow Rose represents "Mental Love for the Divine." Pink or pale rose are the colors of the psychic as with the redbud bloom. The red Rose represents "Human Passions Turned into Love for the Divine." The darker blue, violet and red colors denote vibrations of the vital or nervous and physical centers in us. The beautifully scented Narcissus flower, whose story was told by the Latin poet Ovid, represents the "Power of Beauty."

Daisies are a symbol of innocence and the violets, now withered, mean faithfulness. Rosemary is particularly associated with remembrance of the dead, and pansies get their name from pensées, the French for thoughts.

Let's end with an exercise. Please meditate on what your experiences are with your favorite plants and flower colors.

From The Old Farmer's Almanac 2020

SUMMER COLOR ALL SEASON LONG PLUS TIPS AND FAUX PAWS

So folks, as we continue with summer, I want to share some ideas on how you can have blooms all season long. First off, choose plants with different bloom times. People shop for perennials during May or early June and then take a breather. This means flower gardens tend to have lots of early summer flowers such as bleeding heart, lupines, iris and Asiatic lilies and then there is a lull.

Mix Annuals with Perennials - Most perennials bloom at a certain time during the season - peonies in May/June, delphiniums in June, phlox in July, August and into the fall. Annuals, on the other hand, bloom steadily all season long, especially if you remove the spent flowers. Combining annuals with perennials makes it easier to keep the color going strong.

Stretch the Garden with Bulbs - Planting daffodils, tulips, grape hyacinth and other spring-flowering bulbs in fall will fill your garden with color long before your neighbors' gardens are in bloom. Plan to continue the show right through October by adding summer-flowering bulbs such as dahlias, Oriental lilies, elephant ears, caladiums and cannas. These plants don't mind the heat and most of them are at their best as summer turns to fall. They are planted in early summer.

Drought Tolerant Late Season Perennials - They include echinacea, sedum, yarrow, lavender, salvia, Russian sage, rudbeckia, asters and ornamental grasses. You can also grow annuals that are drought tolerant such as cosmos, California poppy and nicotiana. Calendula drops seed and amaranth comes back as well in my gardens.

Tips - Primp and Prune as You Go - Make a habit of keeping a pair of scissors or a small hand pruner in your pocket. Removing spent flowers and cutting back lanky foliage helps gardens stay tidy and focuses attention on what looks good rather than what doesn't.

Deadheading encourages annuals to keep flowering and will sometimes get perennials, such as achillea, campanula, dianthus and phlox to bloom again.

As I've said many times, plan out your garden and don't take on too much. Before you know it, your to-do list of planting, weeding, watering, thinning, mulching, and pruning can be overwhelming.

Know your soil. Make sure and get a soil test and that could make all the difference in the world. Enrich your soil with compost - the black gold of the gardening world plus plant cover crops like buckwheat, oats and annual rye grass in mid-summer. Add grass clippings and mulch around young plants as well as in the fall.

Some gardeners think it's easier to grow plants in containers. That's not true with some plants, especially ones that grow in direct sunlight and need constant watering. The roots of plants grown in pots become quite hot on warm days, but the same plants grown in enriched beds enjoy cooler roots. I've found this to be especially true with dahlias.

Not giving plants enough space is a common problem. A little plant is a solar being, and each new leaf is part of an expanding solar array. When plants grow too close or are crowded by weeds, reduced sunlight and competition for water can stunt their growth. Spacing has been a challenge for me in my perennial garden beds.

Faux Paws - The biggest problem that many gardeners have is that they don't leave enough room for plants to grow and then they fret and either move them to a different location or throw-um in the compost pile.

This is my biggest faux paw. I needed to leave more room for shrubs and perennials as they grow larger, like with obedient plants, which spread via rhizomes. This has been a challenge, but I'm slowly getting it. I knew that taller plants go to the back of the beds. That was an easy one. The "Chuckster" added, "Yah sure! I've been telling you to read about the spacing requirements and spreaders, but you wouldn't listen, would yah."

For the past 5 years, I've planted pollinator plants in my community garden like butterfly bush, New England aster, geranium, obedient plant, bleeding hearts, milkweed, Aronia and many more. Spacing them is certainly a learning process.

Don't be afraid to break the rules now and then. Create a garden that reflects your tastes and works best for your individual space. If you can't find a spot in the garden for a plant you fall in love with, put it in a container and place it on your porch or patio.

Some people say, "Be careful not to overwhelm the space with Garden Art." Statues and figurines should never be the center of attention. They look best when tucked among the plants." I'm not so sure. What do you think?

P.S. My goal in summer and fall is to fill up a 5-gallon bucket with weeds every time I'm in the garden and pour it on my compost piles. By fall, I'm filling up two 5-gallon buckets of weeds.

Monarch Butterfly and Milkweed

June in Antonia and Ricardo's Garden

In their front yard is a giant silver maple. Underneath are *periwinkles, a ground cover with blue flowers along with *hostas, *ferns and *astilbe. A couple years ago, only grass grew underneath the tree.

Shrubs now grow along the sides of the house including a *daphne 'Carol Mackie,' noted for its variegated foliage. This dense, slow-growing, deciduous shrub typically grows 2-3' tall with fragrant clusters of pale pink flowers in late spring. Later on in summer, Japanese willows are stunning with white blooms. This cultivar was introduced to the west by the great Dutch hosta breeder, Harry Van der Laar in 1979. Not long ago, hey! Another favorite are the *hydrangeas with white and blue flowers, which bloom in early July. Trees include a corkscrew willow, oaks, maples, and basswood.

Summer Rolls Along

So folks, summer is-a-movin along with plants that fill your garden with their fragrances from spring to fall. Do you remember spring's first scents of lilac and azalea? Later came the spicy scent of daphne and the sweet citrus fragrance of mock orange. Roses can be relied upon to perfume the garden throughout summer. Below are many flowering perennials and shrubs with blooms and various aromas.

FLOWERING PLANTS IN JUNE & BEYOND

I want you to follow me through summer with my favorite blooming plants in their order of bloom time: Orange Poppies, Spirea, Red Ossier Dogwood, Iris, Geranium, Roses, Comfrey, Chives, Peonies, Baptisia, Coral Bells, Rhododendrons, Salvia, Elderberries, Lupines, Beauty Bush, Mock Orange, Basswood, Red Poppies, Evening Primrose, Bellflowers, Foxglove, Delphinium and Mountain Laurel.

The "Chuckster" just said, "Does Ron's have the correct order of blooming?" "What's your take after reading below?"

*Orange Poppies - I have large orange poppies that bloom in early June in my front yard garden. I don't know the variety. It looks like the 'Prince of Orange' Oriental Poppy (Papaver orientale), which has huge bright-orange flowers with crepe paper-like petals that light up the late spring garden. It is easy-to-grow and long lived. It thrives in clay and loves cold winters.

FYI - The Oriental poppy has become the 20th century war flower.

The poppy has been associated with war since at least the Battle of Waterloo in 1815 when Duke Wellington of England and the Prussian General Blucher defeated Napoleon on this battlefield in modern day Belgium. It was following WWI that this flower became an official symbol of war. The story goes that, after heavy fighting in the area had ended, graves were dug, and soldiers interred. The following spring when the graves were visited, they were awash in a sea of red poppies-plants that had not been seen in the region for years.

*Spirea - There are many different types of spirea. Some, like the well-known Vanhoutte spirea, often called "bridalwreath," can grow to be more than 8 feet tall. But most of the rest of the types stay under 5 feet, or shorter with a little pruning. They're a perfect fit in most anyone's garden.

Japanese spirea (Spiraea japonica) has the widest color range, with foliage in shades of green, blue, gold or chartreuse. Flowers bloom from late spring into summer in colors of pink, purple, red or white.

Summer blooming spirea has a delicate cascading habit with large clusters of white flowers poised on arching branches. They are among the easiest flowering shrubs to grow. These attractive shrubs are fast growing and should be grown in full sun for best flowering. They can, however, tolerate partial shade.

They are used in the landscape for hedges, shrub border, mass plantings, and as a foundation plant. Since spirea is an early summer blooming shrub, the best time to prune it is after the flowers have faded. Thinning older spireas is also recommended. My favorite spireas have white and blue blooms, a lovely combination. I always have an image of the shrub as an elegant older lady with flowers in her white hair.

Dogwoods

First cultivated in 1731, dogwood trees are among some of the prettiest trees used in landscaping today. Their beautiful white flowers give off a lacy appearance, though some varieties have pink flowers. The dogwood is native to several continents including Europe, Asia and North America, where its uses throughout history date to Native Americans and early settlers.

Founding father Thomas Jefferson was enamored of dogwoods and grew them at his home, Monticello, in Virginia in the late 1770s. This later led to the state naming the flower of the dogwood tree as its state flower in 1918 and its state tree in 1956. In 1941, the dogwood flower also became the state flower of North Carolina. Missouri named the dogwood its state tree in 1955.

*Cornelian-cherry dogwood, one of the first trees to flower in spring, is a small, 20- to 25-foot-high tree or large shrub. I described it earlier.

*Red Osier Dogwood - I planted one in my community garden three years ago and it started to bloom on May 20 in May of 2021. Other common names: Red twig dogwood, dogberry tree, American dogwood, shoemack, redstem dogwood, red dogwood, harts' rouges, kinnikinnick, red willow, squawbush, red-rood, gutter tree, creek dogwood, and red osier. Wow! Lots of names plus it has lovely red stems in winter and spring and white flowers in summer.

Other Dogwoods - Of all the dogwoods, few can match the picturesque beauty and multi-seasonal interest of the Korean or Kousa dogwood (Cornus kousa). Large, white, or russet pink flowers appear in June in Vermont followed by ornate, round, edible fruits of coral red that appear in fall. The birds love them. Its pointed, dark green leaves turn shades of red, orange and purple in fall, and beautiful, mottled bark adds interest to the winter landscape. It's sometimes called the Chinese dogwood or Japanese dogwood and is widely cultivated as an ornamental.

Disease-resistant American dogwood (Cornus florida) hybrids have giving new life to this exceptional landscape tree. Most were developed at Rutgers University as crosses between the Korean and American dogwood.

*Irises are among the best known and best loved of garden plants. This huge genus contains upwards of 200 species, which range from timid and inconspicuous wildings to splendid tall-bearded iris. Tall bearded Iris and Siberian iris are among the most popular. Both can be relied upon to elevate the June garden with eye-catching flowers, and their upright, blade-like foliage provides a welcome vertical accent for the balance of the season. Iris takes its name from the Greek word for a rainbow, which is also the name for the Greek goddess of the rainbow, Iris.

The most commonly planted iris in the United States is the bearded iris. Height of the bearded iris plant ranges from 3 inches for the shortest of dwarf iris flowers to 4 feet for the tallest of the tall, bearded iris. Tall-bearded iris blossom in a remarkably broad spectrum of richly saturated colors - from golden yellow to velvety red and lavender blue to nearly black. The flowers crown tall stems that emerge from a stand of wide blue-green foliage, and they hover over other spring flowers in the late spring garden. Some tall-bearded irises are rebloomers, flowering in June and then again in late summer. This is not common in Vermont.

The most common mistake is planting them too deeply. The elongated rhizome should be horizontal, with the top at or just above the soil surface. You can make a shallow hole, with mound in the center. Place the rhizome on top of the mound, laying the roots downward around it. Then cover the roots with soil.

Siberian Iris, whose smaller flowers can resemble birds in flight, are available in a narrower but equally compelling color range from classic blue to yellow to pink, and these graceful blooms arrive on extraordinarily tough plants that spread gradually in a site they like, forming nearly indestructible clumps.

Geranium - Marilyn Maddison

*Geraniums just came out in summer in Marilyn Maddison's children's garden. Marilyn is my neighbor, and her garden is within shouting distance. Like me, she grows true, wild perennial geraniums, which bloom throughout the summer and - as the name suggests - will return to your garden after lying dormant over winter.

Perennial geraniums go by several different names. You may have heard these hardy, wild geraniums referred to as cranesbill geraniums. While there are several common names for them, the labels are meant to set this plant apart from one that people commonly think of when they picture houseplant geraniums: pelargoniums. In this instance, dubbing the plant a perennial geranium helps to distinguish it from the annual growing habit of the pelargonium.

Geraniums are a genus of 422 species of flowering annual, biennial, and perennial plants that are commonly known as the cranesbills. They are found throughout the temperate regions of the world and the mountains of the tropics, but mostly in the eastern part of the Mediterranean region.

Geraniums are one of my favorite low-growing hardy perennial plants. They reward us with spring and summer flowers ranging from white to pink too dark blue. Try varieties such as 'Patricia' with its magenta pink flowers on 2 to 3-foot plants and the delicate 'Biokovo' with white flowers on smaller plants that tolerate some shade. Grow perennial geraniums near early iris and late flowering asters to have a good complement of color. They continue to grow, spread some and flower grow throughout most of the summer as they do in my community garden and in Marilyn's children garden.

*Roses - My favorite shrub rose is Rosa rugosa, which blooms earlier than other roses. I planted them as a hedge in my front yard many years ago and they come back every year. Just prune out the old canes. Plus, the rose hips are full of vitamin C and can made into a tea. They bloom in May and June and then sparingly, sometimes coming back in early fall.

A Rose is a Rose is a Rose - I grow five varieties of hardy roses in my home garden - mostly shrub roses and a climber as you enter my front yard, but you must bend a little as the roses grow over and under the arbor. The climbers in dark red and pink shrub roses bloom in June.

You can grow beautiful roses in Vermont especially the hardy shrub roses. Floribunda roses and most hybrid tea roses are tenderer than the shrub roses and require more careful siting and winter protection. Even with excellent summer care and good winter protection you should know that the hybrid teas can be a risk.

You can control leaf diseases in roses with a solution of one tablespoon of baking soda to one gallon of water. Use insecticidal soap to control aphids on rose buds. Help your roses during the summer by spreading coffee grounds into the soil. They will enhance the flowers and brighten the foliage.

Roses in full sunlight are often more prone to too much heat, drought, and stress. The key is to make sure to use lots of water and mulch during the heat of summer. Numerous rose species and hybrids are prized for attractive, often fragrant, flowers, various growth habits and other specific characteristics, such as heat and humidity tolerance. Even well-maintained rose plants are still prone to attack from many different pests and diseases.

If a rose is growing in hot, direct sunlight, neem oil is a viable treatment option. A common rose disease in early summer are spider mites, which can devastate certain varieties of shrub roses. My neighbor Marilyn Maddison showed me the damage done to her roses by these mites. I suggested Neem, the organic insecticide used to control mites, and it worked. Neem comes from a tropical tree originally grown in India. In 1987, I went with a peace delegation from New England to Managua, Nicaragua where we planted young Neem trees as quick growing shade trees.

FYI - Neem oil is a vegetable oil pressed from the seeds in the fruits of (Azadirachta indica), an evergreen tree which is endemic to the Indian subcontinent and has been introduced to many other areas in the tropics. Neem also works on white flies and flea beetles.

FYI - Sweet Briar (Eglantine) or wild rose in French are large and sprawling, with single pale pink flowers in late spring and early summer. They are strongly apple-scented, and their hips are popular for use in tea. This rose may be restrained by growing on posts or trellises to control its long, thorny canes. They were grown at George Washington's Mount Vernon. Pasture Rose, Prairie Rose, Wild Rose, Dog Rose, Eglantine, Sweetbriar, and Scotch Briar are just a few of the very common names for wild roses that mean different things in different places.

The botanical term for wild rose is "species rose", which means just what it says - a species that occurs naturally, with no help from man - a true "wildflower." There are over 100 of these worldwide, some native to North America, many from the Orient and Europe. These true wild roses are all single with exactly five petals - never more, and almost all of them are pink, with a few whites and reds, and even fewer that range toward yellow. There are now over 20,000 hybrids, with about 200 new ones every year. Most all North American native roses are smallish shrubs, with canes no longer than three or four feet.

I wrote about roses in my first garden book, The Woodchuck's Guide to Gardening, which went into its tenth printing in June of 2020. I dedicated the book to my mom whose name was Rosalie.

***Comfrey** - I once cut my hand so I chewed on some comfrey leaves and roots and placed them on the wound, and it healed immediately - believe it or not. It's true. The healing ingredient is allantoin. Don't use on a puncture wound unless you clean the wound first with alcohol.

I often cut up the leaves and place them in the compost pile. I also use comfrey leaves for tea along with raspberry, mint, and lemon balm. I call it Bonzo Punch, named after my first dog - described in my first Vermont garden book.

Comfrey is mostly leaves with some light purple flowers, which bloom early in summer and continue to flower for a while. Russian comfrey is one of the top healing plants in the world.

*Chive flowers - I love to pick the stems of the purple flowers and hang them from the beams in my kitchen. The color lasts a year and brightens my home plus the stems are great cut up in salads and stir-fry's.

*Peonies - The peony or paeony is a flowering plant in the genus Paeonia, the only genus in the family, Paeoniaceae. They are native to Asia, Europe, and Western North America. There are currently 33 known species. I have two peonies on both sides of my front steps leading up to the porch. The aroma of the white flowers knocks my socks off - like getting lightly stoned.

Late May and June is peony time! With their massive blooms in shades of red, pink, and white and yellow, they are one of the most beautiful and venerated garden plants in Vermont gardens. For a match made in heaven, try combining them with some of the blue flowers, like salvia, catmint, or irises, which also bloom in June. Late summer is the perfect time to move peony roots. So I chose a sunny spot in my community garden, enriched the soil with plenty of compost and carefully planted my new extravagance.

Over two thousand years ago the people of China started cultivating peonies as a flavoring for food. During the Tang dynasty (618-907) they experimented by placing them in mountainous wildlife settings. Soon peony cultivation began to flourish in Japan, eventually migrating to England and France in the eighteenth century.

The majority of peonies are herbaceous perennials (meaning they will die back to the ground each winter but re-sprout every spring). This vast genetic pool is the basis of all the beautiful, cultivated varieties-or cultivars- we know today. Back in 1923 the American Peony Society began awarding the society's Gold Medal to exceptional peony cultivars, a practice that still continues today.

*Itoh peonies originated by crossing herbaceous peonies and tree peonies, and they combine the best features of each. While they have the mounded growth habit of herbaceous peonies and die back to the ground in winter, they also produce immense flowers along with undulating petals encircling a froth of yellow stamens. The original cultivars were yellow, but to-day there are many beautiful colors including coral, red, pink, and white, as well as their signature buttery yellow. Plant Itoh peonies in full sun to part shade and in rich, well-drained soil.

After the herbaceous peonies finish flowering, the Itoh peonies burst into bloom about six weeks later thus extending the peony season. Itoh peonies also create an elegant mound of finely divided leaves. Thus, even after flowering, they continue to shine at the front of the border.

In 2000, when Itoh hybrids were still a rarity, the renowned peony grower, Bill Countryman in Northfield, Vermont would show off his peony fields in mid-August- when there was not a flower to be seen. He would share with folks about each and every cultivar, and also recounted the incredible story of how the Itoh hybrids came to be.

Tragically in June 2005- within days of a planned visit of the American Peony Society for their annual meeting - Bill suddenly died. And, without his care, it would not be long before his famous peony fields were engulfed by weeds. Five years ago, Connecticut dwellers Dan and Ann Sivori, decided to purchase Countryman Peony Farm and restore Bill's legacy. Today the plants are all labelled, and fields are almost weed free once more.

Tree peonies, with their spectacular flowers and beautiful colors have long been coveted by gardeners everywhere. But typically their above-ground stems (where most of the buds that make next year's flowers are produced) will not survive our harsh winters.

*Baptisia - False or Wild Indigo - No flower fills your garden with brilliant true-blue flowers like blue False Indigo. False Indigo (Baptisia australis) is a native American beauty. In fact, Europeans used to pay Americans to grow this plant, for the dye they made from the blue flowers. True indigo was expensive and Baptisia, which made a similarly colored dye, grew like a weed.

These large, long-lived perennials provide an extended season of interest from flowers and foliage. The botanical name Baptisia originates from the Greek word bapto - to dip or to dye.

Baptisia australis, commonly known as blue wild indigo or blue false indigo, is a flowering plant in the family Fabaceae (legumes). It is native to much of central and eastern North America and is particularly common in the Midwest, but it has also been introduced well beyond its natural range.

*Coral Bells (Heucheras) In recent years, coral bells have becoming increasingly popular among gardeners. They have been going through quite a breeding frenzy. The focus has been on creating varieties with more colorful leaves. While the tall, delicate flowers add a touch of whimsy to a perennial flower border, and are loved by butterflies and hummingbirds, it's the leaves that provide color all season. New cultivars and hybrids are being introduced regularly, giving us stunning new colors to use in our gardens that range from silver and gold to lime, burgundy, chocolate brown, purple, green and more.

The foliage of these plants is their most striking feature just like with lungwort. The leaves are often large and heart-shaped or rounded, and many are variegated or ruffled. Because most heucheras are evergreen, they bring year-round interest to the garden, even under a dusting of snow.

The multi-colored leaf varieties give this plant versatility grown in rock gardens, shade gardens, woodlands, or even containers. The leaves can be rounding, lobed or hairy in shape and texture. The flower stalks give a nice touch to flower arrangements.

Heucheras may be evergreen or semi-evergreen. Most are cold hardy in Zones 4 to 9. Graceful, bell-shaped flower clusters open in late spring through summer; the pink, red or white flowers are actually inflorescences, or tiny clusters of blooms, along a flower stalk that can be two to three times as tall as the leaf mound. Plant size ranges from 12 to 36 inches tall and 12 to 18 inches wide.

Coral bells are versatile in the garden and landscape. Plant in masses, for edging, as a specimen plant and in containers. Use in a mixed perennial border or in a woodland shade garden. An added bonus for planting heucheras? Hummingbirds often visit the delicate flowers.

*Rhododendrons & Azaleas - The Jewels in the Crown - Just three miles from my home is the rhododendron and azalea collection located at the University of Vermont Horticulture Farm in South Burlington - planted over 60 years ago. The reason they are so successful is because the shrubs are protected from the north wind and winter sun by nearby tall evergreen forest. If you visit the "Hort" Farm in late May and early June, you'll see the best collection of colorful rhododendrons and azaleas in Vermont. The curator of the collection was Dr. Norman Pellett.

This book is dedicated to Dr. Pellett who has provided me with much support over the years. He is the Emeritus horticulturist at the University of Vermont and is now retired. I visit him and his wife, Dorothy, a garden writer - every year in Charlotte, Vermont along with Fred Schmidt, a fellow gardener.

There are 15 species of rhododendrons growing at the University of Vermont's Horticulture Farm. It can be said that we live at the end of the rhododendron world. Three of the four species native to Vermont are small colonies at their northernmost range. The collection of rhododendrons at the Hort Farm offers to students and the public a view of plants that are mature and successfully grown in a harsh environment. This is certainly a collection of merit that displays a color in bloom that is not outdone anywhere in northern Vermont.

Volunteers at the Annual Plant Sale at the Horticulture Farm

FYI- All azaleas are rhododendrons, but not all rhododendrons are azaleas. Most azaleas are deciduous, but true rhododendrons are usually evergreen. Azaleas have funnel shaped flowers. Rhodi flowers tend to be bell-shaped. Rhododendron is a genus of 500 to 900 species and includes both of what we commonly call rhododendrons and azaleas. Most are evergreen but some are deciduous.

Rhododendrons

Rhododendrons come from the Ancient Greek "rose" "tree." It is a genus of 1,024 species of woody plants in the heath family (Ericaceae), either evergreen or deciduous, and found mainly in Asia, although it is also widespread throughout the lowland and mountain forests of the Pacific Northwest, California, and the highlands of the Appalachian Mountains of North America. It is the national flower of Nepal, as well as, the state flower of Washington and West Virginia in United States, the provincial flower of Jiangxi in China and the state tree of Sikkim and Uttarakhand in India. Most species have brightly colored flowers which bloom from late winter through to early summer.

Rhododendrons can be found throughout the world. Just under 20 species are native to North America, with the vast majority of these being deciduous azaleas. There are more than 1000 different natural species in the Genus (group) rhododendron. These wild types, called species (as differentiated from hybrids), are native to the temperate regions of Asia, North America, and Europe, as well as to the tropical regions of southeast Asia and northern Australia. No rhododendron species are indigenous to Africa or South America. By far, the largest number of wild species rhododendrons are native to Asia. Wild rhododendrons are found from sea level to 16,000 feet in elevation, and they occur in a variety of habitats, including alpine regions, coniferous and broadleaved woodlands, temperate rain forests, and even tropical jungle conditions.

Rhododendrons exhibit an enormous diversity of size and shape, from prostrate ground covers growing no more than a few inches high to trees more than 100 feet tall. Between the prostrate alpine forms and large trees are a variety of shrubby forms in all shapes and sizes. Leaf sizes range from less than 1/4 inch to almost three feet long, and they also appear in a variety of shapes: rounded, lance-shaped, and elliptical. The flowers may be white, red, pink, yellow, almost blue, purple, magenta, orange, and shades and mixtures of most of these colors.

There is diversity, too, in bark texture and color. And while March, April, and May represent the peak months for flowering, some rhododendrons can flower as early as January in an ideal climate and others as late as October. Again, they flower in Vermont in late May and early June. The actual beauty of many is supreme - in flower, in decorative new growth, in foliage, in bark, in structure, and even in fall color, the latter is noted particularly with deciduous azaleas.

Rhododendrons, not surprisingly, are among the most popular shrubs that people grow where conditions are suitable. They grow best in climates that avoid extremes in temperature and have substantial rainfall. They also require a slightly acid soil.

For rhododendrons to thrive in the wild or in the garden, two main conditions must be met - suitable location and soil condition. Rhododendrons don't like temperature extremes of cold or heat. In the wild they're found in mountainous terrain growing in the shadows of overstory trees. The right location needs to be cool and wet, with specific soil pH levels. The soil also needs to be well drained and high in organic matter. In growing these plants, attempts should be made to have high organic matter.

For best growth, soil should contain 50 to 80 per cent organic matter (anyone or a mixture of the following materials); Decayed oak leaves, humus, woods' earth (fibrous leaf mold from pine, hemlock or spruce woods), ground spent tanbark, peat moss of the coarse acid type, decayed pine, hemlock and spruce needles. To give this some perspective, an average cornfield will have organic matter of 3 to 5 percent, and a good garden soil will be 8 to 10 percent, which is very high. Many gardens don't have anywhere near that much organic matter content. *Go to My Woodchuck's Garden Website for a complete explanation of Organic Matter. This is critical in understanding healthy soil.

Azalea

Azalea is the common name for various flowering shrubs within the plant genus Rhododendron. They make up two subgenera of Rhododendron and are distinguished from "true" rhododendrons by having only five anthers per flower.

They are related to rhododendrons, blueberries and pieris. Azaleas date back to an ancient group of plants dating to 50 million years ago. Most azaleas we are familiar with today are descended from Asian shrubs, and were originally cultivated by monks in Buddhist monasteries.

Eastern North America has more wild azalea species than any other region of the world. These native species have spawned many hybrids. In May and June, the mountains, upland valleys, moist woods and swamps glow with azalea bloom. They bloom earlier than rhododendrons.

Native azaleas are some of the most spectacular native plants, yet are seldom seen in gardens. They evolved slowly - adapting to their local habitats. Most evergreen azaleas originated in Japan, but some came from China, Korea or Taiwan. Several deciduous azaleas are native to North America; others originated in Eastern Europe, Japan, China and Korea.

Most gardeners consider the azalea shrub as an easy plant to grow, if located in the most suitable environment. Azaleas can be divided into two recognizable groups, the evergreen azalea and the deciduous azalea, which drops all of its leaves in the fall during cold weather. Many deciduous azaleas grown in an ornamental garden are native plants of the American forests. The group consists of approximately 16 species that vary in color from: white, pink, yellow, red and bi-color.

*Flame Azalea - William Bartram first described the flame azalea in 1773 and recorded his observations in his famous book, Travels, when he explored the Southeastern U.S. with his father John Bartram, both being natives of Philadelphia, PA. Bartram described the flame azalea in full bloom at the banks of the "Chata Uche River". He said that the name, "fiery", best expressed the appearance of the azalea flowers. The colors include red, orange and bright gold, as well as yellow and cream colour." Bartram stated that every one of these colors could sometimes be found flowering on a single plant.

Bartram vividly described the beauty of these virgin primitive plantings in the original forests of America. He said, "the clusters of the blossoms cover the shrubs in such incredible profusion on the hill sides, that suddenly opening to view from dark shades, we are alarmed with the apprehension of the hill being set on fire."

Flame Azalea (Rhododendron calendulaceum) is tall and produces orange blooms (occasionally yellow or red) with no scent. It is a good background plant and is the orange azalea often seen in the Great Smoky Mountains.

This species is native to the Appalachian Mountains in the eastern United States, ranging from southern New York to northern Georgia. This deciduous shrub has large flowers. It even grows in some spots of Vermont but is not a native.

Flame azalea is an upright-branched deciduous shrub, 6-12 ft. tall and equally as wide, with large, showy, funnel-shaped flowers in clusters of 5 or more. Summer foliage is medium green, and the fall color is subdued yellow to red.

The non-fragrant flowers, appearing before or with the leaves, vary in color from pale yellow to apricot to brilliant scarlet red. A deciduous shrub with terminal clusters of tubular, vase-shaped, orange, red, or yellow flowers. Like most members of the heath family, it does best in acid soil. They bloom in June. Flame azalea shrubs are grown in shade.

*Salvia - Salvia is the largest genus of plants in the mint family, Lamiaceae, with nearly 1000 species of shrubs, herbaceous perennials, and annuals. It is one of several genera commonly referred to as sage. They have square stems for the most part, but some varieties have round stems. Some salvias start with square stems that become rounded with age, much like us humans. Some people plant salvias just for their foliar interest.

Salvias are upright plants that produce colorful flower spikes from summer into fall. Clothed with often-aromatic leaves, sages carry dense or loose spires of tubular flowers in bright blues, violets, yellow, pinks, and red that mix well with other perennials in beds and borders. Provide full sun or very light shade, in well-drained average soil.

Salvias can be annual or perennial, sub-shrub or herbaceous, and evergreen or deciduous. Leaves are opposite and carried on square hairy stems and are often aromatic when crushed. Flowers are tubular with a split lower petal. They are a pollinator magnet, drawing bees, hummingbirds, and butterflies.

Perennials - One of several genera are commonly referred to as culinary sage, a great herb for teas and baking with meats. Some sages have attractive flowers and foliage to make nice additions as edible landscape plants in the garden. I use culinary sage in a tea for tummy ailments with a little maple syrup.

Among the purple salvias often found in gardens is perennial salvia (Salvia nemorosa), also known as meadow sage, and its many cultivars. It resists heat and drought, though it prefers regular watering during the dry summer season. Purple salvia is a hummingbird magnet as it displays spikes of rich cobalt-blue flowers that emerge from purple-black buds on dark stems. I find when looking at flower gardens, they stand out from the rest. It's my favorite.

Blooms appear on this plant in spring, summer, and fall. Strongest flowering occurs in early summer and fall, with more sporadic blooms during the heat of summer. Salvia greggii usually opens blossoms in shades of red, although varieties exist that have flowers in pink, purple, white and orange. My favorites are blues and purples.

Some perennial salvias will bloom twice if you do nothing, but if you dead-head them (remove the old, spent flowers) you can get more in a season. The first flush of bloom is the most robust, but the flowering will linger on all season if you give it a proper pruning after the first bloom.

One of the best perennial sages in Vermont, is the purple-flowered verticillata cultivar Purple Rain. It maintains a tidy habit without cutting back after flowering, as most perennial sages need. Cutting back most perennial sages right after first bloom (except Purple Rain, which remains tidy) keeps them compact through the season. With nice upright spikes of early summer bloom (usually blue to purple), they rebloom in fall in most years.

A couple of other cultivars that maintain a good habit without cutting back included May Night and Vesuvius. May Night has deep violet flowers, shorter than Purple Rain, and blooms a little earlier. Vesuvius is similar, but it blooms later, similar to Purple Rain. These two cultivars are hybrids from the species sylvestris that also was hardy in Zone 5 and has violet-blue flowers. May Night was honored as a top perennials for 1997. These vigorous plants bear lance-shaped leaves and many spikes of purplish-blue blooms. Removing the spent flowers keeps the plant looking tidier.

Blue Hill Sage (Salvia sylvestris) is a superb selection grown for its late spring display of clear blue flowers held over sturdy compact mounds of green foliage. It is extremely cold hardy, Other sylvestris hybrid cultivars are hardy include Blue Queen, and Snow Hill. These are much shorter than others, getting only six to ten inches high. Blue Hill has fairly true-blue flowers, Blue Queen purple-blue flowers, and Snow Hill, white flowers. One problem with Blue Hill that the plants start out compact but fall open prior to bloom, thus making them appear untidy.

Blue Hill has the advantage of being a perennial for most of the temperate zone and it does a great job of drawing bees to the landscape. This perennial plant is a mainstay in the flower garden as they are hardy in our region, and some are native to North America.

Annuals - Although perennials in their warm, native lands, salvias are treated as annual plants by a large number of gardeners, that is, people living in more northerly regions like mine. Salvia splendens is best known as an annual plant with scarlet blooms, but these flowers do come in other colors. Victoria Blue salvia is a highly sought-after color in annual flowers.

Try combining salvias in fronts of borders with ornamental grasses, yarrows, daisies, daylilies, coreopsis, or the silver foliage of artemisias.

FYI- History - The New England Wild Flower Society notes that Lyre leaf Sage is the region's only native sage. Early colonists introduced Old World medicinal and edible plants, such as Clary sage and Culinary sage, both of which escaped into the wild, according to the New England Wild Flower Society.

*Elderberries - Sambucus genus - The elderberry is a member of the honeysuckle family. Fully grown elderberry plants yield delicate white flowers during June, but they change into berries. I planted elderberries in my community garden in 2019. There are many reported benefits of elderberries. Not only are they nutritious, but they may also fight cold and flu symptoms, support heart health and fight inflammation and infections. I drink elderberry syrup when I'm feeling a little ill along with echinacea.

Elderberry harvest season generally occurs from mid-August to mid-September, depending upon your region and the cultivar. The dark clusters of berries ripen over a period of between five to 15 days. Once ripened, harvest the fruit and strip it from the cluster.

In addition to their landscaping value, elderberry bushes produce purple or black edible berries that ripen in mid-to-late summer, depending on the variety. Although the berries don't taste that great, they are often used in jams, jellies, pies and syrups. The berries have more vitamin C than oranges and were used historically to treat colds, fevers and respiratory problems.

Elderberries prefer full to partial sun and well-draining, slightly acidic soil. The plants produce fruit most abundantly when planted with another variety such as "Adams" (Sambucus canandensis "Adams") with "Johns" (Sambucus canandensis "Johns"). Elderberry plants' mature size ranges from 6 to 20 feet, depending on the cultivar.

*Lupines - One of my most joyous moments comes from seeing a field of purple lupines in June. Perennial lupine, also known as Lupinus perennis, is a medium to tall perennial that is native to North America, and hardy in Zones 3 to 9. It will grow in most soils but prefers well-drained, loose, sandy soil. This plant has an extensive root system that depletes the nutrients of the soil yearly. Add compost every other year.

By the way, the lupine plant fixes nitrogen in the soil and is a great addition to your vegetable garden or any area where nitrogen loving plants will be grown.

A member of the pea family, lupines are beneficial in many ways.

Lupines are a plant that many gardeners would love to grow. I would suggest growing them from seed. They are kind of like daffodils which will be pop up here and there near your home. Lupines are like hollyhocks with long roots that don't like to be disturbed. Again, start some each year by placing seeds in large peat pots and once they germinate, plant them carefully into the ground without challenging the roots. Soak the large seeds for a day and then place the seeds in a soil-less mix and they will germinate well. If you want a field full of lupines, direct seed them into the soil but dig out the grass and weeds with shovel size holes before planting.

For many people, especially those who grew up in Maine, the word lupine is synonymous with the name "Miss Rumphius." The beautifully illustrated book by Barbara Cooney was based on a real-life "lupine lady" who scattered the seeds from her pockets and car windows. At Acadia National Park, botanists attempted to eradicate the plant, but visitors protested so vociferously that the effort was halted.

One of the most popular lupine locations is Sugar Hill, N.H. where the 26th annual Fields of Lupine Festival takes place in June. The Franconia Range makes a pretty nice background for oceans of purple flowers. Albany, N.Y., and Stonington, Maine, also have lupine festivals, and there may well be others. In the Concord pine barren habitat in New Hampshire, you can see the native lupine, and the hundreds of tiny, fluttering Karner blue butterflies, an endangered species.

Russell and his hybrids

The one problems with lupines is that they are aphid magnets. So if you like lupines, pick up a package of seed and get them started in mid-April. They can be planted into the Vermont garden by the first of June, earlier if you live in warmer areas.

The Russell hybrids are legendary. They were developed by George Russell of Yorkshire, England, who, as a railroad guard at a quiet crossing, worked out their great flowers, now grown all over the world in temperate climates.

***Beauty Bush** (Kolkwitzia) bloomed profusely in Lisa Yankowski's yard near my home in June. `Pink Cloud' is a lovely variety of beauty bush. This dense, tall, and wide mountain shaped shrub/tree with tubular flowers blooms in late May. They grow in full or partial sun. It originated in China. This fountain shaped shrub with tubular flowers was often seen in the 1930s and 40s and is now making a comeback. Why not plant beauty bush with an underskirt of peonies in the sun. Thin out branches and remove some of the oldest branches after it blooms.

***Mock orange** (Zone 4) is a very hardy shrub with rich green leaves and sweet citrus fragrance of mock orange, white, and pink blooms. I am wowed by the sweet perfume that doesn't overwhelm you like peonies. They are some of the prettiest flowers I've ever seen. Mock Orange do best on patios where the citrus scent can be easily being encountered. It will last for years. Again, my neighbor, Lisa Yankowski, told me she played underneath her Mock Orange tree when she was a child and it's still growing even though the trees have grown up around it and shaded it some. My other neighbor, Marilyn Maddison has a lovely Mock Orange on one side of her cottage and shrub roses on the other side.

***Basswood** - American basswood is a large and rapid-growing tree of eastern and central North America. It is also known as linden or lime in Europe where it is commonly planted in towns and cities as an ornamental. You often see Linden Boulevard or Linden Street.

The flowers are hardly noticeable, but, oh, the scent. Linden is also called "lime blossom." It's a beautifully bright, sunny, sweet, and sharp scent. It's reminiscent of honey, honeysuckle, and grass. The ornamental lindens are often planted on tree lawns, and their fragrance is enjoyed morning and evening by humans and insects. You can actually hear the buzzing as you pass a linden in bloom. Their warm sweet scent often drifts low in the air - even some distance from the tree. The essence of summer has been distilled into this aroma welcomed eagerly by the bees. Some beekeepers cultivate lindens for honey production. A popular use for the wood is carving, as the wood is lightweight and soft.

Linden flowers appear in Vermont in July. Made from the flowers, leaves, and bark of the tree, linden tea has been used in folk medicine for hundreds of years. A popular use for the wood is carving, as the wood is lightweight and soft.

The basswood tree (Tilia americana) makes a bold addition to any yard but may overwhelm smaller parcels of real estate with its broad, dense canopy and large, sturdy trunk. Songbirds and blue jays are attracted to its seeds and use the tree for shelter.

Red Poppies in Flanders Fields

Red Poppies - A month after the large orange poppies bloom in my front yard, the red poppies bloom throughout my community garden.

They spread like crazy, but I don't mind as I love to see the bees and butterflies doing their work with the poppies.

The red poppy (Papaver rhoeas) is an annual herbaceous species of flowering plant in the poppy family, Papaveraceae. The red poppy is a wild weed in Europe. The paper-thin petals grow on 1-to-2-foot-tall plants. The Shirley poppy is a modern, more refined version of its wild cousin, while the Icelandic poppy has a mix of white, orange, red and yellow flowers that are slightly scented. And then there is the California poppies, which self-sow.

This red poppy is notable as an agricultural weed and after World War I as a symbol of dead soldiers. The Flanders poppy as it's called lay dormant on the front lines of France until 1915 when they were disturbed by the soldiers fighting. Coincidentally, the weather was perfect conditions for them to germinate in the fields of Flanders. Every year for the next four, the poppies grew, and their flowers lay like a red blanket across the fields on which the soldiers fought.

Before the advent of herbicides, red poppies sometimes were abundant in agricultural fields. As we enter August, my red poppies and German chamomile are beginning to diminish in my community garden. The dill has since gone to seed. They all grew together as mentioned earlier.

Evening Primrose - These plants grow in my front yard and spread. Evening primrose is a plant native to North America with yellow flowers that bloom in the evening. Evening primrose oil contains the fatty acid gamma-linolenic acid (GLA). Native Americans used the whole plant for bruises and its roots for hemorrhoids. The leaves were traditionally used for minor wounds, gastrointestinal complaints, and sore throats. Today, people use evening primrose oil as a dietary supplements for eczema.

*Bellflower - Campanula - This perennial gets its name from the flared bottoms of the flower blooms that give them the appearance of colorful bells. With varying plant heights that reach anywhere from 1- 6 feet (depending on the variety planted), these hardy plants make great additions to rock gardens and cottage gardens.

This plant is native to many regions where cool nights and moderate temperatures prevail, creating ideal conditions for growing bellflowers. Bellflowers will bloom heaviest in June and July but can delight later on too.

Bellflowers are a diverse group of plants that come in many sizes and varieties. From diminutive alpine species to upright woodland varieties perfect for cut flowers, there are many plants to choose from. There are 420 annual, perennial, and biennial herbs that compose the genus Campanula. Bellflowers have mostly blue flowers, and many are cultivated as garden ornamentals. They do like to spread, popping up the next season in various spots in the garden.

*Foxglove - Digitalis purpurea (foxglove, common foxglove, purple foxglove, or lady's glove) is a species of flowering plant in the plantain family Plantaginaceae, native to and widespread throughout most of temperate Europe. It is also naturalized in parts of North America. The plants are well known as the original source of the heart medicine digoxin, also called digitalis.

This tall and stately foxglove plant with tubular blooms has long been included in garden areas where vertical interest and lovely flowers lie.

Most varieties are biennials that live for only two growing seasons, but some species can survive as perennials in some climates. There is another fact to aware of. Foxglove plants are among the most poisonous plants commonly grown in home landscapes.

Foxglove has dry fruit containing many seeds. Both the beautiful flowers and berries attract children. All parts of the plant are extremely poisonous. The sap, flowers, seeds, pollen, and leaves of foxglove are all poisonous, even when dried.

In spite of the danger of poisoning, these plants are well loved, but they can be fairly short lived and picky when it comes to garden conditions. One of the most important things to keep in mind is that delphiniums don't like hot summers. They perform best in mild weather. When it does get hot, plants die back to the ground. If you're lucky, they may return as it cools down.

*Delphinium - Larkspur - These perennials are grown for their showy spikes of colorful summer flowers in gorgeous shades of blue, pink, white, and purple. They are popular in cottage-style gardens and cutting gardens. Delphiniums are a favorite of many gardeners, but can sometimes be a challenge.

Delphinium is good in borders, containers & as a cut flower. They attract butterflies, bees, and hummingbirds. Wiry stems bear loose branched spikes of single light blue flowers which grow upright, branching with deeply lobed leaves. These tall hybrid delphiniums are an outstanding element of every well-bred garden.

FYI - Belladonna delphinium should not be confused with atropa belladonna, more commonly known as Deadly Nightshade. In spite of its high level of toxicity, delphinium is food to various larvae like the dot moth. This toxic plant is dangerous, especially the younger parts of the plant. If consumed by humans, it will cause severe digestive issues, and if touched, it can cause severe skin irritation. All parts of the plant contain poisonous chemicals, including alkaloids. So please be careful.

*__Mountain Laurel__ - Kalmia (latifolia) - Mountain laurel is a lovely evergreen shrub or small tree that produces lovely pink and white flowers in June. This gnarled, multi-stemmed, broadleaf evergreen shrub is native to Eastern North America. This shade-tolerant North American shrub has gorgeous white flowers that bloom in early summer. A close relative of rhododendrons and azaleas, it's an excellent choice for a shady garden. Even after the blooms have faded, its leathery deep green foliage provides a welcome sign of life. Even in the coldest winter weather, when rhododendron leaves have curled in on themselves, mountain laurel remains bravely open to the elements.

Though not commonly grown in Vermont, I have seen woodlands filled with hundreds of mountain laurel in southern New Hampshire. One exception is Paul Wieczoreck who is growing mountain laurel in the foothills of Vermont. I'm sure there are other places where they grow in the Green Mountains.

During a long-ago canoe trip on Squam Lake in Holderness, New Hampshire, I was surprised and delighted to chance upon forests of blooming mountain laurel. The glorious diminutive blossoms (each an inch or less in width) were blooming in large clusters along the water's edge and visible from a half-mile away.

Mountain laurels are the Connecticut state flower.

Ron's Favorite Annuals

Fill your garden with annuals that are beautiful to look at in the garden while also supplying an abundance of blooms for making bouquets. Highlighted here are some of my favorite varieties for vases - from springtime's fragrant sweet peas to the colorful summertime blooms of cosmos and zinnias. By the way, sweet peas are planted early in May and the soil must be kept damp for germination.

JULY

JULY BLOOMS: DAYLILY, OBEDIENT PLANTS, MONARDA, POWDERY MILDEW & HUMMINGBIRDS

*The Common Daylily - I'm referring to the common daylily of which there are thousands of registered cultivars. This flowering plant is in the genus Hemerocallis. Gardening enthusiasts and professional horticulturalists have long bred daylily species for their attractive flowers.

Daylilies come in many and shapes. The best way to see them is to visit one of the many daylily farms in your region. One of my favorites is Olallie Daylily Farm in South Newfane, Vermont that I described in my first garden book, The Woodchuck's Guide to Gardening.

Some suggestions include the reblooming varieties such as `Stella D'oro', the `Happy Returns' variety, `Joan Senior' and `Barbara Mitchell'. Did you know that you can eat those wild tawny orange daylily flowers? Pick the flower buds as they color and sauté them, stuff the open flowers or use the petals in salads. You can even dig up the roots and roast the tubers. Daylilies are not only edible; they are great to look at.

In early July when I look out my window, I see lots of tiger daylily's. They are everywhere. Hemerocallis fulva, the orange day-lily, tawny daylily, tiger daylily, fulvous daylily, or ditch lily (also railroad daylily, roadside daylily, outhouse lily, and wash-house lily), is a species of daylily native to Asia and very common in Vermont.

They differ in the shape and colors of the flowers, when they bloom, the growth habit of the plants and the root systems. Tiger lily is a single species, while daylilies contain a number of species, also native to Asia, that have many cultivars and thousands of hybrids.

It's easy to breed daylilies because of the high success rate of pollination. Just remove the pollen from the anther and daub some on the end of the pistil. By crossing the different species, a large range of colors can be produced - near white shades, and some purples. There are no true pinks or blues, but rosy pinks, oranges, yellows, coppers, golds, and reds with sickle/sword shaped green leaves. There is also a lot of variation in their size, height of bloom and time of bloom. If you choose carefully for bloom time from different varieties, you can have many weeks of daylily blooms.

I call these tuberous roots, "Queens for a Day," as the blooms of the flowers last only one day. However, some varieties have high bud counts. It's possible to have multiple flowers on the same stalk, each opening on a different day. Some daylily blooms stay open in the evening and others re-bloom most of the season.

Arlow Stoudt was the first person in the US to hybridize daylilies on a large scale. Considered by many to be the father of American daylilies, he published the first book on them in the 1930s.

True Lilies - What I am most definitely not referring to are bona fide true lilies, like the Asiatic and Ornamental lilies. True lilies belong to the genus Lilium and grow from plump, scaly bulbs. They are magnificent flowers that command attention wherever they are planted.

*Obedient Plant or False Dragonhead - This plant grows easily and spreads quickly. Obedient plant (Physostegia virginiana) got its common name because you can bend the individual flowers in any direction. Unfortunately, obedient plants are not so obedient in the garden, where it can spread quite aggressively, by rhizomes. I have learned this so well in my perennial garden bed in my community garden where they would like to take over. Growing obedient plants in the garden adds a bright, spiky flower to the from mid-to-late summer and fall.

*Monarda (Bee Balm) Plant of the Year 2021

This classic North American native is known by its botanical name of monarda or its common name of bee balm. Many Vermont gardeners grow bee balm in their gardens.

Growing them isn't hard if you keep their soil evenly moist. Plant them in spring or fall in a sunny spot. Bee balm tolerates partial sun, but you'll get fewer flowers. Space them 18 to 24 inches apart in organically rich soil with a pH of 6.0 to 6.7 that drains easily. Once established, bee balm is very trouble free and requires very little maintenance.

This native has pale purple nectar-rich flowers that are loved by bees and butterflies. They grow about two to three feet tall. Some varieties have tubular flowers in colors of red, pink, white or purple. My favorite are the reds, which I grow in my community garden.

This popular perennial flower was until recently, more known as a tea and medicinal plant than an attractive ornamental. It was used to cure ailments such as upset stomachs to infections and called Oswego tea by early colonists.

One of its problems is that bee balm loves to spread, so it's best to give it plenty of room by planting it away from other plants. You can also dig up clumps each spring and give them away to your neighbors. If you have a small space garden, consider growing some of the less aggressive, dwarf bee balms. 'Fireball' is a red flowered variety that grows only 1-foot tall with compact flowers and is perfect for small spaces or containers. 'Petit Delight' is another dwarf variety, but with rosy, pink colored flowers.

One other trick to keep bee balm's size manageable and extend the flowering season is to pinch the new growth when plants are 10-to-12 inches tall. This forces the plant to bush out and stay smaller than the usual 3+ feet tall. It also forces the plant to flower a little later, so by pinching some plants and leaving others, you'll be able to have flowers blooming for a long time.

Two other tricks: Bee balms begin to bloom in July and will continue to bloom throughout late summer. As the flowers wilt and fade, cut just above the next flower bud. Continue to cut throughout the season as needed until the stem has finished flowering. Once a stem is finished flowering, trim it back to the ground.

Deadheading spent blooms will prevent seeds from self-sowing and will encourage the plants to continue to flower longer. The "Chuckster" just said, "I don't want to say anything, but those other tricks are the same."

Oops! I forgot to mention that along the roadways in July you'll see amazing sky blues of chicory, white tapestry blooms of wild carrots (Queen Ann's lace) and yellow buttercups. What a lovely combination. They are them the ultimate wild plants of summer. I should write a poem. The "Chuckster" just said, "Please, not another poem."

And beware of the wild parsnip you see along the ditches along the highways. It will burn your skin if you happen to brush against it. It's a highly dangerous invasive. Encounters with wild parsnips can result in a sunburn type rash, discolored skin and even blisters. Symptoms occur after contaminated skin is exposed to sunlight.

Powdery Mildew

This fungus disease can damage bee balm. If you live in a humid climate, you'll notice mildew on its leaves. It can be a difficult disease to control. One of the best solutions is to look for disease resistant varieties, such as 'Jacob Cline', a favorite of many gardeners with fragrant red flowers. It tolerates clay soil and deer damage. The traditional recommendation is to plant bee balm in areas with good air circulation, which will dry out the leaves sooner and reduce the incidence of powdery mildew. Windier locations do better.

Powdery Mildew 2018 - In mid-summer, the conditions were ideal for powdery mildew as we were coming off a cool wet week - especially for bee balm and tall phlox. Greyish/white patches (powdery mildew) can also be seen on asters, goldenrod, lilac and squash later in the season.

With temperatures between 60 and 80 degrees and high humidity, powdery mildew spores start to take hold. By mid-August, the nights are cool and the dew heavy creating the perfect environment for this disease. Powdery mildew not only makes leaves turn gray or white colored and eventually die, but it can also weaken a plant causing it to succumb prematurely.

Besides bee balm, here's what to do to thwart powdery mildew on other plants. First grow disease resistant varieties such as 'Europeana' rose, 'David' and 'Orange Perfection' phlox. Keep the plants well weeded and not crowded so the leaves dry quickly.

A great preventative spray, mixed in a one-quart spray bottle is the formula of one tablespoon baking soda, one-quart water and a few drops of liquid dish detergent. Why? Powdery mildew thrives in an acid environment that much of our rainwater provides. The baking soda nullifies the acidity on the leaves so mildew can't grow. Spray once per week. Baking soda changes the pH on the leaves making it less inviting for disease spores.

You can also spray Bacillus subtilis AKA Serenade to control the disease at the onset. Bacillus subtilis is a bacterium that fights the fungal growth. Another method to control fungus on plants is used in Biodynamic Gardening and Farming. Horsetail (equisetum) is brewed up into a tea. Cook up a large container stuffed with horsetail and water to the boiling point and then let it simmer. The tea is sprayed on the plant. Horsetail has more silica than any other plant and is able to slow down the effects of fungus diseases. I've been using it for years.

Late in the season, there's little you can do to stop powdery mildew. You can remove the diseased leaves and flowers. If it starts on your healthy squash, pumpkins, and melons when they are producing fruit, don't worry. The plants are winding down anyway, and it shouldn't hurt production. But on phlox, roses, bee balm and other flowers it can shorten their flowering period and just look plain ugly.

Hummingbirds

Do you know which hummingbird is a magnet for Monarda? The Ruby-throated hummingbird is the only breeding hummingbird commonly found in the central and eastern half of the United States; and it is the most common species in Vermont.

The Ruby-throated hummingbird (Archilochus colubris) is named after the "humming" sound its wings make as it hovers in the air.

Hummingbirds are the smallest of all birds, and the only bird that can fly backwards, as well as hover in one place. It averages 70 wing beats per second.

The Ruby-throated hummingbird returns to Vermont in the beginning of May and is gone by the end of September. In summer, it will nest in gardens, orchards, roadside thickets, and woodland clearings, and often chooses habitat near running water in open woodlands. In the fall, it will migrate south, travelling 2,000 miles or more, to reach the wintering grounds in Central America and Mexico.

Rufous Hummingbirds (Selasphorus rufus) - Uncommon, but regularly reported in this state. These hummingbirds are usually found in gardens and at feeders. These birds are fearless, and are known for chasing away other hummingbirds and even larger birds, or rodents away from their favorite nectar feeders and flowers.

Margie and Sonny - Gone But Not Forgotten

When I think of summer, two "Woodchuck" gardeners stand out: Margie Rice and Sonny Martin. Many summers ago, I worked at Alice Holway's Nursery in Putney with Margie Rice. We shared the task of caring for rich people's gardens from morning to early summer evenings. I learned a lot from Margie about landscaping, balling trees, transplanting perennials, and life. We'd work hard all day and on the way home stop at Dewey Newcomb's in Westminster West for a glass of moonshine, which put a nice buzz at the end of the day. Margie was a real "Woodchuck" gardener in the way that she lived her life being close to the land, plants, and animals. She loved to hill potatoes with me as the sun began to hide. That's where my passion for growing spuds began. Margie passed away many years ago.

Six summers ago, I learned that Sonny, also known as the Weed Whacker, took off to the higher world and met up with Margie. I was told of his passing by his garden neighbors, the Johnsons, who gardened next to him for many years at the Tommy Thompson Community Garden in the Intervale. Sonny Martin had been homeless for a number of years before he found a place that provided housing for him and others who once lived "on the streets."

Sonny "The Weed Whacker"

I worked closely with Sonny over the years as the coordinator at the Tommy Thompson Community Gardens. We have three acres of community garden plots, the largest in Vermont. If folks didn't weed their gardens, they got two more chances before I asked Sonny if he would whackum down. He always got a big smile on his face when I made the announcement. Sonny proceeded with the task at hand with speed and endurance. He also kept the greenways mowed and created a parklike appearance to the gardens. Sonny donated vegetables to the Chittenden County Food Shelf. It's not the same without Sonny, the Weed Whacker.

Jewels in the Sky

There are nighttime jewels fluttering about in the summer sky. Moths are much more than the pesky insects attracted to porch lights in the spring, summer, and fall. Did you know that Vermont has about 2,500 species of moths? Or that they have ears on their abdomens? Go outside after sunset to turn on the UV lights in hopes of attracting lots of moths!

> FOUR ANNUAL VINES, RUNNERS & CLIMBERS
>
> *Mandevilla - I grow these annual tropical vines in my front yard. They take off like weeds with heat and humidity and die back in the fall when the frosts come. Mandevilla produces trumpet shaped flowers in yellow, pink, red and white. Transplant from a container into the soil next to a south facing fence where it will climb up rapidly. Don't plant until the soil warms up in June. Two varieties are 'Alice du Pont' a pink flowered variety and 'Parfait Series" with pink and white flowers. Use Neem oil to protect the plants from aphids and other insects. I bought a potted madevilla plant with red flowers on sale in mid-summer

and it took off like wildfire. I'm going to bring it inside in the fall and see how long it lasts unless it begins to take over my house. The "Chuckster" just said, "He's not very good with houseplants and eventually the madevilla died."

Morning Glory - I've been growing the annual vine, morning glory, for many years. They are special because there are so many blooms with colors ranging from white to blue to purple. `Granpa Otts", an heirloom, has deep, purple, velvety flowers. `Scarlett O'Hara', a heirloom, has unusual red blooms. Two others are `Royal Blue' and `Glacier Star'. Plant morning glories after all danger of frost  has passed. They love to grow up a trellis and will drop seed (self-sow) and come back the next year. I've grown them up giant sunflowers and the clematis vine in my front yard. To ensure quick germination of morning glories, nick the dark seeds with a nail file and soak seeds in warm water the night before sowing.

Morning glories are one of the first blooms in the morning flower clock. The "Chuckster" just chimed in with, "Perhaps, that's why they're called morning glories. Hmm! `Linnaeus' Flower Clocks was a garden plan hypothesized by Carolus Linnaeus that take advantage of several plants that open or close their flowers at particular time of the day to accurately indicate the time. He proposed the concept in his 1751 publication, Philosophia Botanica. Other blooms include chicory 5 a.m., dandelion 5 a.m., morning glory 5 a.m., pinks 8 a.m., calendula (pot marigold) 3 p.m., Iceland poppy 7 p.m. and daylily at 8 p.m.

Scarlet Runner - Another great vine I've grown for many years are scarlet runner beans, which originated in the mountains of Central America. Most have lovely scarlet/red flowers and artistic multicolored seeds. They are often grown as ornamentals and the hummingbirds love them. I can't wait to eat their fresh, soft beans in summer casseroles or dried beans in soups in winter. I save scarlet runner's and share with friends.

Climbing Honeysuckle (Lonicera sempervirens) is also called trumpet honeysuckle. Honeysuckles are arching shrubs or twining vines in the family Caprifoliaceous, native to the Northern Hemisphere. Approximately 180 species of honeysuckle have been identified.

Although climbing honeysuckle will grow and flower in part shade, the more sun the vine has, the more flowers you'll get in colors of scarlet to orangish red on the outside and yellowish inside. This native honeysuckle is deer resistant. Plant vines in well-drained, compost-amended soil. Space plants 3 to 5 feet apart. I have one in my sunny yard on a trellis against the front of my home next to the foundation. They are non-fragrant, narrow, and trumpet-shaped flowers.

Climbing honeysuckle is a vigorous, deciduous, twining vine which typically grows up to 10-15' - not that high in my garden. It is one of the showiest of the vining honeysuckles. This vine is evergreen in the warm winter climates of the deep South. The species is native to the southeastern U. S., but there are populations in New England where it reaches the northern edge of its range. It gets its common name from its long, tubular flowers, which attract a wide variety of visitors including long-tongued insect pollinators.

Honeysuckle flowers appear in summer at stem ends in whorled clusters. They are attractive to hummingbirds, butterflies, and bees. Inedible red berries form in late summer to early fall and can be ornamentally attractive. The small red berries are attractive to birds. Oval, bluish-green leaves are glaucous beneath.

Why not plant two native climbing honeysuckle vines on either side of your porch steps? Let them twine up the metal railings so that visitors would be welcomed by cascading red flowers. You know that old adage about vines - the first year they sleep, the second year they creep, the third year they leap.

Keep climbing honeysuckle plants well-watered and mulched with bark mulch to keep the soil consistently moist. The mulch will help to control weeds. Add layers of compost and an organic plant food for fertilizer each spring.

Climbing honeysuckle has the toughness of the bush honeysuckles, with a climbing habit that makes it a great plant to grow up pergolas, arbors and walls. The small flowers often have two colors in one flower and bloom in early summer. They will repeat bloom throughout the growing season, especially if the plant is deadheaded. Some species of climbing honeysuckle are fragrant, too. The small red fruit that emerge after flowering are favorites of birds. However, unlike Japanese honeysuckle (L. japonica), this vine isn't invasive. This fast growing, twining vine is deciduous in our climate, but an evergreen in warmer southern locations of the country. It's an attractive plant for bees, butterflies, and hummingbirds as well.

Prune climbing honeysuckle after blooming to keep it in bounds and looking attractive. Climbing honeysuckle leaves can get ratty looking by midsummer, especially under hot dry conditions and from insect and disease attacks. Plant in part sun and keep the vine well-watered to prevent the leaves from dying back. Reduce the number of insects feeding on the leaves to keep them looking attractive in summer. Climbing honeysuckle is a haven for aphids, mealy bugs and powdery mildew disease. Control aphids and mealy bugs with sprays of insecticidal soap. Control powdery mildew with proper pruning and sprays of Serenade organic fungicide or use a mixture of baking soda and water.

The vine will twine around a pole, post or wire or grow down a bank or rock wall, letting it cascade down the slope as well. It looks great as a backdrop to other tall perennials, such as peonies, coneflowers, and bee balm.

Try 'Alabama Crimson' and 'Magnifica.' These popular red flowered varieties flower throughout the summer. 'Cedar Lane' is a red flowered variety that's more disease resistant. 'Blanche Sandman' is a vigorous orange-red flowered variety. 'Sulphurea' has yellow flowers, but is not as vigorous a vine as 'Blanche Sandman'. 'Gold Flame' is a yellow flowered cross with fragrant flowers.

Trumpet Vine (Campsis), Japanese honeysuckles (Lonicera japonica) and Morrow's honeysuckle are three invasive - hard to get rid of. Please see My Woodchuck Garden Website for more info on these plants. Be careful what you wish for with them as they love to take over.

Other vines include *climbing roses, *wisteria, *kiwi and *grapes. I grow climbing roses in my front yard, training them over an archway from the crab apple branches. Wisteria is a long-lived vining plant with cascades of blue to purple flowers that look spectacular hanging from a pergola in early summer.

Wisterias are slow to mature and may not begin flowering until three to five years after planting. While growing wisteria is easy, you should take caution, as it can quickly overtake everything without proper care. Wisteria's perfumes are almost impossible to resist. It will grow in Zones 5 and up. They need protection from the cold north winds.

Kiwi and grape vines need especially strong supports. They are essential in growing vines and must be sturdily constructed of durable materials. It's discouraging to see a beautiful, healthy vine ruined after several years' growth because the structure on which it is trained has collapsed.

The grape is probably the best known of the vines that climb by means of tendrils although it is not reliably hardy in much of the far north, which includes much of Vermont. Tendrils are slim, flexible shoots or, in some cases, leaf-like parts that act as tendrils. They quickly wrap themselves around anything they come in contact with to support the vine for further growth.

I grow Concord grapes, which got its start in Concord, Massachusetts. Horticulturalist, and Concord resident Ephraim Wales Bull (1806-1895) spent years working with thousands of seedlings before finding a vine worth keeping - a derivative of a wild Vitis labrusca grape that could withstand the harsh New England weather. He propagated it for five years before bringing his crop to market, thus making the Concord grape one of just a handful of edible fruits native to North America. I love to crush the grapes for the juice with my feet just like my grandfather once did.

Hedgerows

Hedgerows create boundaries in your garden. They can be a substitute for a stone wall or wooden fences. Tall hedgerows of Rugosa roses and blackberries can keep animals from invading your gardens. Elderberry and viburnum hedges provide fruits in summer both for humans and birds as well as habitat for birds, animals, and insects. In my yard, I have hedgerows of rosa rugosa, forsythia, and lilac. Traditional hedgerows include privets, hemlock, and cedar. They can either grow wild or be trimmed.

Edible hedge plants include currants, Aronia, elderberries, gooseberries, and high-bush blueberries. Blackberries with their thorns create a real barrier. They keep deer and dogs out and perhaps your neighbors.

The taller evergreen hedgerows include cedar and hemlock. They act as windbreaks to stop cold winds from harming your plants and create microclimates. Shorter hedgerows of boxwoods make lovely boundaries in your garden. American arborvitae (Thuja occidentalis) is a native evergreen. The narrow, pyramid shape makes it a natural choice for windbreaks. It requires almost no care when used as a hedge or screen.

Thuja is a genus of coniferous trees in the Cupressaceae (cypress) family. There are five species in the genus, two native to North America and three native to eastern Asia. They are commonly known as arborvitaes (from Latin for tree of life) or Thujas; several species are widely known as cedar but, because they are not true cedars (Cedrus), it has been recommended to call them red-cedars or white-cedars.

A thing of beauty is a joy forever.
Its loveliness increases; it will never
Pass into nothingness.

-John Keats 1818

In summer, the song sings itself.

-William Carlos Williams

The Earth Laughs in Flowers

-Ralph Waldo Emerson

THE GARDEN
I have a garden of my own,
But so with roses overgrown,
And lilies, that you would it guess
to be a little wilderness.

-Andrew Marvell (1621-1678)

JULY MOVES ON
summer is about rain, sun and sweat
and flea beetles, black flies, and mosquitoes
and honey and bumble bees
and leaky faucets, rain barrows and rain gardens
and mulch and more mulch
and weeds of course
and getting down and dirty
and would we do without lawns?
except do without them

-The Woodchuck Gardener

SUMMER NOTES & TIPS: 2019

Native Plants Help Support Wildlife - Gardeners are learning that they are never alone in the garden. Insects, birds, earthworms, deer, moles, voles, and many other creatures live among the plants and in the soil. In other words, the greater the diversity of plants in your garden, the greater the amount of life. By including native plants in your landscape, you can provide wildlife, such as butterflies and bees with the food and habitat they need for survival.

Examples of Native Plants: Goldenrod: 'Fireworks' and 'Golden Fleece' are two standouts valued for their late summer yellow flowers. Asters: A favorite selection originally found in the wild is 'Purple Dome,' a New England aster. An aster relative that has proven itself as a valued source of long-lasting cut flowers is the white daisy flowered "Snowbank". Joe Pye Weed: 'Gateway' is a wonderful example. Monarda: Bee Balm cultivars like 'Violet Queen' has mildew tolerance and thrives in drier conditions. Liatris (Blazing Star or Gayfeather): Liatris ligulistylus is a superb gayfeather with long showy purple flower spikes. Coneflowers (Echinacea) reign supreme in the summer garden. Echinacea purpurea and its various cultivars ('Magnus' and 'White Swan') are well known.

Heat and Rain - Today, our summers bring too much heat or too much rain or both or not enough. You just never know any more. June of 2014 was the third wettest month on record in Vermont. The summer of 2020 was very hot and dry. So how do we cope in these times of climate change and the weird weather it brings? Even the rhythms of bees, butterflies and other insects are off kilter because of a changing climate.

Weeds and Invasives - In June and July, we need to prevent weeds and vines from taking over our gardens and protecting plants from harmful insects. The invasive shrubs on the fencerow near my home have taken over again along with the wild grape vines, both of which I battle every year. I just whack-um down. On the other hand, the wild roses intertwined amongst the forsythia are quite pretty together in red and yellow and green. A statue of Saint Frances sits nearby in a bird bath, so all is well.

In my front-yard and community garden, there is another battle that continues. Some years, I'm not sure who wins the war between the weeds and flowers. Just when you think you are ahead, you relax for a few days and then, the weeds come back with a vengeance. And then you go at it again until fall when you clean up your garden a final time before putting it to bed. And then you can rest, perhaps.

Insects - Because there was so much rain in June of 2015, the slugs and snails had a heyday. They attacked the hostas and other perennials they love to chew on.

*Golden Glow is a lovely tall flower that blooms in July and August. They grow in my front yard garden. Its botanical name is Hortensia `Rudbeckia'. My neighbor, Marilyn Maddison was freaking out as snails were devouring her Golden Glow plants. I suggested four solutions: spray a mixture of coffee and water on the plants, which she used. It was the cheapest method. She could also have used thin-rolled copper or pennies around the plants. Copper carries an inherent electrical charge which will shock snails and slugs. There is also a commercial product called Sluggo which contains iron phosphate. Once slugs and snails ingest it, they won't bother your hostas or Golden Glows any longer. Finally, you can place round plates filled with beer at ground level. The slugs will slurp up the beer, get drunk and drown. I use Budweiser Light. No fancy beer for me.

Watering - Another concern is how to deal with the hot, dry summer weather. Watering is key, especially if you have new plantings. The way to water is long and slow. Spraying overhead will lead to fungal issues. A slow hose aimed at the roots for the count of ten is optimal. Water plants thoroughly and only when needed. I've seen gardeners at the community gardens bring out a hose and water their plants at midday, the worst time to water as much of it is lost to the heat and transpiration. The best time to water is in the morning and second best in the evening, even though evening watering can potentially cause fungus problems. Make sure and water the soil around the plants, not directly on the plants. Using drip irrigation or a soaker hose uses less water. See below on the plusses of mulching around plants.

Composting - Adding several inches of compost to the soil will help it to absorb and retain water so you won't need to water as much. Trees, shrubs and groundcovers will help slow the flow of rainwater and increase the amount of water that stays in your landscape and filters water before it enters the groundwater.

Fred - Fred Schmidt, my friend and next-door neighbor at the Tommy Thompson Community Garden is the "Super Compost Guru." He's the ultimate scrounger of grass clippings, newspapers, burlap bags, shredded leaves, horse manure, cardboard and whatever - like bed springs for growing peas and pole beans. Fred must have ten different types of cold frames in various sizes and shapes. One can't simply walk through his garden. You have to meander right and then left and then center left and then retreat back and it goes on and on and on like a corn maze. The "Chuckster" told me he once got lost in Fred's Maze.

In the fall, Fred puts shredded leaves, food scraps, grass clippings and water in black plastic bags and lets them sit for a year or longer before mixing them with the soil. By then, the materials are well broken down and ready to be added to the soil as compost. What's amazing is how well his plants grow. Fred builds garden beds in various sizes and shapes, some vertical and some horizontal. We teach composting workshops at the community gardens.

You wouldn't believe how different my garden is from Fred's. Mine has long rows of garden beds, with five cold frames and paths in between. Interspersed are four compost piles where I grow pumpkins and winter squash. In the fall, I spread compost from the piles onto the beds. Burlap bags cover the paths between the garden beds. Vegetables are grown in the beds along with perennial flowers, a sweet cherry tree, Concord grapes, blueberries, rhubarb, a grape vine, red currants, and Aronia berries plus perennial flower beds and shrubs and ...

Mulch - Mulch the soil around trees, shrubs and other plants with several inches of woodchips, evergreen needles, or other organic materials. Mulching reduces watering frequency and prevents soil compaction from heavy rainfall thus increasing water absorption. Apply mulch around plants and shrubs to conserve water.

Rain Barrels and Leaky Faucets - Place rain barrels beneath the downspouts on your house and why not plant a rain garden? Repair leaking faucets and garden hoses. A slow leak of one drip per second can amount to nine gallons of water per day. Collect rain water with rain barrels as an effective way of managing water in your landscape. See if there is a way to collect grey water from washed clothes, dishes or even yourself. Hmm said the "Chuckster."

Lawns - The author, Michael Pollan says "A lawn is nature under totalitarian rule." When mowing your lawn if you still have one, avoid cutting more than 50 percent of the height as the health of the roots is dependent on the food in the leaves. If tall grass is cut too short, it will upset the balance between root and leaf growth and will weaken the roots. That's what happens when sheep overgraze pastures. Lawns need regular deep watering that goes down to the roots, not light sprinkling which evaporates quickly. Don't water during the middle of the day but in the evening.

The "Chuckster" just said to me, "How come after telling gardeners to get rid of their lawns, you provide information on how to care for their lawns." I responded by saying that I am a "pragmatic hypocrite." I live in the world and realize that there will be lawns as long as there are people, unless the goats and sheep take over the planet, which would be okay with me as they have been around for centuries.

Lawns, as we know them, have become an expected part of a home's exterior and many homeowners feel obliged to maintain one. However, there are many options other than square beds of grass. Some folks are shrinking their lawns and planting vegetables, fruits and berries for bountiful harvests. They are also planting trees, shrubs, ground covers and perennials plus adding interesting patterns of gravel and stone walkways, ornamental garden beds, sculptors, rain gardens and perhaps a bench beneath a flowering dogwood.

The benefits of lawn alternatives include relying less on fossil fuels for mowers, eliminating the use chemical fertilizer, pesticides, herbicides, fungicides, and lessening chemical contamination of our water resources from storm water runoff from chemically treated lawns. Time is another commodity we can save by not spending our weekends mowing the grass and bothering our neighbors. Folks are now using push mowers and electric powered mowers as well. Just as important is the conservation of water. So if you must, mow your grass when it is high to encourage deep roots that are more drought resistant and allow your lawn to go dormant during the hot dry weather in the "Dog days of August."

Hoses - By the way, your garden hose may be toxic. And did you know that the hose you occasionally drink from might contain harmful chemicals. *HealthyStuff.org* found that water from garden hoses contained dangerous toxins including lead in the brass fixtures, neurotoxins, and endocrine disrupters. Of the 90 garden hoses tested, 33 percent contained levels of lead not considered safe for children. Hoses aren't regulated by the Safe Drinking Water Act.

Older hoses, especially those that are yellow and green, carry the most risks. It's best to choose a hose made from at least recycled materials. Typical materials are rubber or polyurethane or a combination of the two. A light hose that's flexible and weighs much less than old models will likely be made from recycled polyurethane. Also, look for a hose with a UV protective coating to protect it from the sun. There are ecofriendly hoses labeled for safety with labels such as "drink safe," or "safe for potable water," "lead free," "Eco Smart" and "family safe." Three safe hoses are Water Right and Armadillo. So with summer here, please replace old, cracked hoses with new ones.

The "Chuckster" just told me a Mexican hose joke. He began with the question, "Do you know the name of a Mexican fireman? The answer he gave was Jose. And then he asked, "Do you know his brother's name? The answer was Jose B." Hmm!

JUNE AND JULY

Midsummer & St. John's Day

The last day of Gemini, June 21st, is the start of the Summer Solstice, the longest day of the year. Modern-day Druids and others celebrate this event at mid-summer. This is the same time as the Christian Festival of St. John's Day or St. John's Tide, one of the four major Christian festivals along with Michaelmass (September 29th), Christmas, and Easter. This day is said to be the day of birth of John the Baptist.

The Summer Solstice is the time when the sun is at its zenith blazing away as we are being lifted into the cosmos in mid-summer. Ancient peoples, watching the sun reach its high point, lit bonfires to encourage it to shine and ripen their crops. Humans spend much time outdoors enjoying the element of fire with campfires and barbecues; loving the element of water with swimming, boating, and fishing and savoring the summer breezes of the forest, mountains and the sea.

Long ago, people spent time gazing at the bright summer stars. They were connected to the heavens and led their lives according to them. Back then, before people became self-conscious, there was a lot of spontaneous singing and dancing to be had. Today, we have to work harder to create these experiences, but they are still worthwhile such as a grand bon-fire on St. John's Day.

Midsummer traditions are full of fertility beliefs (and practices) and divinations of future (and not so future) lovers. Babies conceived during this time would be born in the spring, the time of new life. In many ancient cultures this was the preferred time for "mating" allowing for gestation over the winter and the new birth in the spring.

More Color and Plant Tips

Here are some TIPS to help you put together a color show that will delight from June on.

As I enter July, I hope for a garden full of color with waves of blooms. *Red poppies, *green dill and *yellow calendula drop seed and mature in hues of red, yellow and orange in my community garden. These are some of my favorites. I plant *nasturtiums by seed. They flower later. Their petals overlap, nestling in glowing green disks like a musical score. Each fold and stamen speaks in various hues.

A few late summer annuals include pansy, viola, ornamental kale, and pansy. The seeds need to be started in May. Annuals bloom steadily all season long, especially if you remove the spent flowers. Combining annuals with perennials makes it easier to keep the color going strong.

You can also grow annuals that are drought tolerant such as cosmos, California poppy, and nicotiana. I start them from seed, and they bloom in my community garden later in summer. These annuals are easy to grow and will keep your annual flower garden colorful without running up your water bill. Added to the list is the reddish-purple amaranth, which self-seeds as a biennial. Other annuals include cleome, salvia and impatiens.

*Sweet Williams make their presence known in late June. Like most dianthus, they have a spicy clove scent in colors of red, pink, and pure white. They originated in the mountains of Europe. Sweet William (Dianthus barbatus) is a colorful, biennial flower. It grows for two years, blooming in the second year. It is a heavy reseeder and comes in a multitude of colors from white to deep burgundy running in the shades of pink. Great for pots, containers and cut flowers. They are hardy in Zones 3-9, and need more shade in hotter climates. They grow in my community garden.

Perennials - Perennials bloom at a certain time during the season: peonies in May/June, *delphiniums in June, *phlox in July and August into September. Gardeners shop for perennials during May or early June and then take a breather. This means flower gardens tend to have lots of early summer flowers such as bleeding heart, lupines, iris, and baptisia. Plan for late season drought tolerant perennials including echinacea, sedum, yarrow, lavender, salvia, Russian sage, rudbeckia, asters and ornamental grasses.

Celebrating American Grown Flowers in All 50 States
June 28 to July 4, 2019

Bulbs - Stretch the Garden with Bulbs

In July, my *gladiolas are blooming. Plan to continue the show right through October by adding late summer-flowering bulbs such as *dahlias, *Oriental lilies and *cannas planted in early summer. These plants don't mind the heat and most of them are at their best as summer turns to fall.

Primp and Prune as You Go - Make a habit of keeping a pair of scissors or a small hand pruner in your pocket. Removing spent flowers and cutting back lanky foliage helps gardens stay tidy and focuses attention on what looks good rather than what doesn't. Deadheading encourages annuals to keep flowering and will sometimes get perennials, such as achillea, campanula, dianthus and phlox to bloom again.

High Summer

Soon it will be "High Summer" when my lettuce goes to seed, and woodchucks begin checking out my garden for flowers in eat. Raccoons are waiting for the corn to ripen into those sweet milky kernels before ravaging what I've worked so hard to grow.

Insects and diseases are continuing to do damage. I noticed the  Japanese beetles on my raspberries in July. I deal with them by throwing those pesky creatures into a pail of soapy water. I don't use traps as there are many gardens around me and all the beetles would come to visit my berries. If I lived on the moon, it wouldn't need to worry.

You can spray the beetles with the organic product Neem by mixing a gallon of water, an ounce of neem oil and a teaspoon of mild liquid soap. Mix the soap and water and then add the neem oil slowly while stirring constantly. A hand spray bottle is ideal for applying the mixture to the plants. You can also apply beneficial nematodes on grassy areas where they feed in early summer and early fall to kill Japanese beetle grubs.

Kaolin clay is used on grapes and fruit trees to deter the beetles. It creates a white film that beetles hate to feed on. Bacillus thuringiensis BeetleJUS is a new form of B.T. that kills grubs and adults without harming pets and bees and us humans. It works well on canna, roses, and many other flowers. After it rains, you need to spray it again. Let me know how it goes?

While all of this is going on, I've come face to face to one of the ironies of gardening. I call it "perseveration." I can't stop looking back at my garden when I leave. It's like an obsession and I don't believe it affects only me. It probably has something to do with my dark side as my blood type is B-negative. The Chuckster just said, "You've gotta a problem and need garden counseling." Perhaps he's right. On the other hand, I believe a lot of folks have this problem.

ADDED SUMMER TIPS & NOTES
- Cut blighted shoots on lilacs.
- Control aphids on rose buds by spraying insecticidal soap.
- Cut back perennials after they have finished flowering and take cuttings to start new plants.
- As perennial chrysanthemums begin to grow, encourage bushy plants and more flowers by pinching the stems back. You may get the second flowers coming.
- To keep annuals and perennials flowering over the season, remove some of the flowers as they fade. Letting them go to seed reduces flower production. Of course, we need to leave some for the birds and insects.
- Transplant groundcovers including English Ivy, myrtle, pachysandra and ajuga.
- Deer like shrubs such as false indigo, bleeding hearts, primrose, Autumn Joy Sedum, New England asters, coneflowers, and phlox. They don't like lungwort and daffodils and avoid herbs like mints, rosemary, catmint, oregano, and lavender plus some of the ferns.
- Harvest early fresh leaves of herbs like lemon balm, mints, sage and other herbs. Pick chamomile blossoms and tie them up with twine and hang the herbs up to dry in my back room. You can continue to harvest lemon balm and mints more than once.
- The phlox, bee-balm and echinacea in my community garden are just starting to bloom in July. There is even a rare plant you rarely see in Vermont in my neighbor's yard, the Gittelson's. It's called *yucca and is a genus of perennial shrubs and trees in the family Asparagaceae. Its 40-50 species are notable for their rosettes of evergreen, tough, sword-shaped leaves, and large terminal panicles of white or whitish flowers. They are native to the hot and dry parts of the Americas and the Caribbean. Early reports of the species were confused with the cassava. Consequently, Linnaeus mistakenly derived the generic name from the Taíno word for the latter, yuca. You rarely see it growing in Vermont.

Summersweet Gardens at Perennial Pleasures is a retail and mail-order nursery located in East Hardwick, Vermont, a beautiful part of the state known as the Northeast Kingdom. These gardens are one of my favorite places to visit.

Phlox at Perennial Pleasures Nursery

The nursery, greenhouse and display gardens are sited on the sunny fields behind the family home, an 1840s brick house at the edge of the village. Over 900 varieties of flowers, herbs and shrubs, specializing in heirloom and medicinal plants, and a special fondness for phlox. Plus you are welcome to partake of tea and pastries on certain days. Call ahead for reservations. Rachel Kane owns and manages the nursery. 1-802-472-5104 or email annex@perrennialpleasures.net

Perennial Pleasures Nursery throughout the seasons

SCENT
My favorite phlox scent
If this surprising fact is true,
I wonder of the creator knew;
And did he dip the Lily and the Rose
And every other scented flower that grows
In some sweet Heavenly dew,
Whose secret He alone, The Great Creator, knew.

-Reginald Arkell 1882- 1959

Arkell

HOT WEATHER IN JULY OF 2018

Jesum, 2018 was a very hot summer with some 90-degree temperature along with dry weather and little rain. The grass is parched in many places. The heat wave began in mid-June, continued through the summer and into fall. The average temperature in July was 76 degrees Fahrenheit. July in Burlington, Vermont was the hottest on record. That's a whopping 5.2 degrees above the norm for July. We normally get just a rare 90-degree day time temperature, but not this summer. The drier conditions in addition to the persistent high pressure over the Atlantic Ocean helped make July much hotter than average. 2018s' heat wave tied for the second hottest heat wave in Vermont history. The brutal heat and humidity continued well into August along with muggy nights. We need good soaking rains and cooler temperatures. By the way, 2020 brought hotter temperatures and dry conditions as did 2021.

Dry weather may mean a reduction in Lyme disease in our region. Over the past decade, black legged tick populations have grown exponentially. I'm sure all you know someone with Lyme disease caused from tick bites. The number of ticks depends on the number of deer and small animals around. There is a connection between high acorn years, which spike in the mouse and chipmunk populations. Most tick species show reduced host seeking behavior when it's dry. Their Achilles heel is desiccation - a fancy word for drying out. Ticks need moisture which is why you find them in moist leaf litter. None of these preliminary findings should warrant you to not be extremely careful when walking through woods, fields, and back yards. Check your pants and socks after walking, strip down at home and let your partner check you out. I got a tick bite on my arm in the summer of 2020 and removed the tick.

I've been using washrags dunked in cold water on my neck to cool off, but it doesn't take long for the rags to dry up, so I dunk my head in a water barrel at my community garden every hour or so. I keep my dog Herk cool by going down to the lake in the evening for a mutual dunk. He's also my companion at the community garden in the morning where he lies in the shade in the grass with his water bowl close by.

I'm watering container plants in my front yard garden once a week. The containers are placed five inches below the soil. They containers include marijuana CBD and THC plants. Vermonters are allowed to cultivate a total of six plants per home, including up to two mature female plants that have flowered.

AUGUST

The Dog's Days of August

Hello, August! Can you believe that in less than six weeks we'll officially welcome Autumn? Where did the year go? And yet, the gardening season is not over by a long shot. Fall is the time for planting more plants and fretting as well. I need a break. Too much harvesting, canning tomatoes, weeding, watering. It's just too much.

Oops I just saw a hummingbird sucking up nectar from a purple flowered butterfly bush in my community garden. They use their aerial agility to supplement their nectar diet with insects, which they snatch from the air. While many birds can do that, they typically have short beaks and wide gapes. Hummingbirds, by contrast, have long flower-probing bills. I watched the hummingbird for some time and was entranced as I always am with them.

I have hummingbird feeders hanging off my front porch. In early August, I noted how they were going to town on the sweet water. I guess they were getting prepared for their long trip west and south. I was changing the sweet water every two weeks. I love to listen to their humming sound of wings, fluttering in the air - before I see them.

In early August in 2020, I saw a profusion of bee balm in the garden of Richard Foye's, an old friend from southeastern, Vermont. There were hummingbirds taking nectar from the red flowers of the bee balm and from his two homemade plastic hummingbird feeders.

Richard, seen here leaning over his 51 Chevy truck, fashions his own homemade hummingbird feeders.

Shrub Tips

Low maintenance and easy to grow, shrubs can be used to hide unsightly views, add privacy, and buffer noise on tight properties, and can help divide your yard into garden "rooms". Take a look around your garden. Make note of where you might need to add a shrub to fill in an empty spot and identify plants that need replacing.

Shrubs can also provide cover for birds and other wildlife. Hydrangea, rose of Sharon, potentilla and wiegelas are easy to grow, and they bloom beautifully. They do well in Zones 3 through 9.

Two Favorite Late Season Shrubs - Hydrangea and Rose of Sharon

*Hydrangeas - Hydrangeas have a special place in our gardens. These lovely old-fashioned grandma shrubs stand out, especially the ones with large white blossoms. As they ripen, the blooms begin to dry. If you snip off the blossoms and hang them, they will hold their hues. They grow in my front yard and my community garden. My whitish-pink hydrangeas bloom in August and September.

The color of hydrangea blooms can be changed by the soil pH. A somewhat acidic 5.5 should turn them blue, a more alkaline 6.0 should turn them pink with the effect being more intense the more extreme the pH. Hydrangeas will turn blue or purple in acid soils. They will turn pink or red in alkaline soils. One of my favorites are the 'Endless Summer' blue hydrangeas.

Hydrangea paniculata, better known as panicle hydrangea, typically offers a flowering season from late spring to early summer, but plants retain the blossoms until they shatter, which can occur as late as winter.

French hydrangea's blooms sooner in warmer, Southern or coastal gardens than they do in cooler New England gardens. Popular hydrangea quercifolia, oakleaf hydrangea, flowers in late summer. These are the ones I grow from midsummer to early fall.

Hydrangeas are excellent for a range of garden sites from group plantings to shrub borders to containers. Varieties abound (every year, it seems, breeders present us with more options!), and gardeners' expectations of bloom size and color are boundless.

Another common name for hydrangea is Hortensia. Charlie Nardozzi, the Vermont garden writer, is excited about the new panicle and smooth leaved hydrangeas that give our gardens bountiful blooms in late summer to fall. The panicle hydrangeas are best known by the tall standard 'Pee Gee' hydrangea. But new varieties are smaller and better flowering. Charlie likes 'Little Lime' which grows only 3 to 5 feet tall with white fading to pink- and burgundy-colored blooms. 'Bobo' stays 3 feet tall as well with pure white colored flowers.

Charlie says that for a twist on the taller panicle hydrangeas that grow to 6 feet tall, try 'Quick Fire' with its rosy colored flowers or 'Little Lamb' for its small airy petals on large flower heads. A smooth leaved variety is 'Invincibelle Spirit'. Like the common 'Annabelle' hydrangea it has massive flowers in summer. But 'Invincibelle Spirit's' flowers are pink instead of white, offering a nice color alternative. All these hydrangeas are hardy in Zone 3, have few pests or problems and flower every year. They last well into early fall.

*A great book is, "Hydrangeas for American Gardens" by Michael Dirr, the famous horticulturist.

*Rose of Sharon - (Hibiscus syriacus) This erect, deciduous shrub produces colorful, cup-shaped flowers. The blooms are most welcome since they come during the latter half of the summer. Other common names include shrub althea and Chinese hibiscus.

Colorful, showy flowers appear in summer in shades of white, red, pink, and purple on the rose of Sharon bush. Growing rose of Sharon is an easy and effective way to add long lasting summer color with little fuss. The large, showy flowers attract birds, butterflies, and other useful pollinators.

After planting rose of Sharon, this attractive specimen may thrive with neglect. However, some care, especially pruning for shape, will likely be needed for this showy shrub to add value to your landscape display.

Flower colors include blue, pink, red, lavender, purple, and white, depending on the variety. Most varieties grow 6 feet tall or less even though they are not as large in Vermont. The plant shows good pollution tolerance.

There is a rose of Sharon called 'Tri-Color' that has pink-, red- and purple-colored flowers all on one shrub. 'Sugar Tip' has double pink flowers on a variegated plant. 'Lil' Kim' only grows three-to-four feet tall, while most rose of Sharon shrubs reach up to 8 feet. And the 'Pillar' rose of Sharon only grows two feet wide, but straight up.

These native plants of eastern Asia are well adapted to grow in most USDA plant hardiness zones. They can be used as part of a privacy border. It leaf's out late in spring, so don't worry if it's still bare when other shrubs are growing. Since it's big show is late in the growing season, rose of Sharon is often paired with other earlier blooming full sun-loving shrubs to provide continuous color.

LATE SEASON PERENNIALS

Fall planting gives perennials a head start over their spring-planted counterparts. Roots continue to grow even as air temperatures cool, so plants are rarin' to go in spring. To give plants time to get established before winter, plan to plant at least six weeks before the ground freezes. Root systems will start to grow as soon as the ground thaws, long before the soil can be worked, and any new plants can be put in. This means first-season perennials can actually show their flowers in the first season! That's not always the case. Also, the cool fall weather makes planting much less stressful for the plants. Some examples include butterfly bush, ornamental grasses, black eyed susan, New England aster, lobelia, and Russian sage.

Bulbs and Late Season Color from my community Garden

*Dahlias - Few plants can compete with the flowering power of dahlias. They deliver some of the garden's biggest and most spectacular blooms! Dahlias are a reliable source of color for late summer flower gardens, and it takes just a few bulbs to transform even the simplest cut flower arrangement. I've been growing them for ten years and all my neighbors are wowed and happy when they bloom, especially when I give them bulbs in early summer.

This genus of bushy, tuberous, herbaceous perennial plants are native to Mexico. They are a related species to the sunflower, daisy, chrysanthemum, and zinnia. There are 42 species of dahlia, with hybrids commonly grown as garden plants.

My first dahlias bloomed on August 5th in 2019. In cooler parts of Vermont, dahlias began to show buds. When they bloom, reach for your shears or a garden knife to cut bunches of the colorful stems and flowers for a vase. On October 12 in 2021, my dahlias were still "bloomin like crazy." The American Dahlia Society is a wonderful resource to use to learn more about growing dahlias.

And then there are other summer-blooming bulbs including gladiolus, lilies and cannas. *Cannas bloom 8 to 12 weeks after they are planted. This means in most places they bloom later in summer through the fall. Gladiolus bloom first.

Let's Continue with of a Profusion of Color in Late Summer and Fall with: Hostas, sunflowers, coneflowers, phlox, peonies, astilbe, joe pye weed, veronica, false obedient, sneeze weed, sedum, thistle, mallow, bee balm, rudbeckia and milkweed.

***Hostas** - Fall is a good time to plant hostas in your shade garden. Be careful with hostas as they can get out of hand in terms of size. Some of the smaller hosta varieties are `Halcyon' and `Aureomarginata'. They stay a little smaller and don't need dividing as often. They begin to bloom at the end of July.

Years ago, I visited a garden along the Otter Creek, not far from Lake Champlain. There were many hostas in shades of green and even some in blue/green and others with yellow tips. There were large and small hostas. Scattered throughout the gardens were sculptures and evergreens placed amongst the hostas. I'm sorry as I can't remember the name of this hosta garden along the Otter Creek.

Up to now, I've focused a lot on flowering plants, however, you shouldn't just choose plants only for their flowers. Many of my favorite plants are attractive to me because of their foliage like hostas. It's amazing how colorful and textured a plant bed of various shades of green can be.

***Sunflowers** - In the Tommy Thompson Community Garden, large sunflowers drop their seeds and sprout up in early summer. I dig them up when they are a three-inches tall and give them away to friends. I leave some where they stand, and they grow tall and large. Eventually, the squirrels try pulling them down and eating the delicious sunflowers seeds. I also allow myself to partake in the gathering of the seeds and drying them for winter snacks.

I don't know the sunflower variety that grow in the community gardens, but I guess they may be the tall and large "Mammoth" variety. Some ornamental, multi-headed varieties are `Moonshadow' and `Cinnamon Sun.' Sunflowers attract bees for their heavy pollen. I've noticed how the yellow finches love to hang out on the plants and eat the seeds.

These "Flowers of the Sun" lift my spirits. As they mature, it's a reminder that summer is moving on. The sunflowers bloom in their tallness and strength in August. They are so strong that the stalks can be cut up and used as kindling. I leave some for the snow to hang out on. I don't need to plant sunflower seeds in my garden as they drop their progeny in the fall and germinate in early summer.

AH! SUN-FLOWER
Ah Sun-flower! Weary of time,
Who countest the steps of the Sun:
Seeking after that sweet golden clime
Where the travellers journey is done...

-William Blake 1757-1827

Eagle of flowers! I see thee stand,
And on the sun't noonglory gaze:
With eye like his, thy lids expand
And fringe their disk with golden rays:
Though fix'd on earth, in darkness rooted there,
Light is thine element, they dwelling air,
They prospect heaven.

~From The Sunflower by James Montgomery 1771-1854

*Echinacea (American coneflower) are blooming with the heat of summer. A member of the Aster family, its disc flowers, which make up the cone of the flower, provide loads of pollen late summer for bees and butterflies as well as nectaries to feed beneficial predatory insects. Some of the favorite Native varieties are Echinacea paradoxa along with native cultivars such as 'Magnus' and 'Solar Flare.'

Echinaceas are native to the prairies of North America and their roots are excellent for busting up prairie clay as well as New England soils. Echinacea purpurea is the most common native and is known as Purple Coneflower. You can grow Echinacea paradoxa, with bright yellow petals, as a good pollinator.

A favorite is the "nativar" 'White Swan' grown at Full Circle Gardens in Essex Junction, Vermont. A nativar is a cultural variant found growing within a natural grouping of the same species of plants. It is not hybridized, and pollinators can derive nectar and pollen from it. The problems with hybridized echinaceas is that they are sterile and do not set seed and therefore cannot provide nectar and pollen to pollinators. While Full Circle Gardens remains committed to growing pollinator perennials, it also believes in a little balance with some of the colorful hybrids.

Echinacea's are hardy to Zone 4. They require full sun and drier conditions. "Think prairies" when contemplating American cone flowers.

FYI - An echinacea tincture for winter colds is easy to make. Use a wide mouth canning jar and add some dried echinacea roots until the jar is half full. (The roots and above-ground parts of the echinacea plant are dried and used to make teas, extracts, capsules, and tablets.) Add vodka (with at least 40% alcohol - 80 proof). Pour vodka to the top of the jar so there is a little room at the top. The dried herbs will swell over the coming weeks. Label jar with the date and the expected date your tincture will be ready.

Perennial Pleasures Nursery in East Hardwick, Vermont has the best collection of garden phlox in Vermont.

***Phlox** - Another of my favorite perennials are phlox which provide a myriad of colors. There are many varieties in hues of pale blue, violet, white, pink, and red. I grow them in my front yard and community gardens.

***Creeping phlox** come in May and the other phlox begin to bloom at the end of July and last until early fall. They make wonderful bouquets and have been favorites in American gardens for well over 100 years.

Phlox are a favorite choice of gardeners - from ground cover blooming in early spring to the tall phlox blooming in mid- to late summer. They are a genus of 67 species of perennial and annual plants in the family Polemoniaceae. They are found mostly in North America and even one in Siberia. Phlox come in two forms - there is Garden phlox (Phlox paniculata), which is an upright flower that grows to about three feet and Creeping phlox (Phlox subulata) just mentioned above.

In the Northeast, purchase mildew resistant varieties like "Lavender" and "Blue Lagoon" You can spray a baking soda solution to control fungus plus provide full sun and plenty of spacing between phlox. -See more on mildew controls below.

***Peonies** - They bloom earlier in summer. Mid-to-late August is when peonies set buds on their root stocks. In order to insure a good blooms next season, make sure that your peonies are well watered. They need water below the surface so that the buds can be swelled. And remember when planting peonies, never plant the root deeper than 1.5 to 2 inches. Planting lower will created lots of foliage but not much in the way of blooms.

Early September is a good time to plant peonies. They should be settled in place before the first hard frosts. If you must move an established plant, this is the time. Spring planted peonies just don't do as well; they generally lag about a year behind those planted in the fall. Dig a generous sized hole, about two feet deep and two feet across in well-drained soil in a sunny spot. If the soil is heavy or sandy, add compost and one cup of bone meal to the soil. Set the root so that the eyes face upward on top of the firmed soil, placing them two inches below the soil surface. Then backfill the surface, water thoroughly and add a little mulch on top.

Peonies take time to develop - usually a few years to establish themselves - to bloom and grow. Spare the fertilizer or in my case, the compost. In other words, don't fertilize every year. On the other hand, if the soil is poor add bone meal, and compost after they have bloomed.

Astilbe - Thia is a great late summer and fall shade plant. Some varieties bloom later such as 'Visions' and 'Gloria'. They provide a late spark to a shady border. Even when not in bloom, the lacy green or bronze colored foliage adds interest to the shade and contrasts well with other shade flowers. Astilbe come as a small or large plant so do a little research to get the variety that will best fit your landscape situation. And don't be afraid to give both hostas and astilbes a little sun.

Joe Pye weed (Eutrochium)- This popular native that is loaded with butterflies this time of year. While the species version has pink flowers and can grow 6-feet tall, there are smaller varieties. 'Baby Joe' only grows 2- to 3-feet tall, but still produces an abundance of flowers. 'Chocolate' Joe Pye Weed produces white flowers and burgundy-colored stems on a 3-to 4-foot-tall plant. Joe Pye weed likes a wet soil and can thrive in part sun. It's a good plant for a meadow or hedgerow.

As the story goes, there once was an Indian medicine man named Joe Pye who used concoctions from a wild plant found growing in the nearby woods to cure typhoid fever. His brew is said to have halted an epidemic that raged in Colonial Massachusetts. Hence this local plant became forever known as joe pye weed.

Veronica - Speedwell - Butterflies and hummingbirds love veronica. It produces colored flowers, which comes in a wide variety of heights for you to choose from, but they are all easy and undemanding to grow. These perennials prefer full sun and average, well-drained soil. I see them everywhere in purple red.

These neat tidy plants that are beautiful in or out of flower. Their blossoms provide rich blue, purple, pink or white shades of long-lasting color. I prefer the purples. Speedwell are carefree perennials that prefer well-drained soil with full to part sun.

On the taller side is Giant Ironweed. It is similar to joe pye weed as it thrives on wet sites. Giant Ironweed (Vernonia gigantea) is a member of Asteraceae, the Sunflower family. In older manuals and guides, this family is called the Compositae because the 'flowers' are a composite of many flowers, often of different types. The purple flowers bloom in August and on into November.

The plant is native to the eastern United States, north to New York state and Ontario. Tall Ironweed prefers wet soil conditions and full sun exposure. This plant spreads by rhizomes to form clumps. Because it can spread aggressively, Tall Ironweed is often categorized as a common pasture weed.

And then there is Blue Reflection Speedwell (Veronica), a vigorous groundcover that covers its garden space with handsome evergreen foliage and a profuse late spring display of small blue flowers.

*False Obedient Plant (Physostegia virginiana) - is the next plant to blossom. It begins to flower in early August and is called obedient plant or false dragonhead. This species of flowering plant is in the mint family, Lamiaceae. It is native to North America, where it is distributed from eastern Canada to northern Mexico. It is known as the obedient plant because a flower pushed to one side will often stay in that position unless it falls over, which I find so common at my community garden in the perennial bed.

Obedient is considered a good plant for adding late-season flowers to a garden. Fertile soils produce robust growth and wide spreading, and the plant may require staking. When it grows tall it has a "tendency toward floppiness" that can be controlled with pruning, which I find necessary in my community garden as it tends to take over. They do spread via rhizomes, so be careful and give them lots of room. I know this from personal experience.

*Sneeze Weed - A native that's a charm in fall is Helenium or sneeze weed. It has an unfortunate common name, but the plant is beautiful in fall and carefree. It's also known as the Mexican hat for the shape of its flowers. The Mariachi series only grows 2-feet tall with rosy, red- or yellow-colored flowers depending on the selection. 'Mardi Gras' grows up to 4-feet tall with bright, orange-colored flowers. 'Ruby Tuesday' has deep red flowers on dwarf 18-inch-tall plants.

Helenium is an adaptable garden perennial because of its size. It does like well-drained soil. It will spread over time, but stays manageable. Like the previous flowers mentioned, Helenium is a butterfly magnet, blooming from late summer until frost. Plant these fall bloomers in a garden setting, hedgerow, meadow or edge of the woods.

The best way to keep butterflies happy and around, is to plant flowers that bloom into fall for them to feed on. Select native plants that are easy to grow and bloom in fall. Three of the best are joe pye weed, helenium and ironweed.

***Sedum** (Stonecrop) - This graceful and charming plant, Sedum sieboldii offers blue-green leaves that are often tinted purple. They look great against the clusters of pink flowers that appear in autumn. It needs full sun and well-drained soil. This native plant grows 4 inches tall. Its loved for its evergreen foliage that turns pink in winter. I have sedum plants in my perennial beds in my community garden.

There are few succulent plants more forgiving of sun and bad soil than sedum plants. Growing sedum plants is easy, so easy that even the most novice gardener can excel at it. Sedum plants come in a wide variety of heights, colors, and forms. Showy Stonecrop, the taller plants in the genus Sedum, are popular garden plants. Although lovely, sedums are often taken for granted in the garden, partly because they don't bloom until the fall, but also because they require so little care from the gardener.

***Thistle** is the common name of a group of flowering plants characterized by leaves with sharp prickles on the margins, mostly in the family Asteraceae. Prickles can also occur all over the plant - on the stem and on the flat parts of the leaves. These prickles are an adaptation that protects the plant from being eaten by herbivores. It came out in mid-July.

Besides the plants described above, chicory and Queen Ann's lace have been showing off in blue and white for close to a month. What a lovely combination they are. I consider them the ultimate wild plants of summer. I should write a poem. The "Chuckster" said, "Not another poem." "Enough already."

***Mallow** - It's hard to keep count of all the plants blooming in late summer. Many of them were described above. In late July, the common mallow was in flower. Every year the lovely pink mallow shows up in new places from its spreading seeds. This flowering plant is in the hibiscus, or mallow, family (Malvaceae. Hibiscus species include the great rose mallow (H. grandiflorus), with large white to purplish flowers.

Echinacea -Full Circle Gardens

The common mallow was once highly regarded as a medicinal plant by Native Americans. They chewed on its tough root to clean their teeth. Common mallow was also used to treat wounds, toothaches, inflammations, bruises, insect bites or stings, sore throats, and coughs as well as urinary, kidney or bladder infections.

***Rudbeckia** - Rudbeckia is a plant genus in the sunflower family. The species are commonly called coneflowers and black-eyed-susans; all are native to North America and many species are cultivated in gardens for their showy yellow or gold flower heads. I've been growing a tall one called 'Golden Glow' in my front yard for many years. Rudbeckia "Goldsturm" is the standard for rudbeckia. It is long-blooming and virtually pest free. (2 feet tall) rudbeckia hirta "Cherokee Sunset" has double and semi-double flowers in shades of yellow, orange, red, bronze and mahogany. It is short-lived but re-seeds itself.

*Milkweed - Fill your garden with spectacular fall color, and support monarchs at the same time. Native asters and goldenrods are an important source of nectar for monarch butterflies as they fuel-up for their fall migration - keep your garden blooming and the pollinators humming throughout the fall!

If you're growing the more ornamental butterfly weed, plant it in full sun in the middle of your flower border on well-drained soil. It has a strong taproot so be sure you plant it in the right place since it will be hard to move later. Plant it in a pollinator or butterfly garden with other plants such as butterfly bush, Shasta daisies, salvia, and zinnias. Butterfly weed tends to grow in a clump, so they don't readily spread.

The butterfly weed (Asclepias tuberosa) is a cultivated version of the wild milkweed species. It comes in a yellow flowered version called 'Hello Yellow' that has narrow leaves and grows 2 feet tall. The classic orange butterfly weed grows 3 feet tall and wide.

Another way to grow these plants is in a meadow or "wild" area of your yard. Plant milkweeds, depending on the species, in well-drained, dry areas or wet areas. Choose the right milkweed for your soil and location. Plant transplants in spring or fall. Sow seeds in fall with the cooler, moist weather. This is when native milkweeds will be spreading their seeds, too.

Milkweed plants will spread over time. Simply brush hog the meadow once a year in fall, after a frost, to keep the desired milkweed and other pollinator flowers coming back and keeping out invasive brambles and trees. The common milkweed grows throughout my community garden, Every year, it expands to every corner of my garden.

Wild milkweeds grow in meadows and abandoned fields. There are a number of different milkweed types. The Soulmate Swamp milkweed features cherry colored, sweetly scented flowers that attract not just butterflies but other pollinators as well. There's a white version of swamp milkweed called 'Ice Ballet,' too.

Every spring and summer, the monarch butterfly migrates thousands of miles in search of the ideal milkweed plant. When she finds it, she lays her eggs on the plant, so when each egg hatches, the baby caterpillar can feed on the milkweed leaves. The milkweed plant then provides the perfect protection as the caterpillar turns into one of nature's wonders, a chrysalis, before transforming into an even greater wonder: a monarch butterfly. And once the newborn butterfly soars away, the milkweed seeds fly away on the wind and start this cycle over again.

Butterfly Cottage Garden

In 2021, I planted a Butterfly Cottage Garden with seeds which will turn into masses of flowering plants from late spring on. This garden will eventually capture the essence of the cottage style perennial border. Massing the individual perennial species into groups magnifies their impact and creates a bold grouping that pleases with color, flower form, and foliage. Sedums, achillea, coreopsis, veronica, rudbeckia and echinacea are my favorites.

Coreopsis Full Circle Gardens

    RAIN
    a soaking rain
    we pray
    dryness prevails
    desperate we are
    for puddles
    finally
    rain pours
    walking through my garden
    the fern-like leaves of asparagus
    glowed with water droplets
    sparkling in prisms of color
    curled water on thin leaves
    of the corkscrew willow
    seen out my window as I compose

    -The Woodchuck Gardener

AUGUST

August Jitters 2019

Well, folks, August has been hot and sunny like July with little rain. Thankfully, the sun goes down earlier. It's cooler in the mornings; there is dew on the grass as I walk Hercules.

And yet, I get nervous when the eighth month of the year arrives and moves on to September. Actually, it's more like "freaking out." The "Chuckster" concurs as he has seen me go into conniption fits. I haven't gone canoeing enough or hiking as well or taken in many concerts on the green or … How am I going to fill up my life with all of these activities and care for my garden? Well, I need to take a breath. I'm finally getting ahead in the garden. Of course, in a week or two, I'll be behind. That seems to be the rhythm in my garden (and my life)!

> AUGUST IS
> Yellow slopes
> of goldenrod plumes
> spires of mullein
> and evening primrose:
> fields with golden grass,
> Black-eyed Susan's
> and by-gone buttercups;
> gardens of pumpkins,
> marigolds and swallowtails;
> dooryards of giant sunflowers
> and tiny, lemon-featured finches,
> And, through the fading trees,
> Shafts of flaxen light
> In the early morning fog.
> August is yellow,
> fading,
> except for lacy white
> of Queen Anne's,
> and now,
> audacious crimson
> of dogwood leaves,
> drops of summer
> blood.
>
> *-Ann Day, Fayston, Vermont*

CARING FOR PERENNIALS IN AUTUMN

Fall is a great time to tune up your perennial flower garden. Many perennials need to be cut back as they fade and die. But there's other reasons for cutting back perennials. Some, such as echinacea and rudbeckia, self-sow seeds rampantly in the garden. You won't notice the seeds in fall, but come spring you'll be weeding out lots of seedlings.

One downside of cutting back these self-sowers is that many are food for birds. Gold finches and chickadees love to feast on the sunflowers, echinacea and rudbeckia seeds.

Other perennials self-sow seeds. Hollyhocks are actually biennials or short-lived perennials. They drop seed and young plants grow in fall. Next spring these young plants send up flowers for summer. So, after the seed pods have dropped seed, cut back these lovely perennials.

Separate old perennials and plant new ones in your garden beds. This will give time for perennials to increase in root size and store food for the cold months.

Cut back leaves of bearded iris to two inches before digging and dividing crowded plants. Clip back daylilies, peonies and other earlier bloomers whose leaves are yellowing in late September and fading now. But don't clip them all back as insects need places to overwinter.

Many perennials get cut back to the ground or at least to about 6 inches tall. In cold winter areas, leaving some stubble in the gardens helps collect snow which can insulate the plants. And then weed well. It's an opportunity to find weeds lurking in between plants and digging those out. Using a sharp hoe or pointed trowel cut back annual weeds and dig out perennial weeds. You'll be surprised if you don't weed, how fast the weeds will emerge in spring.

After weeding add compost to the gardens. A 2-inch-thick layer should be fine. Compost will not only feed the roots of perennials for next year, but it will also help hold soil moisture if you have a dry fall. Adding mulch around the plants helps with water retention.

Rosemary, Scented Geraniums & Lavender

If you're growing rosemary, lavender, scented geraniums or any perennial herb that may be tender in your climate, October is the time to have a plan for overwintering them.

Rosemary is a plant that needs to be dug out and brought inside in Vermont by November. Pot up the herb plant, place the pot in a shady area outdoors to get used to the reduced light levels and check for any insect pests on the leaves. After a few weeks, move your rosemary indoors to a partial sunny window - away from cold drafts, and continue to monitor for pests. In the winter, rosemary plants grow much more slowly and need much less water than they do in the summer. Watering too often will cause root rot, which will kill the plant. So keep the soil moist, but not wet, and the herb should make it to spring. On the other hand, if the soil is allowed to dry out completely, the roots will die back, and the plant will not have enough life to support itself. That's been my experience.

You can use the same process for other perennial herbs, such as thyme, oregano, chives and mint. While these might be hardy in your area, they will go dormant outdoors, but stay green and alive indoors so you can use them in cooking.

Scented geraniums are not frost tolerant and must be protected in most areas. Move these plants indoors using the same process described above for rosemary. If you have a large geranium or herb plant and no room for it indoors, take cuttings and root them in smaller containers filled with moist potting soil. Dip the cut ends in rooting hormone powder first, then stick them in the pots. Keep the soil moist and in a month or so they should root. Then transplant the young plants into potting soil.

Yarrow and Lavender

Lavender is hardy to Zone 5, depending on the type. English lavender is the hardiest while Spanish and French lavender need warmer winters. If you're growing lavender and the type, you're growing is borderline hardy for your area, protect the plants in the ground come December. I've had success placing bark mulch or wood chips on top of lavender plants in late fall. You don't have to cover the plants completely, but certainly cover the base of the plants. You can also use evergreen boughs on top and around the plants. That should help them survive cold weather. In spring, remove the mulch, chips and boughs, cut back the plant to live growth and they should take off and grow.

Enjoy the cooler days and evenings, watch out for frost in colder regions and keep gardening. Water new plants if its dry, cleanup gardens removing dead and diseased plants and make notes about what grew well and what struggled this year in the garden. It will help you plan for next year when you turn your attention back to gardening in winter.

With the passing of the autumnal equinox, we are officially into fall. While many perennials have lost their blooms, fall beauties such as *Japanese anemones, *monkshood and *hibiscus are shining.

FINAL TIPS BELIEVE IT OR NOT!

Heat Wave Gardening - Now that we're into August and later, many gardeners are experiencing heat waves and less-than-average rainfall. Water more frequently in the morning and mulch plants to reduce evaporation. Consider heat and drought-tolerant perennials next year. Deadhead perennials, but not all as snow adds beauty to the tops of plants and again, insects need places to hibernate in winter. Remove spent flowers from roses.

Trees - Mow grass around fruit trees to deter deer and moles. You can also spray red pepper as a deterrent. Place tree guards around young fruit trees. It's good time to remove any dead branches from the trees around your garden. Deadwood is not only hazardous and unattractive, but it's also a host for insects and fungal diseases. For information on Planting Trees Ecologically, go to My Woodchuck Garden Website.

Compost - Early fall is a good time to turn your compost piles. After turning, add shredded leaves, vegetable scraps, grass clippings, garden weeds, dried-up old plants, animal manures, newspapers, human urine and other organic materials to new piles. Make sure the pile is well watered after you turn it. The "Chuckster" just said, "Did you just say, urine. Sounds disgusting to me." I answered "Yes! I save my urine to as it adds nitrogen to the compost piles. Just make sure to mix in lots of water to the urine (5 to 1) and each to his own."

Hummingbirds - Make sure your garden has a season's worth of hummingbird favorite plants to keep them coming back from spring through fall. Learn which nectar-rich flowers will draw them to your garden. Hummingbirds love the color red but will feed on flowers of any color that have a good nectar supply like the purple blooms of butterfly bush. They particularly enjoy hummingbird mints, lobelia (cardinal flower), salvia, pink azalea, delphinium and sage. These beautiful, summer-blooming perennials are also full of nectar for bees and butterflies. They love butterfly bush in early fall.

Monarchs Need Fuel For Their Migration - Fill your garden with spectacular fall color, and support Monarchs at the same time. Native asters, milkweed and goldenrods are an important source of nectar for Monarch butterflies as they fuel-up for their fall migration. They also keep your garden blooming and the pollinators humming, through fall!

The Minor Spreaders - I've noticed many landscape perennial beds have been taken over by a number of some of my favorite plants including geraniums, irises, wild phlox and squills (gooseneck), which is the most invasive of the group. I don't consider the others to be as invasive, but when planning your garden, you should be aware of the spreading tendencies of these plants.

Let's not forget bellflowers. Some spread by seeds, which is a desirable trait when they are planted in a naturalized environment, but it becomes a problem in small, highly managed flowerbeds. The bellflower groundcovers spread by underground rhizomes and can slowly colonize an area where growing conditions are ideal, Korean bellflower being most notorious for this trait. Some gardeners don't mind them spreading and others do. If course, nothing is as noxious as gout weed.

My dog Hercules (Herk) said he needed more of a part in the book, so here he is!

SEPTEMBER

FALL PLANTING OF NOT-SO-COMMON WOODCHUCK SPRING BULBS

The key to getting a parade of spring flowers is to plant bulbs that bloom at different times. Here are some not-so-common suggestions: Glory-of-the-Snow in periwinkle blue and white bloom early grow and multiply for many years. Why not brighten wooded areas, rock gardens and garden beds with snowdrops, another early blooming bulb. Winter aconites add a slash of yellow, while Siberian squill and Harmony iris bring a touch of blue and white. Checkered lily comes in cream, lavender and burgundy. Japanese Anemone windflowers bring beauty to your early garden and will attract bees and butterflies.

Of course you can add the familiar crocus, daffodils, hyacinths and tulips. Let's not forget the alliums, which provide a wonderful bridge between spring bulbs and early summer perennials. Fill in shady areas with sky blue, white and pink Spanish bluebells, also known as wood hyacinths. Order your bulbs early for the best selection. Go to your garden center or order spring flowering bulbs online to plant in late September or early October. Make sure and add bone meal to soil.

FYI - Do squirrels or other rodents eat the tasty bulbs you plant? You can protect your favorite irises, lilies, daffodils, and tulips with an underground steel mesh enclosure. The openings are small enough to keep the rodents out but big enough to allow the roots and shoots to grow through. You can make your own or purchase them. Go online for instructions.

Walking Herk

I was just hummin' Richie Haven's song. "Mornin, mornin - feel so lonesome in the morning." His melancholic tune rings true early in the dawn. Haven's was the first performer at Woodstock. I heard him sing a long time ago. He's now taken off to higher worlds.

I walk Herk and listen to the honkers honk and acorns as they hit metal rooftops. Herk chews on a piece of wood and the day moves on. The hummingbirds are drinking lots and lots of sugar water preparing for their long trip.

I'll work in the garden transplanting iris's and a peony, make applesauce and tomato sauce and take out my canoe for an evening paddle.

The cicadas will welcome me home. These prehistoric creatures with bug eyes, a scaly body and nearly transparent wings are seldom seen, but their buzzing song can pop up anywhere there's a stand of trees.

The "Chuckster" just said, "Jesum Crow, will the plants ever stop a-blooming? I hope Ron won't be spending any more of your time and mine in idle plant banter."

LATEST FLOWERING PLANTS: HIBISCUS, MOUNTAIN ASH, MONKSHOOD, TURTLEHEAD, NEW ENGLAND ASTER, JAPANESE ANEMONES, CHINESE LANTERNS PLUS FERNS

***Hibiscus August 2019** - Late summer flowers are in their glory, and none are more beautiful than hardy hibiscus. Unlike the tropical hibiscus that grows outdoors in warmer climates, the hardy hibiscus dies back to the ground in fall and reemerges in early summer. My red-flowering hibiscus in my front yard began to bloom on August 25th.

Hibiscus is one of the hummingbird's favorite flowers. The genus of this plant is in the mallow family, Malvaceae. The genus is quite large, comprising several hundred species that are native to warm temperate, subtropical and tropical regions throughout the world. Member species are renowned for their large, showy flowers and those species are commonly known simply as "hibiscus", or less widely known as rose mallow.

***Native American Mountain Ash** (Sorbus americana) began to show its orange berries in late August. It's easy to identify in late summer and fall by its wide clusters of bright red-orange berries. Its European cousin, sometimes called Rowan tree, has orange-red berries in a more rounded cluster. The compound leaves of the American Mountain Ash resemble the leaves of sumac and are more pointed than those of the European tree.

In the spring it is loaded with clusters of snowy-white flowers. In summer it is covered with feathery, fern-like leaves that turn red in autumn. This fast-growing tree reaches heights of 20-30 feet tall. Because of the pretty fall berries, and the lovely spring flowers, mountain ash has been planted in many landscaping settings. Mountain Ash rival's dogwood as it is one of the most beautiful flowering forest trees in spring. Unfortunately, the tree isn't long lasting. Out of its natural habitat and ecosystem, it appears vulnerable to pests and diseases, fire blight and borers.

The American Mountain Ash was first cultivated in 1811. The bark was used as an anti-malarial medicine by pioneer doctors because of its close resemblance to the quinine tree.

*Monkshood - Aconitum also known as aconite, monkshood, wolf's-bane, leopard's bane, mousebane, women's bane, devil's helmet, queen of poisons, or blue rocket, is a genus of over 250 species of flowering plants belonging to the family Ranunculaceae. It gets its common name from the flower shape; it resembles a helmet or a hooded cloak of a monk.

Monkshood has become popular as a garden addition because of its purple/blue flowers and attractive dark green foliage in September. Monkshood grows well in full to part sun. It's a good woodlands edge plant and a nice addition to a perennial flower border. It's not invasive and deer and other animals seem to leave it alone. It grows two to four feet tall so it may need staking especially if grown in a part shade location where the stems might reach for the light. It grows best in moist, well-drained soil and once established doesn't like to be moved.

The drawback to this sturdy perennial is that all parts of the plant are poisonous. In fact, in medieval times, it was often used to poison enemies or unfaithful spouses. So be careful with animals and young children around and wear gloves when cutting it to keep the sap off any wounds and cuts.

*Turtlehead (Chelone obliqua) - These native wildflowers adapt beautifully to garden conditions such as the ornamental purple ones my community garden. Plants form an upright, bushy mound of green foliage, bearing upright stems of large bright- rose, pink, or white with hooded flowers beginning in late summer. It does best in heavy, moist soils. Turtleheads get their name from the shape of its unusual flowers, which resemble the heads of snapping turtles. It spreads to form dense colonies from late summer into fall. Years ago, I noticed native wild white turtlehead in wet areas while collecting wild herbs. They grow next to New England asters in my community garden.

*New England Aster - These asters are a Missouri native perennial which occurs in moist prairies, meadows, thickets, low valleys and stream banks in well-drained soils. It is a stout, leafy plant typically growing 3-6' tall with a robust, upright habit. I especially love the wild purple ones, which you see everywhere in the wild.

Aster wildflowers are members of the Asteraceae family and native to the eastern and central United State. New England aster's rich color highlights the late season landscape with magnificent blooms ranging in color from blue-purple to lavender-pink, with yellow-orange centers. These tall perennials are not only hardy and low maintenance, but also provide vibrant displays of color in the fall.

Like most asters it blooms late in the season and provides a critical fall nectar source for pollinators, especially Monarch butterflies as they stock up for their fall migration. The bees are also going crazy feeding on the purple blooms. I love to hear their buzzing as I weed nearby plants.

'Hella Lacy' is a 3- to 4-foot-tall plant with dark purple blooms. 'Honeysong Pink' has yellow centered pink flowers on 3 ½ foot tall plants. 'September Beauty' blooms a deep red on 3 ½ foot tall plants. 'September Ruby' flowers are rosy-red atop 3- to 4-foot-tall plants.

*Japanese anemones - (Wind flowers) - This time of year, it's often hard to find fall flowering perennials that will put on a show besides the usual mums. An exception is the Japanese anemones. These plants throw great sprays of fresh, spring like flowers in late summer and early autumn and bring new life to the garden. Come late summer, flower stalks emerge with dainty white, lavender or pink colored flowers seemingly dancing in the breeze above the foliage providing a splash of color. What I love about Japanese anemones is they flower for weeks in fall, right up to frost sometimes.

There are some specific varieties to try as well. Most are hardy to zone 5. "Honorine Jobert" is an heirloom, white colored variety that blooms for weeks in fall. "Bressingham Glow" is a double, rose-pink variety. "Whirlwind" is a white variety that only grows 2 feet tall. For a touch of lavender, try "Kriemhilde". "Max Vogel" has semi-double pink flowers.

Japanese anemones grow best in part shade in well-drained, moist soil. If they have too much shade, the flower stems may get leggy and flop over. They grow fine in full sun in our area as long as the soil is kept consistently moist. I like growing them near hostas, ornamental grasses, monk's hood and asters to provide some color contrast with the foliage or with the late blooming flowers.

The only downside to Japanese anemones is their penchant for spreading by underground rhizomes. Once happy in a garden, they can spread around. So, each spring we do a little selective editing and remove those Japanese anemones that have strayed too far. I grow them in my community garden, and I don't find they spread too far.

p.s. I also grow earlier blooming anemones in my community garden in summer. For example, there is anemone sylvestris, an Old-World perennial that bears masses of glistening white, fragrant blooms in May.

There are several different types of anemones. Some grow from bulb-like corms like anemone sylvestris, and others are herbaceous perennials like the Japanese anemones. They feature a clumping habit and spread by rhizomes once established in the garden. As stated above, they will happily naturalize to form colonies. While their rhizomatous habit may be desirable in larger landscapes, they may out-compete other surrounding herbaceous plants.

*Chinese lanterns (Physalis alkekengi) and tomatillos or husk tomatoes are closely related in the nightshade family. The spring flowers are pretty enough, but the real delight of a Chinese lantern plant is the large, red-orange seed pod. These papery pods enclose a fruit that is edible though not very tasty. While the leaves and unripened fruit are poisonous, many people like to make use of the pods in dried flower arrangements.

Chinese lanterns are invasive perennial plants grown again for their colorful and delicate orange pods, which, true to the common name, remind one of those paper lanterns sometimes used to decorate with an Oriental theme. They do spread in my front yard, but I am able to control them. I often share them with my neighbors. The pod comes out in its glory in early fall.

Watch this plant regularly for pests and disease and be prepared with neem oil or insecticidal soap. It is bothered by a number of destructive beetles. Fungal and bacterial disease are often a problem for potted Chinese lanterns. Plant so there is airflow between the plants to help avoid such issues.

Ferns - Although many ferns are starting to die back in fall, it's still a good time to identify the ones you like the best. One way is to get a handy guide, such as the new guidebook called, Identifying Ferns the Easy Way by Lynn Levine. It's a simple pocket guide that features 28 of the most common ferns in the Northeast.

Ferns are great shade plants that are underappreciated in the garden. While most gardeners think of ferns as those green plants in the forest, many actually make great garden plants. By the way, I call them foreigners.

Certainly, some ferns spread by underground rhizomes and can take over an area. That can be a good thing if you're looking for ferns to create a patch of greenery. But many ferns aren't so aggressive. The Japanese painted fern has colorful silver fronds with red veins, is low growing and tame in the garden. Maidenhair ferns only grow 1-foot tall and have elegant, bright, green, finger-like fronds with shiny, black stems. They do spread, but not as aggressively as other ferns. Christmas ferns grow 2 to 3 feet tall with dark green fronds and stay green all winter in the North.

If you like edibles, the ostrich fern is otherwise known as the fiddlehead fern. In spring these ferns are eaten when small and unfurled as fiddleheads. They're tasty! Fiddleheads will spread and form numerous clumps in a shady, wet area. I grow tall ostrich ferns along the eastern and western sides of my home in garden beds. Their green colors create a nice contrast to the blue siding, and they keep my house cooler in summer. I spread leaves as a mulch over them in late fall, providing nutrients for the ferns. Please check before harvesting them as they are protected in most areas.

Brunnera

Depending on your location you can pair ferns with other perennials such as astilbe, brunnera and lungwort. I once planted green hostas and ferns together and they made a great, dark green, low maintenance foliage bed.

THE END

Zarathustra is said to have tended a paradise-like garden from an otherwise barren landscape. The word paradise comes from the old Farsi word for exceptional gardens, pairi-daeza, which means a heavenly place on earth.

One of the earliest gardens dates back to Persia, present day Iran around 1500 B.C. It was called a garden of Paradise and was located within a walled enclosure. The garden was of a four-square design and was used for poetry, music, meditation and included fruits and flowering plants. The central feature was a fountain that symbolized milk, honey, wine and water.

The Greeks and Romans took up the four-square design as did the monks and nuns throughout Europe. During medieval times, monasteries were cloistered enclosures with high walls made of stone and thick hedges. Medicinal and culinary herbs were cultivated for the wider community. Prayer was balanced by physical labor of which gardening took a large part of the monk's day.

Let us remember the great agricultural heritage of the Native Americans. The Four Sisters- corn, beans, sunflowers and squash - were grown throughout the Americas. The tradition of calling these crops the sisters originated with the "People of the Longhouse," also known as the Iroquois.

Just like in yesteryears, gardens of today provide us with a sanctuary, and maybe even a bit more than that in our world of consumption and stress. They are a place of beauty and utility, a place to refresh our spirit, a place to be in touch with the seasons and a place where soil, rocks, plants, light, shade and water and people intermingle. How easy it is to lose oneself before you know it.

Kneeling in your garden with a trowel in hand watching a butterfly hover over a dandelion conjures up the word idyllic, which translates to please in natural simplicity. According to the Bible, a garden was where it all began. Perhaps we've been trying to find our way back ever since.

The Garden of Ann and Fred Schmidt

APPENDIX:
USEFUL LINKS, ORGANIZATIONS & OTHER VALUABLE INFORMATION

WILD ONES is one of the oldest if not the oldest organization solely devoted to replacing portions of home landscapes with regional native plants. Wild Ones Presents *"The Nature of Oaks: The Rich Ecology of Our Most Essential Native Trees"* by Dr. Doug Tallamy. You can watch YouTube him talking on their home page. Another presentation - *Wild Ones Presents 'WASPS: Their Biology, Diversity, and Role as Beneficial Insects and Pollinators of Native Plants'* by Wild Ones Honorary Director, biologist, pollinator conservationist, and author Heather Holm. www.wildones.org

THE GARDEN WEB FORUMS is onee of the largest community of gardeners on the Internet. Whether you're a new gardener or an old master, you'll find like-minded folks and friendly discussions on subjects dear to your heart. www.gardenweb.com

GOOD GARDENING VIDEOS.ORG - A 501(c)(3) nonprofit, ad-free educational campaign to find and promote evidence-based gardening videos. Two of the founding sponsors are Garden Design Magazine and the employee-owned Gardeners Supply Company of Burlington, Vermont.

GARDEN GONE WILD is a garden/landscape design and maintenance company happily established in 2003. www.gardeninggonewild.com

THE HARDY PLANT CLUB of Northern Vermont has an informative quarterly bulletin and many summer outings and workshops. Contact Robin Worn Huntington, Vermont robin@gmavt.net for more information.

PERRY'S PERENNIAL PAGES - Dr. Leonard Perry's Web pages provide online perennial and related horticultural information. They serve the Green Mountain State of Vermont. See Perry's Perennial Pages - University of Vermont www.perryspserennials.wordpress.com

CHARLIE NARDOZZI has a monthly Vermont newsletter and garden blog. Charlie is also the host commentator of *The Vermont Garden Journal*, a gardening series on Vermont Public Radio, which can be found online. www.gardeningwithcharlie.com

FRIENDS OF THE HORTICULTURE FARM - This grassroots volunteer organization is dedicated to protecting, enhancing and promoting the significant plant collections and natural areas of the University of Vermont's . The Friends provides many workshops to the community including how to grow pollinators. .The University of Vermont Horticultural Research Center, also known as the "Hort. Farm," is home to many local trees, shrubs, perennials, apples and small fruit. 65 Green Mountain Dr, South Burlington, VT 05403 (802) 658-9166

HORITICULTURE MAGAZINES - My two favorite horticulture publications are: *"Fine Gardening"* and *"Horticulture - The Magazine of American Gardening."*

GEORGE AFRICA'S VERMONT FLOWER FARM, MARSHFIELD, VT - George has a garden blog. Check it out. He tells stories about his farm, weather, and muddy roads in spring and throughout the year in a colder zone than mine. www.vermontflowerfarm.com

NEGOTIATING WITH NATURE - "As someone who has spent some 25 years in my garden, I've come to realize that the earth itself is a garden, and that we need all the help we can get caring for it." -Stefan Van Norden *See more Norden's film in #2 My Woodchuck Garden Website.

NEW FLORA OF VERMONT - Written by Arthur V. Gilman, is a guide for those who have an interest in learning the names - and studying the botany - of Vermont plants. The 600-page manual, published in 2015 by the New York Botanical Garden Press, calls plants by their scientific, or Latin, names and by their common names. Vermont is a small and a well-botanized state - beginning with a list of Vermont's trees and other economic plants in 1795 continuing with four editions of the Flora of Vermont. Go to Part I of My Woodchuck Garden Website for more information on the book. For a copy, go to New York Botanical Garden Press website at www.nybgpress.org.

STORIES FROM THE NORTH - This six-part webinar series covers growing medicinal herbs and organic apples in the North Country of New Hampshire, to embracing no-till farming on a high slope in the Northeast Kingdom of Vermont to regenerative farming and why mycelium is at the heart of soil health. Email: Vermonthealthysoilscoalition@gmail.com with any questions

MY WOODCHUCK GARDEN WEBSITE:

Access this additonal information at
woodchuckgardening.com
or https://woodchuck37.wixsite.com/woodchuck

1. NATIVE SPECIES PLANTS - THE CONNECTION BETWEEN NATIVE PLANTS & INSECTS
   Dr. Douglas Tallamy's book - "Bringing Home Nature," the origins & loss of native species, genetic diveristy & lists of native species in Vermont

2. NEW FLORA IN VERMONT - BY ARTHUR V. GILMAN

3. NEGOTIATING WITH NATURE - A FILM BY STEFAN VAN NORDEN

4. HORTICULTURE TERMS
   Fi Hybrid, Open-Pollinated & Heirloom, Variety & Cultivar Plant Definitions: Annual, Biennial & Perennial Definitions, Horticulture Terms – Fi Hybrid, Open-Pollinated & Heirloom, Variety & Cultivar, Plant Definitions: Annual, Biennial & Perennial Landscaping Terms

5. HOW TO SELECT PERENNIALS FOR ALL-SEASON COLOR | DRY & SHADE-LOVING PERENNIALS, SUN-LOVING ANNUALS, BIENNIALS, CLIMBERS, GRASSES FOR DRY SUNNY BORDER ROSES & MOISTURE LOVING PERENNIALS

6. SUMMER BULBS & TUBERS & CORMS DAHLIAS, GLADIOLAS, CANNA & CALLA LILLIES & BEGONIAS

7. HISTORY OF SEEDS, SEED ARKS & FAVORITE SEED CATALOGS SEED PLANTINGS IN SPRING

8. THE NATURE OF SOIL, MYCOORHIZAL FUNGI, SOIL ORGANIC MATTER, & COMPOST- BLACK GOLD

9. COVER CROPS & GREEN MANURES

10. PLANT & ANIMAL EXTINCTION

11. GLOBAL WARMING & CLIMATE CHANGE

12. INDOOR HOUSEPLANTS & HOW TO CARE FOR THEM

13. THE MISSISQUOI NATIONAL WILDLIFE REFUGE SUMMER 2016
14. THE GREAT MILKWEED LEAP AUGUST 2018
15. WHAT KINDS OF SHRUBS & TREES HAVE BERRIES IN SUMMER?
16. THE INVASIVES ARE HERE
17. CREEPERS, INVASIVES, & THE EFFECTS OF CLIMATE CHANGE
18. SNAKES & TOADS: BRINGING BENEFICIALS TO YOUR GARDEN
19. MOLES & VOLES
20. DEER YES & NO'S
21. MOSQUITO'S 2018 & 2019
22. TREE PLANTING, RETENTION, & CLIMATE CHANGE
23. BULB FAVORITES
24. PLANT HARDINESS ZONES
25. CUT FLOWERS STRAY CAT FLOWER FARM, BABY'S BREATH & OTHER EVERLASTINGS
26. CREEPING THYME
27. FROM PALLETTE TO GARDENSCAPES - PLANNING YOUR HOME GARDEN
28. DR. NORMAN PELLETT
    Additional biographical information
29. MUMS
30. NATIVE WILDFLOWERS
31. PLANTING WILDFLOWERS IN VERMONT
32. WOOD ASH

OTHER BOOKS BY RON KRUPP

 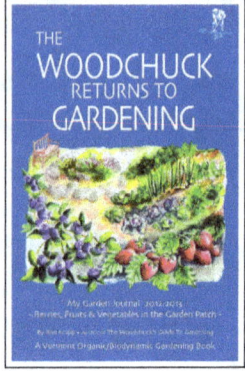 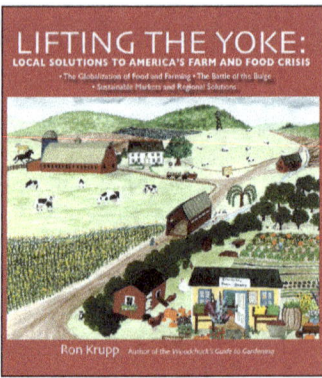

The Woodchuck's Guide To Gardening - $18

The Woodchuck Returns To Gardening - $18

Lifting The Yoke - Local Solutions To America's Farm And Food Crisis - $20

To purchase a copy of any of these books please contact Ron at *woodchuck37@hotmail.com* or call 1-802-658-9974

THE WOODCHUCK TRAVELS THROUGH THE GARDEN SEASONS

Need a copy of this book?

Ron Krupp
8 Lyons Avenue
S. Burlington, VT 05403

woodchuck37@hotmail.com

1-802-658-9974

If you have any questions or comments on the book, please email Ron